A Tiny Universe

A Tiny Universe

Astrology and The Thema Mundi Chart

Joy Usher

To order additional copies of this book, contact:
Xlibris
1-800-455-039
www.Xlibris.com.au
Orders@Xlibris.com.au
520648

Contents

Acknowledgements

With thanks to the various astrological communities, students, friends, colleagues and clients who have supported my journey over the past twenty five years.

My appreciation goes to Mari Garcia, Janette Leibhardt, Tom Pommerel, Anne Fryer, Elaine Kane, Brenda Moss and Deborah Houlding for their constant encouragement and helpful feedback on the ideas presented in these two books. A special thank you to Alan Usher for his patience and expertise in navigating the IT snares that threatened to ambush me along the way.

To the warm and loving Usher Clan who surrounds me – thank you for patiently listening and loving me for the past three years – I couldn't have done it without you.

And lastly, with deep gratitude and respect for their dedication to this project, I give thanks to both Ian, and Jessica, who read every single word of countless drafts, and whose comments and suggestions enabled me to get to this page.

"Man is a microcosm, or a little world, because he is an extract from all the stars and planets of the whole firmament, from the earth and the elements; and so he is their quintessence."

Paracelsus (1493-1541)

"In the first place, we must be aware that God the Creator, copying nature, has made man in the image of the universe, a mixture of four elements – fire, water, air, and earth – so that a well proportioned combination might produce the living being as a divine imitation.

- *Julius Firmicus Maternus, Matheseos (c. 334 C.E.)*

CHAPTER ONE

Thema Mundi: The Birth of the Universe

Thema Mundi is a mythical chart which pinpoints the alleged positions of the seven original planets at the time of Creation.

Sometimes known as the Birth of the Universe, it has been reproduced throughout the ages, not because it is a true reflection of an actual event but because it is identified as the principal source, or origin, of astrological lore.

As such, Thema Mundi is the fountainhead from which most astrological principle flows and is the initiator of the rules which so many astrologers abide by when delineating a horoscope.

The archetypal chart of Creation (or *Genesis Cosmos)* has many variations in its form and in the arrangement of the planets, and it is not my intention to promote one version over another, to prove the chart's historical authenticity, or to discuss the differences between the various Charts of the Universe.

Rather, I have followed the model from the textbook of fourth century astrologer Julius Firmicus Maternus who wrote *Matheseos,* a collection of eight books on the theory of astrology.

In *Matheseos,* Firmicus adheres to the Stoic doctrine of *'sympatheia',* the belief in a kinship between all parts of the universe including the stars in heaven and mankind on Earth.

This man, like a tiny universe, is sustained by the everlasting fiery movement of the five planets and the Sun and the Moon."[1]

When Firmicus calls man 'a tiny universe' in his introduction to Thema Mundi he is referring to the relationship between the macrocosm, heaven, and the microcosm, man.

Firmicus states that the legendary Hermes Trismegistus has provided the chart as a bridge between the immense Universe, and the millions of tiny universes, each of which is a human being.

Furthermore, if an astrologer follows the example of the Thema Mundi chart, they can learn the laws of astrology and by using this, they can decipher the destiny of one human being and how they differ from another with a similar birth chart.

The First Chart gives important information such as signs in which a planet is comfortable, and where it can best express its own unique essential qualities.

These signs are known as Rulership or Domicile signs, and from these signs are born the idea of Essential Dignities.

The twelve divisions of Thema Mundi show the twelve signs of the zodiac, and the twelve segments are the houses, which together form the basis of a chart.

The birth chart takes the planets as they move through the Universe and makes a map that describes such individual experiences as parents, lovers, marriages, children, careers and money matters.

Thema Mundi is the astrological tool of yesteryear, but it is still as relevant today as it was in the days of Greek philosophers such as Socrates, Plato, and Aristotle.

Each time a practitioner of astrology picks up a chart, reads an article, talks to a client, thinks about a planet's position, or merely looks up at the night sky, they are accessing information which began with Thema Mundi.

Thema Mundi's beauty lies in its balance between theory and practical application and as such it is a perfect teaching model to promote the connection between the divine and the mundane.

True to the Stoic's 'sympatheia' where a macrocosmic universe is capable of creating individual charts to imitate nature, each individual becomes their own tiny universe and a living duplication of the infinitely greater celestial movement at the time of their finitely small birth.

The Thema Mundi Chart

Thema Mundi presents itself as a chart with an ascendant at fifteen degrees of Cancer with the Moon rising at an identical degree (known as partile). The Sun follows the Moon one full sign later at fifteen degrees of Leo.

Each of the five planets follows in consecutive signs beginning with Mercury at fifteen Virgo, followed immediately by Venus at fifteen degrees of Libra. Mars is the next planet at fifteen Scorpio, Jupiter is on the heels of Mars at fifteen Sagittarius, and finally, the last of the visible planets is Saturn in Capricorn at the middle degree of the sign.

The two luminaries lie side by side in the chart, Mercury and Venus follow the Sun and are placed roughly in positions of astronomical possibility, with Mercury being thirty degrees from the Sun (maximum distance is 28 degrees), followed by Venus two signs away from the Sun at 15 degrees of Libra (maximum distance is 47 degrees), and whilst Venus is a stretch at sixty degrees, these two planets lie close enough to the Sun to maintain the illusion of celestial viability.

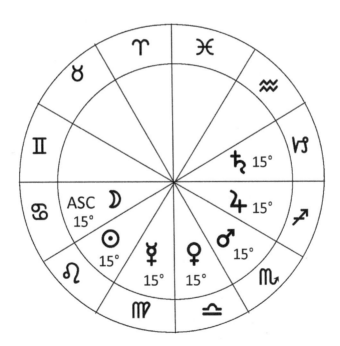

Fig. 1 Thema Mundi

Completing the Circle: Aquarius Through to Gemini

'And so, from events which actually occurred in the history of mankind, the hypothetical birth chart of the universe was put together with allegorical meaning. It has been handed down to us as an example to follow in the charts of men.' [2]

Firmicus Maternus, 334 C.E.

In the text following the introduction of Thema Mundi Firmicus explains how the continuation of the Moon's passage through the remaining five signs of the chart creates the rulership of the five remaining signs by a planet which reflects humankind's progress through the passage of Time.

Fig. 2 Thema Mundi's Time Periods (Aquarius to Gemini)

Ideally the Moon is well qualified for this task.

Firstly, the ascendant's degree is identical to the Moon's degree and she takes the honour of being the first planet to cross the horizon in Thema Mundi.

As such, the Moon becomes symbolically the initiator of birth and life on the ascendant.

Secondly, as the signifier of all things physical the Moon will be the first planet to truly experience this living world.

And thirdly, as the fastest moving planet, the Moon traverses the zodiac in the shortest period of time, and her movement through the remaining five signs becomes an emblem for five successive periods in humankind's development.

Firmicus comments that after the creation of Thema Mundi, humankind's journey on Earth coincides with the Moon's arrival in Aquarius, and befitting his nature, Saturn becomes the inaugural ruler of Time.

Firmicus describes Saturn's period as being a time when the universe is rude and uncultivated, when the world was inhabited by crude men who have just taken the first unfamiliar steps toward enlightenment.

He reasons that Saturn is the most appropriate governor for this earliest period, simply because Saturn is a hard task-master, and human life will need to harden itself by means of 'uncivilised ferocity' if it is to survive and move forward to its next development period.

When Moon moves to the following sign of Pisces she gives the rulership of Time over to Jupiter, so that humankind can leave the barbarism of Saturn behind in order to grow into a more enlightened and refined civilization.

Under the guidance of Jupiter, humankind experiences a period of tolerance, knowledge and wisdom.

Arriving at the third place of Aries, the Moon assigns Mars as the next ruler of Time.

Now humankind, civilised by the previous lord, Jupiter, may dedicate itself to learning the arts and refining their martial skills.

With the Moon's movement into the fourth sign of Taurus, Venus now receives control over Time, and she occupies her period by training humankind in learned speech and educating in the sciences of the humanities.

Having come this far in their rudimentary development, humankind is now ready to learn the more refined aspects of human culture such as languages, literature, philosophy, religion, art and musicology, so that this species can become skilled in debate and observe good manners in their social gatherings.

Firmicus adds that the wise men gave Venus rulership over this period because they wanted men to be *protected by a joyful and health-giving divinity*. [3]

Finally Mercury claims the fifth and final period of Time when the Moon passes over Gemini on its return to Cancer.

During Mercury's term the human race is purified of crude habits and is at its optimum in skills and learned sciences.

Unfortunately, humankind appears to have lost its way during Mercury's duration and instead of reaping the benefits from the previous time periods, it has become divided in customs and beliefs and has turned to wicked and evil ways.

Dissent, friction and strife are the order of the day as *'different institutions and customs arose, and wickedness and evil appeared and men invented and handed down wicked crimes'.*[4]

A Summary

The following chapters begin with Aristotle's Model of the Universe which commences at Saturn and finishes with the Moon.

This model is based on the Chaldean Order of the planets; it is a heliocentric model with the Sun at the centre of the spheres and Saturn (as the slowest visible planet) is furthest from the Earth.

An examination of the Chaldean Order is necessary to understand how the ancients viewed the universe and to appreciate that this is the beginning of our interpretation of the original seven planets.

In earlier times an astrologer's skill lay in being able to accurately judge whether a planet was in good condition or in poor condition, as this information was directly related to what the practitioner might expect from a planet in terms of its strength and its ability to express its true essence.

If a planet has the ability to express itself and if it is comfortable, then it is capable of being authentic, that is, true to its own nature, and hopefully this will work to the native's benefit.

A planet's condition is judged according to both the Essential Dignities and the Accidental Dignities as this will provide the necessary information on the planet.

Essential Dignities describe a planet's placement in a sign whilst Accidental Dignities describe environmental impacts on a planet, such as house placement, the joys, planetary sect, and the relationship between a house and its ruling planet.

Thema Mundi lays out the planets' relationships with one another, and both friendly and hostile relationships are explored in a future chapter, as the inaugural link between planets has left an indelible mark, one which is repeated in every astrological chart. Chapter Four reproduces al-Biruni's Table of Friendship and Enmity of the Planets and the on-going impact of the planets' relationships.

Chapters Five and Six list the contributing factors which form the basics of a sign's constitution, such as the four qualities (hot, cold, wet and dry) which make up the elements, the aspects which connect the signs, and the planets which rule the signs that ultimately creates the conditions under which a planet thrives (or merely survives) in a chart.

The connection between Accidental Dignity and the twelve houses is explained in Chapter Seven on houses.

Chapter Eight discusses the differences between the quadrant style house systems and the whole sign house system.

Throughout the book there are a number of diagrams to accompany the text and to illustrate certain techniques and ideas originating from the Thema Mundi chart.

A number of the terms are unusual to our modern ears but re-instating them into our language is important as these were common to traditionalists and deserve to be resurrected and included once more in the astrological vocabulary.

Terms such as

'native' describes the individual or chart owner;

'sect' is the name given to the division between night and day;

'dispositor' means the owner of a sign (as in Mars is the dispositor of Aries);

'benefics and malefics' are categories used to describe planets from which we hope to gain essentially good or fortunate experience (benefics), and planets that we often handle badly or perceive to result in troublesome or painful experiences (malefics), and

'passive or debilitated' apply to certain houses in a chart.

For the most part, these expressions are explained in detail in future chapters with the hope that they begin to filter back into our consciousness, as the techniques of traditional astrology become integrated with modern ideas and its practice becomes widespread within the broader astrological community.

CHAPTER TWO

The Chaldean Order of the Planets

"The nitrogen in our DNA, the calcium in our teeth, the iron in our blood, the carbon in our apple pies were made in the interiors of collapsing stars. We are made of star-stuff."

- Carl Sagan, *Cosmos*

The term 'tiny universe' seems to be somewhat of an oxymoron. Universes are huge, not tiny, but astrophysicists agree that our link to the greater Universe is physical and that our bodies actually do contain *"star-stuff"*.

Without knowledge of this scientific fact, the ancients made the link far more substantial and real by reinforcing the philosophical and spiritual tie between the heavens and the physical world.

They believed that each person was made in the image of the universe using the same elemental materials of fire, air, water and earth, and humans were a reflection of the planets' energies and their essence.

Humans may be tiny in comparison to the heavens but the connection between the macrocosm and the microcosm was believed to be strong and irrefutable and astrology was the bridge which bound each small universe to the greater cosmos.

Thema Mundi's activation begins at the ascendant, with the Moon on the rise concurrent with the ascendant's degree, and is followed at thirty degree intervals by the Sun, Mercury, Venus, Mars, Jupiter and Saturn.

The planets in the Thema Mundi chart follow a particular order, as six of the planets are ranked from the fastest moving (the Moon) to the slowest moving (Saturn), with the exception of the Sun which should rightly be placed at the centre of the other planets if all seven planets were to obey the rule of movement.

The sequential speed of the planets is known as either the Ptolemaic System, after Claudius Ptolemy, or the Chaldean Order, in honour of the Chaldeans of Babylon, and is the philosophical basis of a number of techniques practised in astrology *(Fig. 3 and Fig. 3a)*.

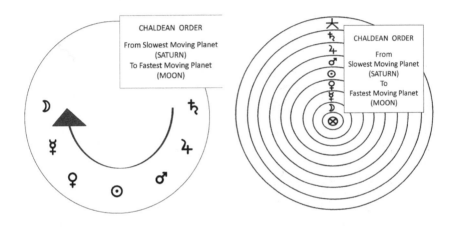

Fig. 3 Chaldean Order
of the Planets

Fig. 3a Chaldean Order
of the Planets

The Chaldean Order was adopted by the Greek philosophers and in its day became known as Aristotle's Model of the Universe. It has had a deep and lasting effect on astrological principles, as according to Aristotle, the soul descended through the heavens by alighting at each of the planets' spheres on its descent to the earthly realm.

With the pure essence of each planet collected on its downward movement the soul arrived at the Moon where it waited for the correct moment of the native's birth where physical manifestation took place and the soul joined with the body.

When the native's birth took place, the natal chart reflected the planets' celestial involvement with the soul through their zodiac signs and the aspects created by the signs, and whatever resulted from the fusion of energies, was then experienced by the chart owner during their lifetime on Earth.

The Descent of the Soul

Roman writer Macrobius Ambrosius Theodosius (390-430 CE) is famous for his classical *Seven Books on Saturnalia,* a series of dialogues conducted between learned philosophers at a fictional banquet during the holiday of Saturnalia and composed in the early part of the fifth century.

Macrobius also wrote a Commentary on Cicero's *Dream of Scipio,* a discourse on the nature of the cosmos and the constitution of the universe from a classical point of view.

In his Commentary, Macrobius discusses the soul's journey through the spheres of the seven planets as it descends from the highest heavens to manifest as physical matter on Earth.

Many Stoics and Neo-Platonic philosophers believed the soul was released from the eighth sphere of the Ogdoad (or the dwelling place of the Prime Mover of the heavens), and continued its journey to Earth by travelling through the seven descending heavens belonging to the planets, stopping at each of the spheres to collect or extract the planet's essence *(Gr. esse).*

The soul received certain benefits from a planet as each planet bestowed a gift unique to its own nature, in order that the soul gain divine properties and be guided by insight once it was far from its celestial origins.

Even the so-called 'malefics' (Saturn and Mars) provided worthy talents for the soul as nothing created by the Prime Mover could contain an essence of an evil or destructive nature.

Rather it was the individual's own excesses or mismanagement of the malefics which brought heartache or despair, and not the planet itself.

Astrologically, the soul descended through the Chaldean Order in the order of Saturn, Jupiter, Mars, the Sun, Venus, Mercury and the Moon, where it pauses to await the appropriate moment of birth according to the chart chosen by the soul before its descent.

According to Macrobius when the soul encounters Saturn's heaven, the seventh sphere, it gains the powers of reasoning and theorizing.

At the next sphere, one level closer to the Earth, the soul alights on Jupiter where it is shown the manner in which Saturn's gifts of reason and critical analysis can be put into practice so that the soul can direct the body towards worldly success or spiritual enlightenment.

The fifth heaven is Mars' domain where the soul obtains the power of 'ardent vehemence', thereby adding a passionate, courageous or zealous quality to the soul.

Immediately below Mars at the halfway mark, the soul encounters the Sun, where it meets glorious light in its purest form and envisages the potential for its own illumination or enlightenment.

When it leaves the fourth heaven of the Sun the soul absorbs the image of the Sun's spirit and brings with it the instinct for sensing or imagining the soul's full potential during the lifetime.

Macrobius says that when the soul descends to the third realm it inherits the motion of desire from Venus, whilst at Mercury's heaven the soul is given direction on ways in which to process, debate or manage Venus' desires.

At the second level from Earth, Mercury contributes to the soul's journey by bestowing the power of language in order for it to be capable of interpreting human feelings and giving expression to its emotions.

Finally, the soul enters the realm closest to the Earth.

This realm belongs to the Moon and the soul absorbs the Moon's essence which includes the awareness that it will soon experience the changes of physical movement, growth and eventual decay.

Macrobius comments on the soul's reaction to its impeding encounter with the process of physical manifestation and likens it to the human experience of drinking excessive amounts of alcohol.

"When the soul is drawn towards body – in this first production of it – it begins to experience a material agitation, matter flowing into it. And this is remarked by Plato in the Phaedo *(when he says) that the soul is drawn to body, staggering with recent intoxication"*[5].

Plato and Macrobius presume the soul's embodiment is an uncomfortable sensation, yet it is necessary for the soul so that its latent ability can be awakened within the boundaries of the temporal world and through the combined experiences of the body and the spirit.

Maurus Servius Honoratus, a contemporary of Macrobius, was a Latin grammarian, commentator and teacher whose works were deeply respected by Macrobius, and Servius is listed as one of the honoured guests present at the feast celebrated in *Saturnalia*.

Servius was famous for a valuable Commentary on Virgil, but a lesser known work on the descent of the soul talks about the connection between planets and the virtues which affected the psyche.

Servius differs from Macrobius' view that the planets were the soul's benefactors, and on first observation of Servius' text, it seems he believed that the planets were more harmful to the psyche, passing on negative attributes which caused strife and disruption to the soul rather than giving their blessings.

One analyst on Servius' Commentary states that the spheres were regarded as inimical or dangerous to the good of the soul, and that the planets' energies were directly responsible for a soul's struggle between the body's good or bad actions.

> *"The philosophers tell us what the soul loses in its descent through the separate spheres. For which cause also the Mathematici imagine that our body and soul are knit together by the powers of the separate divinities, on the supposition that when the souls descend, they bring with them the sluggishness of Saturn, the desire for rule of Jupiter, the passionateness of Mars, the lustfulness of Venus, and the cupidity of Mercury. And these things perturb souls, so that they are unable to use their own energy and proper powers."*[6]

In Book 12 of his *Metaphysics* Aristotle describes God as the Unmoved Mover, not a contradiction in terms, but rather an immortal unchanging being (Unmoved) who is the directing force of the planets (the Mover), and who is ultimately responsible for unity and order in the mundane world.

The Unmoved Mover is incapable of imperfection or imbalance, and by extension, the planets themselves are incapable of evil in their role as the celestial vehicles of the Mover's will.

Speculation on Servius' words invites discussion over whether the planets were directly responsible for weaknesses which led to the soul's ruin, or in fact, his text is a warning to his readers of a list of possible temptations for the soul, which could best be summed up by each planets' excesses.

It may be that his writing is a direction of the planets' intentions towards acting as the soul's divine councillors, or daemons, who provide their own interpretation of areas where the soul may struggle towards evil-doing on Earth.

The luminaries were exempt from Servius' list, as either they were above such evil doings or spiritual advice was not included in their list of duties, especially considering that the Sun signified the purity of divine light, and the Moon was the keeper of all things belonging to the physical realm.

However, the five planets in order of descent from Saturn to Mercury, may have counselled the soul to avoid specific pitfalls deemed catastrophic when the soul assumed physical form on Earth.

If Macrobius is so public in his praise of Servius' opinions by immortalizing him as an honoured guest in *Saturnalia*, it is hard to imagine that these two literary powers of their day, would disagree on a fundamental philosophy such as the descent of the soul.

However, regardless of how we might interpret Servius' meanings, a comparison between the surviving texts of two writers from the fifth century demonstrates the credence the ancients placed on astrology and the planets' involvement in the soul's experiences on Earth.

DESCENT OF THE SOUL—TWO OPINIONS (from 5th C.)

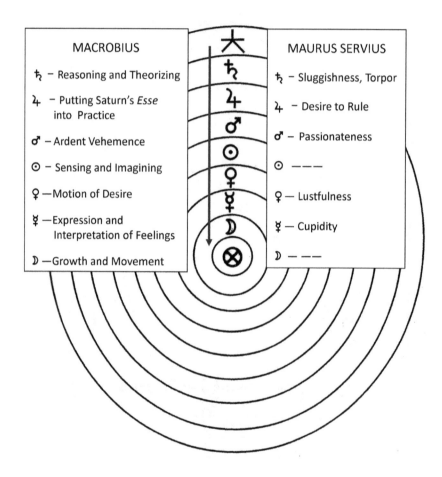

Fig. 4 Comparison between Macrobius and Maurus Servius' Descent of the Soul

Pre-Birth and the Chaldean Order

The Months of Gestation: When Soul Becomes Manifest

The marriage between Aristotle's Model of the Universe and astrology was not a new revelation as it reached backwards in time beyond Mesopotamia (and the Chaldeans), and had a direct effect on several principles and practices when it came to the span of a human's lifetime.

The Chaldean Order was the model used to describe the nine months before birth (Omar's Disposition of the Months), and it provided the skeleton for preordained time periods within a person's life.

The Ages of Man begin at birth with the Moon and end in old age with Saturn, whilst the time period system of Firdaria ran through the Chaldean Order beginning at birth with either the Sun for a day-time birth, or at the Moon with a night birth, and continued in the same vein as the descent of the soul.

When a life on Earth ended, the soul was believed to ascend at the native's death, and on its way back to the highest level of the Ogdoad, to return in opposite order to each planet cleansing itself of the pollution (specific to the planet) which it had accumulated during its time on Earth.

Once it was decontaminated, the pure soul would wait at the Ogdoad until its next descent to its new body and life, thereby repeating the cycle until achieving the highest level of enlightenment, when it would no longer be required to return to a string of temporary bodies for short periods of earthly learning existence.

Classical philosophers were fascinated by the soul, so the question of how and when a soul became manifest (L. *'manifestus'* is *'that which may be laid hold of by the hand'*) was open to interpretation and Omar's text provides an insight into how an astrologer might view the process.

Five centuries after Omar, Guido Bonatti, who was aware of Omar (referring to him as Aomar), and his idea of the planets' influence on the physical growth of the foetus in the mother's womb, also laid out a process of the soul entering a developing foetus in a similar fashion to Omar's text.

Omar of Tiberias from the late 8th century CE, is believed to have translated the first century works of Hellenistic astrologer Dorotheus of Sidon into Arabic text, and for this reason, Omar demonstrated early Hellenistic concepts and their influence on Arabic era astrology.[7]

In his final book of *Three Books on Nativities,* under the added title *The Disposition of the Months* from a later translated edition, Omar discusses the nine months of gestation, offering a more practical perspective than Macrobius and Servius, and commenting on the planets' direct influence on the unborn child.

Omar lists each planet's involvement with the developing foetus chronologically, beginning from the embryo and noting Saturn's involvement at this, the earliest of life's stages:

"When the seed falls into the vulva in the first month, it happens in the disposition of Saturn, and he disposes of the native by means of cold"[8].

Omar looks at the nine months of incubation and dedicates a planet to each month in the Chaldean Order from Saturn at germination, to the Moon at the seventh month, and then returns to Saturn and Jupiter and their engagement in the final two months of pregnancy.

This re-occurrence of Saturn and Jupiter's participation in the eighth and ninth month allows for the seven planets to adequately cover the full nine months of gestation.

Italian mathematician, astronomer and astrologer Guido Bonatti (1210-1296) was the most celebrated astrologer of the 13th century.

Bonatti adopts Omar's ideas when connecting the Chaldean Order with conception and foetal growth:

"Saturn is in the first circle of the planets, and is the first planet in the order of these, and the one which all of the others follow; and he is also the first planet which engages in its own working upon the one who has been conceived after the fall of seed into the womb, binding together and assembling that matter from which is formed the one who has been conceived."[9]

Bonatti is far more detailed in his explanation as he continues to explain that although the fixed stars on the highest Primum Mobile (the Prime Mover's) sphere are the principal agents of the soul's movement, they are *"...not experienced manifestly in these matters"*, and therefore, are not directly involved in the process of the soul's incarnation.

Rather, this responsibility falls solely to the planets beginning at the seventh sphere of Saturn, and continuing by the operations of the planets themselves in their role as secondary agents under the supervision of the Unmoved Mover.

Returning to the order which began with Saturn, Omar says that in the second month, Jupiter projects spirit into the native and: *"...disposes of him with a certain tempered quality"*, whilst Bonatti says that as Jupiter is the second planet, its role in the second month of gestation is to allot spirit and life, *"...according to its own workings"* and on a practical level, to provide warmth and humidity for one who has been conceived following Saturn's month.

Omar's text states that the third month belongs to Mars when life-giving blood strengthens the developing embryo.

Bonatti echoes this sentiment by saying that Mars, as the third planet in the Chaldean Order, is responsible for engaging in the growth process by enriching the blood and reddening it according to Mars' own red nature.

In the astrological model the first trimester of pregnancy is governed by the three superior planets Saturn, Jupiter and Mars.

The term superior refers to their position above the Sun in higher realms of heaven.

It is noteworthy that even with today's medical advancements, the first three months are still considered to be the most dangerous for the unborn child, so much so that the embryo is not technically regarded as a foetus until after the completion of the first trimester.

The fourth month belongs to the Sun, and Omar says that *"God breathes into the native the breath of life, that is, the animating principle"*.[10]

In Omar's model it is the Sun's responsibility in its role as the central figure in the Chaldean Order, to determine whether the soul will continue to descend as at this point the Sun's spirit enters the tiny body and animates the native's soul.

Omar explains the turning point for the soul's embodiment is analogous with the Sun animating the seasons and breathing life into the signs as it passes through each one over the course of a year.

Bonatti confirms the continuance of this belief, saying that the Sun is the fourth planet from Saturn following in the order of the planets, and that the Sun engages in its own working on one who has been conceived, by facilitating the growth of the foetus in the womb *"through natural heat or its like, by giving spirit and functional organs to the one conceived, vital soul, and the lines of the face."*[11]

After the Sun's month Omar says that the fifth month belongs to Venus and during this month God prepares the male or female sex in the native, whilst Bonatti comments that Venus is the fifth planet which engages in its own working on one who has been conceived, namely by finishing the sex of a man or a woman, whichever the sex of the one conceived should be, and by finishing for the native the nose and eyebrows and the entire arrangement of the face.

Omar follows Venus' time with the sixth month dedicated to Mercury whose task it is to bestow the unborn child with the physical attributes to develop language once birth has occurred.

Unfortunately Bonatti's text on the planets' involvement with the unborn child is incomplete.

His text is more concerned with the other planets' influence on Mercury and the Moon, rather than their place in the development of the foetus during the latter months of pregnancy.

Omar, on the other hand, continues through the full nine months with the planets' involvement saying that during the seventh month the Moon sets things in order, the native's image is completed, and should birth occur during the Moon's month, it is likely that the child will survive the birth.

However, if the infant is born in the eighth month belonging to Saturn, Omar warns the disposition of Saturn may cause disaster, *"... and the native will die if born in that month."*[12]

The text finishes with a note on the final month whereby disposition reverts to Jupiter, the natural significator for children in general, and the perfect overseer for a successful birth, and Omar says that the native will live,

"if God wills."[13]

THE CHALDEAN ORDER AND GESTATION

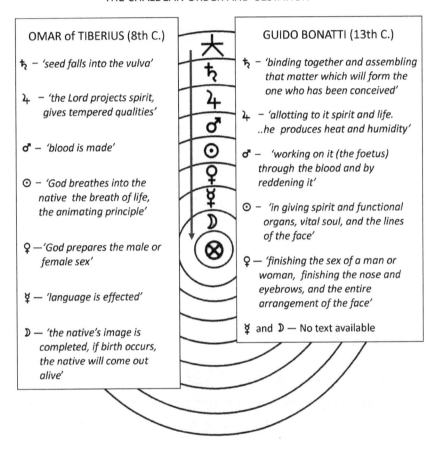

OMAR of TIBERIUS (8th C.)

♄ – 'seed falls into the vulva'

♃ – 'the Lord projects spirit, gives tempered qualities'

♂ – 'blood is made'

☉ – 'God breathes into the native the breath of life, the animating principle'

♀ –'God prepares the male or female sex'

☿ — 'language is effected'

☽ — 'the native's image is completed, if birth occurs, the native will come out alive'

GUIDO BONATTI (13th C.)

♄ – 'binding together and assembling that matter which will form the one who has been conceived'

♃ – 'allotting to it spirit and life. ..he produces heat and humidity'

♂ – 'working on it (the foetus) through the blood and by reddening it'

☉ – 'in giving spirit and functional organs, vital soul, and the lines of the face'

♀ — 'finishing the sex of a man or woman, finishing the nose and eyebrows, and the entire arrangement of the face'

☿ and ☽ — No text available

Fig. 5 Omar's Disposition of the Months and Bonatti's Reference to the Planets' involvement in the Development of Life

The Ages of Man

The Moon to Venus – Birth and Childhood

"Today you are you! That is truer than true! There is no one alive who is you-er than you!"

Happy Birthday to You! By Dr Seuss
Theodor Seuss Geisel (1904-1991)

Echoing the symbiotic relationship between macrocosm and microcosm, Claudius Ptolemy employs the Chaldean sequence of planets in reverse order to describe the progression of different psychological stages in human life, beginning at the Moon and finishing with Saturn.

These planetary periods are known as the Ages of Man.

They are divisions of time which demonstrate a particular focus or experience unique to the nature of a planet, and although the allotted time for each planet is generic in number, the quality and magnitude of the period differs according to the condition of the ruling planet in the native's chart.

Life begins with the Moon symbolising the first Age of Man from birth to four years of age as the human condition in infancy best reflects her own nature.

According to Ptolemy, the Moon's period describes the first four years of life when reason and the mind are not fully developed.

This leaves room for the Moon's emotional qualities to dominate the infant's reactions to external stimuli, and the Moon's instinctive drive toward survival to override conscious development of the intellect during this earliest period.

The Sun's reflected light on the Moon is symbolic of a constant strengthening in the baby's life-force as its own diminutive universe is learning to react by instinct and to acclimatize itself to the enormity of the world which surrounds it.

The child's first years bring rapid change so that it can adapt to an expanding physical environment, and in order for this to happen, the infant requires constant liquid nourishment and temperate living conditions, or at least, protection in extreme climates.

This suits the nature of the Moon perfectly, especially when moisture and coolness, or a reduction in heat, are qualities best suited to the night-time rather than the day, and therefore are the Moon's own intrinsic qualities.

After the age of four the Moon releases the child into the care of Mercury in correspondence with the Chaldean Order, and the planet second from the Earth takes command for a period of ten years, lending its own qualities to the development of mind and character through *"imbibing the seeds of learning, and developing, as it were, the elements and germs of the genius and abilities, and their peculiar quality."*[14]

For a decade, Mercury assists with education, focuses on instruction and feeds the desire for knowledge in the ages between four and fourteen.

During Mercury's period the child is given the opportunity to learn to reason within their own unique framework, and to carry Mercury's seeds for individuation into the future, as personality evolves and other planets get ready to take charge of life.

"Give me the child until the age of seven and I will show you the man", is a quote attributed to Ignatius Loyola, the founder of the Jesuit order in 1540, which refers to the belief that a child's spiritual and moral indoctrination during the early years will remain with them throughout life.

The assumption that the adult's temperament, moral choices and religious affiliations can be moulded in the first seven years of life is not unique to the Jesuits, and in some ways the Ages of Man reflect a similar sentiment when Mercury rules four of the years before the child reaches their eighth birthday.

In a chapter entitled Quality of the Soul in Book Three of *Tetrabiblos*, Ptolemy states that Mercury, and its condition in the chart, is responsible not only for the quality of the mind, but also for the rational and spirited part of the soul, whilst the Moon provides indications as to the sensory and appetitive part of the soul.

If the first seven years of life are under the jurisdiction of the Moon and Mercury, then the Jesuit phrase has some merit, and the combination of these two planetary periods can create an imprint on the adult because of the two planets' impact on childhood experiences.

Both planets are highly susceptible to pressure from other planets, and later authors such as Guido Bonatti (c.1282 CE) note that the Moon signifies the 'quality of the soul' (Ptolemy uses this term as well) according to her commixture with the planets, because if she is joined with a good planet, the native's quality of soul will be good, but if she is with an evil planet, the quality of soul is affected by its maleficence.

Likewise, Mercury naturally signifies the infirmities of the soul such as *"the arrogant (person) belittling great matters, or the timid magnifying little ones, and horrible thoughts, the unquietness of the mind and doubt, such that the native seems out of his mind and similar things."*[15]

Akin to the Moon's signification, Bonatti states that if the planet with which Mercury is joined is well-disposed he signifies a good quality of soul, and if he is badly disposed, he signifies an evil quality of soul.

Ptolemy warns of being hasty in making rash judgements concerning the soul and says that arriving at an opinion of the soul's quality is a complicated task and a thorough investigation of all factors must be made, as *"the mind is liable to impulse in a multiplicity of directions"*[16].

However, Ptolemy did believe it to be possible to glean clues on the quality of the soul as his text is detailed in explaining the differences between the signs of Mercury and the Moon, their dispositors (the owner of the sign), and the other planets who dominate them, as each factor contributes much to the character of the soul.

Several centuries after Ptolemy, Johannes Schoener (1477-1547) also discusses The Ages of Man and remarks that a child's susceptible nature during Mercury's period is reflected by the planet itself as Mercury can mimic another planet's qualities, and will take on their nature if found under a planet's influence.

For instance, if Mercury connects with a planet of a hot and dry nature, then the other planet will stimulate the tongue and speech of the native and sharpen the child's reason and intellect, and they will become keen for the discipline of learning.

Schoener adds that if Mercury should be well disposed in a revolution (solar return) during its ten year period, this will be an excellent year for education, and the child will have a greater propensity for learning.[17]

The third Age of Man belongs to Venus whose eight years of government corresponds with her astronomical cycle covering the same period of time.

Once Mercury and the Moon have played their role in developing the mind, soul and character of the native, the reproductive nature of Venus encourages love, sex and procreation during this particular Age which lasts from fourteen years to twenty two years of age.

Ptolemy says that *"from Venus the movement of the seminal vessels originates, as well as an unrestrained impetuosity and precipitancy in amours"*[18]which is Ptolemy's way of saying: Beware the raging hormones of pubescent teenagers!

Venus still plays an active part in the teenage years today, as adolescents begin to develop intense social and sexual relationships during this third Age, often connecting through social media and cyber-space.

The focus on Venus from fourteen to twenty two years of age may have differed in the 15th century, but Schoener's text indicates that not much has changed when it comes to love: *"If at that time Venus is the lady of a year (solar return ruler), the native will become most fervent in love; he will enjoy scented substances, beautiful ornaments, music, entertainments with lutes, hunts, fowling and similar things which delight the soul."*[19]

The Sun to Saturn – Moving Through Adulthood

"When I was a child, I spoke as a child, I understood as a child, I thought as a child: but when I became a man, I put away childish things."

1 Corinthians 13:11,
The Bible, King James Version (KJV)

In the Chaldean Order the Sun bestows light and divides the planets into three up and three down. By analogy the fourth Age of Man is ruled by the central Sun, and it is this Age which becomes the pivotal point of life, marking the end of childhood and the beginning of adulthood at twenty two years of age.

The Sun holds sway over nineteen years and determines the manner in which the native gains authority and glory, how he distinguishes himself amongst his peers, and how he applies the knowledge and experience he has gained from the previous three Ages belonging to the Moon, Mercury, and Venus respectively.

By leaving behind Venus' Age and entering into the Age belonging to the Sun, the young adult is encouraged to abandon 'puerile irregularities' in pursuit of more orderly conduct, in other words, to concentrate less on love, and more on his station in life.

Schoener comments that the hot and dry nature of the Sun loosens Venus' velvet grip and inclines the native to a desire for glory.

The Sun makes him bold in his affairs, intelligent, sagacious, and avid for the gathering of riches, honours and magistracy.

Childhood is definitely set aside as Schoener tells us that under the influence of the Sun, *"the native will become a lover of justice, and will withdraw himself from jests and sport, and will go towards serious matters, and will seek glory, honour, and a good name."*[20]

Mars is the first of the three superior planets to claim ordinance over the life, and the fifth Age comes at a time when the native, having gained worldly success from the Sun, must apply cunning and tenacity to hold on to any power gained during the Sun's double decade.

The Mars period lasts from forty one to fifty six years of age, and often wears down the native's stamina due to its propensity for trouble.

After the apparent ease of the previous Sun period, the native must draw on their inner strength if they are to be resourceful, resilient or courageous in order to triumph over the stresses brought on by Mars' Age.

Mars shares the same hot and dry qualities as the Sun who directs the native sagaciously and with due care, using its heat to drive enthusiasm and maintain self-confidence, and its dryness to focus on the task at hand.

On the other hand, Mars amplifies the same qualities according to its own nature, and its recklessness can produce destructive traits, inclining the native towards vices such as greed or wastefulness.

Mars 'excess heat triggers anger or argumentativeness, agitating the mind and stirring the soul towards malcontent, and coupled with its extremely dry quality, Mars can inflame or irritate the body creating chronic health problems during its fifteen year reign.

Schoener warns that during the period of Mars' dominance, the body begins to lose its youthful vitality, and that although the native will be inclined to rashly start many projects, he will encounter difficulty when his strength falters and he ignores the signs of aging, preferring instead to use sheer will-power or physical force to bring them to completion.

Jupiter follows in the correct succession of planets, influencing the sixth Age, and taking possession for twelve years to occupy the mind, body and spirit from the ages of fifty six to sixty eight years of age.

The human's tiny universe is now definitely slowing down after the wearisome years of Mars, and the soul is now keen to acquire the mantle of wisdom through the virtues of prudence and temperance.

If Jupiter is well placed in the chart and is in good condition, the native can expect a bountiful period of privilege, at a time when the younger generation will honour them and seek them out to gain favour and advantage for themselves.

Schoener says of this period that because Jupiter's nature is warm and moist, the native will be inclined towards divine and religious concerns, and that they will willingly withdraw themselves from mundane cares and labours in order to direct their minds towards eternal matters.

The native will discipline their mind to abandon shameful thoughts, speeches and deeds, and they will exercise their body leisurely, no longer exposing themselves to dangerous pursuits.

The seventh and final Age in the Chaldean Order belongs to Saturn who, as the custodian of old age, understands that its guardianship will most likely be the last, heralding in the "age of decrepitude", according to Schoener's text.

Saturn's period lasts for thirty years, beginning at sixty eight years and continuing until just short of a century, with its cold, dry nature intensifying over the three decades.

Old bones become brittle, the back bends under the weight of age, and Saturn does its utmost to restrict enjoyment and calcify both mind and body so that any remaining zest for life quietly steals away.

Ptolemy says that during this period Saturn destroys the mind as it weakens mental acumen, rendering the native to become an 'imbecile and dumb'[21]; the encroaching dullness of the mind matching the dullness of the body.

Schoener adds to this by saying Saturn affects not only the body, as it "weakens and bends the body of the native, who, shaking and fastened to a staff will walk with difficulty; but also darkens the spirit, "troubled in everything, the native will not care for joys and comforts."

Schoener says that Saturn makes the mind serious and discerning when it comes to the most important matters in life, *"but he will hold those things which are empty of joy and happiness in contempt, for intent on other things, therefore, he talks about his deeds."*

Ptolemy goes no further than Saturn's period, presuming that death occurs during its three decades, but Schoener adds that if the native should survive past their ninety ninth year, the cycle begins again with the Moon ruling the next four years to the age of one hundred and two years.

Schoener says that once more the native will become moist like an infant, and although few persons live beyond this second period of the Moon, if they should do so he adds somewhat unkindly,

"they become tedious both to themselves and to others."

Planet	Period	Age
☽	4 yrs	0 – 4 years
☿	10 yrs	4 – 14 years
♀	8 yrs	14 – 22 yrs
☉	19 yrs	22 – 41 yrs
♂	15 yrs	41 – 56 yrs
♃	12 yrs	56 – 68 yrs
♄	30 yrs	68 – 98 years
☽	4 yrs	98 – 102 years

THE SEVEN AGES OF MAN

	Planet
Allotted Years	Begins At....
(♄) 30 yrs	68 yrs old (♄)
(♃) 12 yrs	56 yrs old (♃)
(♂) 15 yrs	41 yrs old (♂)
(☉) 19 yrs	22 yrs old (☉)
(♀) 8 yrs	14 yrs old (♀)
(☿) 10 yrs	4 yrs old (☿)
(☽) 4 yrs	(☽) BIRTH / 98 yrs old

Fig. 6 The Ages of Man

The End of Life

The Soul's Ascension According to Hermes Trismegistus

After the soul completed the physical side of life on Earth it returned to the upper reaches of heaven by reversing the order of its descent, this time beginning at the Moon and passing through each of the planet's heavens. Whilst on its upward journey the soul became lighter and pure in essence by depositing any impurities it may have gathered whilst on the physical plane at the appropriate planet's level of heaven.

The *Hermetica* are Egyptian-Greek wisdom texts from the 2nd century C.E. presented as dialogues between a teacher, Hermes Trismegistus (Thrice-greatest Hermes) and his student.

In one such text entitled *Poemandres,* the Divine Pymander or "Shepherd of Men", passes on his wisdom to Hermes and tells him that once death occurs the material body surrenders the habit of life, void of energy, to the Guardian Angel.

The senses of the body separate and are returned to the natural energies of Nature, and the part of man which remains, his spirit, speeds upwards through the Harmony of the Spheres, or the seven zones of the planets, to be reunited with the Powers of the Ogdoad who reintroduce the soul to God and reveal His infinite Wisdom to the soul.

At each of the zones the spirit becomes lighter and is purged as it surrenders negative attributes learned on Earth at each of the seven spheres.

According to Plato, the soul consisted of three separate parts or levels (the Tripartite Soul), which was comprised of the highest level, the Rational soul, the next level, the Spirited soul, and the lowest level known as the Appetitive soul.

Most of the soul's purging involved the Appetitive soul which was inclined to stray from the true and righteous path of Reason and Spirit by pursing every desire and passion with which the body could possibly distract the soul.

THE ASCENT OF THE SOUL

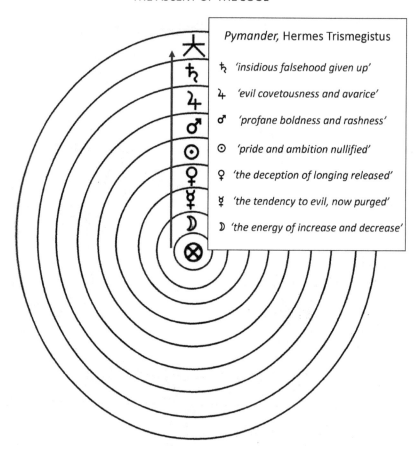

Fig. 7 The Soul's Ascent according to Hermes Trismegistus

At the Moon, the soul gives up the energy of augmentation and diminution (the constant change and corruption of physical matter which is the Moon's domain).

To the second sphere belonging to Mercury, the soul purges itself of the tendency to evil.

At Venus' station, the soul gives up the deception of incontinence, unfaithfulness and sexual longing.

When the soul arrives at the Sun, pride and ambition are surrendered and nullified.

At Mars, the fifth sphere, profane boldness and unseemly rashness are left behind.

At the sixth sphere of Jupiter the soul surrenders evil covetousness and avarice.

Finally at Saturn's seventh sphere the soul abandons insidious falsehood.

After releasing at each of the planets' spheres the soul is met at the eighth sphere by those who have already arrived: *"And then, denuded of all the energies of the seven spheres, clad in his proper power, he cometh to that nature which belongeth to the Eighth Sphere,.....They who are there rejoice at his coming, and he, being made like unto them, hears the Powers of the Ogdoad who are above Nature, hymning unto God in the sweet voice that is their own."*[22]

The Planets' Significations: Past and Present

	Modern Interpretation of Planets
SATURN	Stability; Responsibility; Good judgement; Ease with Authority; Expertise gained through experiment and experience; Self-control; Father
JUPITER	Benefit; Largesse; Self-confidence; Good Fortune; Adventure; Education; Wisdom; Elevated Professions; Success; Ambition; Expansion
MARS	Competitiveness; Confidence; Energy; Excitability; Rashness; Anger; Impatience; Passion; Spontaneity
SUN	Direction; Purpose; Reputation; Vitality; Ambition; Self-expression; Personality; Inner Self; Ego; Father
VENUS	Ease and comfort with others; Social skills; Beauty; Style or grace; Women; Relationships; Music; The Arts
MERCURY	Reasoning ability; The Mind; Business and marketing skills; Cognitive skills; Memory; Communication
MOON	Emotions; Instincts; Physical comfort; Style of nurturing; Emotional security; The body; Mother

Fig. 8 The Significations of the Planets (Modern)

The preceding Table *(Fig. 8)* shows the areas into which each of the planets extends their influence over the native's life.

There has been little alteration in the list since traditional times, and both medieval and modern astrologers will recognise many of the qualities and characteristics listed above.

The Table below *(Fig. 9)* is an extract taken from eleventh century astrologer, al-Biruni, who provided detailed and extensive lists on the planets and their Indications, in his textbook, *The Book of Instruction in the Elements of the Art of Astrology.*

Al-Biruni covered such diverse topics as descriptions on the nature of the planets (Notes 396-401); their individual properties, form, and climates (402-406); places and countries (407-408); metals, jewels and fruits (409-411); plants, foods, states of being and powers (412-417; the animal world (418); the body – humours, vital organs, senses and periods of life (419-426); relations, physical attributes, disposition, morals and disease (427-432); and lastly, religions, pictorial representations of the planets, and professions (433-435).

The Table demonstrates that little has changed over the considerable gap of time, countries of origin, and philosophical differences, between Plato, Macrobius, Servius and al-Biruni, when it comes to the planets' significations.

al-Biruni's Notations	Powers #417	Disposition #429	Activities #430	Morals #430
♄	Retentive power	Fearful, truth-telling, Melancholy, grave	Exile and poverty, Wealth by trickery	Enslaving people by Violence and treachery
♃	Vital, growing nutritive faculties	Inspiring, intelligent, Devout, honourable	Friendliness, Peace-maker, charitable	Responsible, but with Levity and recklessness
♂	Passion	Ignorant, rash, bold, Violent, cheerful	Travelling, litigation, Ruinous at business	Solitary, lustful Spiteful and tricky
☉	Youthful vigour	Patient, chaste, Eager for victory	Longing for power, And government	Hankering after wealth And management
♀	Coition, sensuality	Good-natured, pride, Joy, friendliness	Jesting, fond of wine, Dancing, chess	Well-spoken, laughing, Lazy, cheating
☿	Speaking, faculty of reflection	Sharp intelligence, Longing for reputation	Teaching manners, Theology, logic	Frivolous, slanderous, Busybody, thieving
☽	Natural power (power over nature)	Pure in heart, timid, Forgetful, loquacious	Over-anxious for Health and comfort	Lying, generous, too Uxorious (fond of wife)

Fig.9 al-Biruni's Interpretations (11th C. CE)

The Chaldean Order and The Twelve Houses

Planets as Co-Significators

Johannes Schoener was a fifteenth century astrologer who wrote a concise compendium of astrological principles, ideas, and methods as they were practiced at the end of the Middle Ages entitled *Opusculum Astrologicum.*

Canon Five contains a diagram of the houses, their meanings, their value according to a point system, and also lists the planets which Schoener termed as the house's 'co- significator'.[23]

These co-significators commence at the first house with Saturn, and run in the Chaldean Order through the houses.

For instance, Schoener says the first house *"is called the Horoscope or Ascendant in which is the life of Men, spirit, and the constitution of the body, & whatever happens to the body."*

He then adds *"Saturn is Co-significator".*

THE PLANETS AS CO-SIGNIFICATORS OF THE HOUSES

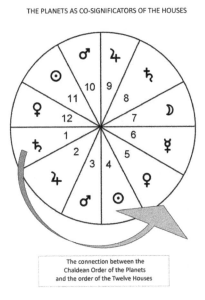

The connection between the
Chaldean Order of the Planets
and the order of the Twelve Houses

Fig. 10 Schoener's Twelve Houses with the Planets in the Chaldean Order as Co-significators of the Houses

The term co-significator is indicative of a type of kinship or a state of harmony or connection between house and planet, rather than a clear case for rulership of the house, but it demonstrates the desire to theoretically link the planet (macrocosm) with the individual's chart (microcosm).

In Schoener's model Jupiter follows Saturn in planetary order, and takes its place as the co-significator for the second house of wealth and substance.

Mars is named as the co-significator for the third house of siblings.

Schoener identified the Sun as the father figure who is in agreement with the fourth house, and so the houses follow with their co-significators identified in descending order through the list of inferior planets which reside below the Sun.

Accordingly Venus is congruent with the nature of the fifth house, Mercury takes the sixth, and the Moon corresponds with the seventh house of partners and alliances.

As there are more houses than planets, the order is repeated.

Commencing the cycle of planets once more with Saturn who co-signifies the eighth house, the planets follow in the correct Chaldean Order with Jupiter as co-signifier of the ninth house, Mars for the tenth, the Sun for the eleventh, and lastly, the twelfth house, where the co-significator role is reserved for Venus (*Fig. 10*).

Two centuries before Schoener, Guido Bonatti mentioned the same planet to house connection, and although Bonatti provides some text to explain the logical thought behind the theory, the text is incomplete and does not follow through to explain each house's relevance to the signifying planet.

Bonatti begins with Saturn's association with the first house and continues for five houses listing Saturn through to Venus, however, there is no further mention beyond the fifth house.

Bonatti writes that Saturn signifies the body, and the first house according to its own nature, that is, in creating a vehicle by which something can exist or come into being, as it signifies: "*the first thing that happens to a human being is the individuality (Latin: 'persona') through which existence is granted to a human being.*"[24]

Schoener's later model lists Saturn as co-significator for both the first and eighth houses, as Saturn signifies the house of birth when the soul manifests in concrete form, and Saturn also signifies the house of death when the same form is discarded and the soul ascends to the Ogdoad.

Logically, Saturn denotes both beginning of the physical journey and the end.

It binds and restricts the soul and imprisons it in flesh, but it also releases the soul from its material trappings when the time is right through the simple act of death.

Jupiter follows Saturn's two houses with the second house of wealth, which Jupiter is connected with in other systems, and the ninth house, the house of God.

In his description of the houses Schoener states that in the ninth house *"we seek piety, truth, the sects of mankind* (religion), *long journeys, wisdom, divination, philosophy, and the interpretation of dreams."*[25], so it would seem natural for Jupiter to correspond with this house.

Bonatti states that Jupiter is naturally the significator of substance (second house) because substance presents itself to the native as the second necessity for their survival, after the generation of the physical body as a result of their birth.

Mars is co-significator of the third house. Brothers and blood relations are require to defend the bloodline by responding to the call to arms and unite kindred to defend the honour or property of the native.

Regardless of their age and circumstances, siblings will fight amongst themselves and even compete for their share of parental attention, but if an external threat materializes, then the clan puts aside all personal grievances and becomes a united force.

Bonatti says that Mars is naturally the significator of travels and brothers, as brothers are the *"third accident that happens to the native after conception, to wit, after birth, and because a native loves the more among those who are able to encounter him first after birth"*, and because Mars is the third planet in the order of the planets after Saturn.

In Bonatti's times travel was potentially dangerous: *"in journeys many inconveniences, many difficulties, plundering, impious sufferings, and similar things happen to those who travel, all of which are like unto those things signified by Mars."*[26]

Mars is also dignified in the tenth house of honours, dominion, magisterial authority or office according to Schoener and this is a house hard fought for and won through courage and tenacity in the pursuit of power and control.

In order to hold on to that power Mars identifies with the need to be original, dynamic, and fearless, especially when others come to challenge the top position or usurp the leader of the pack.

The Sun and the fourth house both signify father so the connection is clear, and by repetition of the Chaldean Order the Sun follows Mars, so if Mars is in harmony with the tenth house, the Sun is a suitable candidate to signify the eleventh house, the house belonging to the Good Daemon.

In a later chapter Schoener says the eleventh house *"is dedicated to friends, counsellors, political supporters, hope and favours"*, so the Sun is free to add its light and warmth to a house both elevated in position and in nature, whilst at the same time avoiding the wear-and-tear of the tenth house which the Sun is happy to leave for Mars to fight the battles.

Bonatti precedes Schoener but adds little only linking the fourth planet (Sun) with the fourth house and noting that the Sun is also the natural significator for father in a diurnal chart.

Unlike the Sun which is the co-signifier for two fortunate houses being the fourth and the eleventh houses, Venus on the other hand, holds the position of co-significator to two houses with very different meanings in the chart.

The fifth planet in the Chaldean Order corresponds to the fifth house, *Agathe Tyche* or Good Fortune, in which is found the condition of children, and of favours, gifts and garments.

Venus is well suited to this house, and in fact, if Venus is physically placed in the fifth house she gains accidental dignity through being in the house of her Joy.

Bonatti says that Venus signifies the fifth house as she is the fifth planet from Saturn, and she is the planet of delight and joy.

Likewise, the fifth house is assigned to children, and Venus signifies children because they are the happenstance in which the native rejoices more than any other house.

However, when the Chaldean Order is repeated, and Saturn co-signifies the eighth house, Venus once more becomes the fifth planet after Saturn, and this leaves her as the co-significator of the twelfth house.

This is no longer a house of joy, but perhaps in the ancients' minds, Venus stands as the bridge between the house of imprisonment, or one's undoing, and silent misery, and ultimately, the weakening or pollution of the soul.

Ancient texts abound with dire warnings of the consequences of dalliances with amoral sexual partners, of excessive eating and drinking, and Pluto's tripartite model of the soul includes the Appetitive part which has the potential to ruin the soul, or at the very least, to distract the more reverent parts of Reason and Spirit through engagement in the base pleasures of life.

In Schoener's diagram Mercury is co-significator for just one house – the sixth house known as *Cace Tyche* or the house of Evil Fortune.

The ancients were understandably cautious when it came to Mercury; it was the spiritual significator for both the mind and the soul, and yet its position alongside the Sun meant that it was often burnt by the Sun, or appearing to move in a retrograde direction.

It was also incredibly unstable, changing gender, sect, dignity and behaviour, as it was constantly subject to the external influence of other planets.

In describing Mercury, first century astrologer Vettius Valens says: *"Mercury will make everything capricious in outcome and quite disturbed. Even more, it causes those having this star in malefic signs or degrees to become even worse."*[27]

When Mercury as the sixth planet after Saturn associates with the difficult and often unpredictable sixth house which indicates accidents, injuries, and illnesses, perhaps it is fortunate for the native that Mercury is robbed of the opportunity to create mischief in another part of the chart.

The Moon is the final planet in the Chaldean Order; as the seventh planet from Saturn the Moon counter-balances Saturn across the East West boundary of the chart and is the co-signifier of the seventh house.

Schoener tells us that the seventh house is *"The West* (and) *shows the dowry, the state of marriage, contentions, dissentions, and damages that come from the foregoing."*

With considerations such as these, it seems obvious for the Moon to be the herald and protector of such matters, for if the Moon is happy, then so too should marriage be a state of bliss, and the success of contentious matters ought to be reflected by the Moon's condition in the chart.

CHAPTER THREE

The Dignities

All men are mortal
Socrates is a man
Therefore, Socrates is mortal

In any introduction to logic, these three statements are used as one example of syllogism (Gr. *syllogismos,* "conclusion"), a method of traditional deductive reasoning that combines two existing statements to arrive at a conclusion.

The first two statements must be factual in order for the logic to be valid.

For instance, both the major premise *(all men are mortal)* and the minor premise *(Socrates is a man)* must be agreed upon to be true statements.

And the two premises must relate to one another in order for the conclusion to be an accurate representation of deductive reasoning.

The minor premise, "*Socrates is a man*" is deemed to be a genuine statement because Socrates is made of the correct material – blood, flesh, and bone – and his form is that of a male human being.

However, there is more to Socrates than his physical appearance.

Socrates is a man because he has the essence of humanity in him, and although his body exists and includes matter, this is not the same as his essence.

It is not enough to say that Socrates is a man because he has man-ness in him; the definition must include room for a special identifying sense of the essential qualities that a man might possess in order to confirm his humanity.

This is generally where soul and essence meet.

Socrates' soul may wish to guide his physical matter towards what it deems to be successful outcomes, but the ease or difficulty by which Socrates can potentially do this is determined by his essence.

Some of Socrates' essential qualities are pre-determined.

They cannot be changed since they are beyond his control and may have occurred even before his birth.

Factors such as genetic makeup, the history of family, the period in which he is born, or his country of birth, will affect the nature of his essence and whether it has the potential to materialise or be fulfilled during his body's time of Earth.

What happens after death can also express a man's essence since Socrates has continued to affect human consciousness for centuries, even though he recorded nothing tangible during his lifetime.

Instead, Socrates was immortalised through the dialogues of his devotees, Plato and Xenophon, and through the plays of Aristophanes.

Socrates was 'a man of his time'. Born in Athens five hundred years before Christ, Socrates belonged to the tribe of Antiochus, a fact which gave him automatic membership to the Athenian executive ruling council.

It can be assumed that the social advantages which Socrates enjoyed in his native city also helped to shape his essential qualities and to inspire Plato's written dialogues on the philosophy behind mankind's morals and virtues.

Other essential qualities are more personal.

For instance, more can be deduced about the nature and strength of Socrates' essence by adding

"Socrates is an ugly man with a brilliant intellect",

given that extant texts describe Socrates as profoundly ugly, resembling a satyr more than a man.[28]

Allegedly, he had wide-set bulging eyes, a flat nose with flaring nostrils and large fleshy lips.

He wore his hair long and wandered through Athens barefoot and unwashed, carrying a stick wherever he went as he walked with a peculiar gait that caused him to swagger like a sailor at sea, all of which did little to improve his physical appearance.

At a time when good looks and proper bearing were important for political advancement, Socrates possessed neither attribute yet his power and influence over Athens' aristocratic youth was both puzzling and alarming for their affluent parents who mistrusted this strange old man.

Socrates was impervious to the effects of alcohol and the cold, he never earned a living, preferring instead to live an austere life bordering on poverty, refusing payment for any service he provided as a philosopher and emphatically denying professional status as a teacher.

These conditions collectively describe Socrates' essential qualities, and tell us not just about the man, but also about his characteristics, his temperament, and his choices in fulfilling his destiny.

Rulership: The First Level of Essential Dignity

If a similar discussion on a planet's essential qualities began with the statement, *"Jupiter is the largest planet in the solar system"* it would provide knowledge towards Jupiter's matter and form, but would do little to describe its characteristics, its temperament, or its ability to perform its duty so far as the significations listed by al-Biruni in the previous Chapter on the Chaldean Order.

"Jupiter is a planet which is travelling through the sign of Pisces".

This statement identifies several factors concerning Jupiter: its matter (*planet*), its movement (*according to the ephemeris*) and the state of its essence (*in the sign of Pisces*).

Jupiter is essentially strong in Pisces because Pisces is one of its domicile signs *(Fig. 11, 12)* along with the fire sign, Sagittarius.

Jupiter's advantage in being situated in a sign which it rules is known as Essential Dignity, and there are five different levels where Jupiter, or any other planet, can profit from its transitory position in the zodiac circle.

PLANET	ESSENTIAL DIGNITY Rulership Signs	DEBILITY Detriment Signs (Opposing Rulership)
SATURN	Capricorn; Aquarius	Cancer; Leo
JUPITER	Sagittarius; Pisces	Gemini; Virgo
MARS	Aries; Scorpio	Libra; Taurus
SUN	Leo	Aquarius
VENUS	Taurus; Libra	Scorpio; Aries
MERCURY	Gemini; Virgo	Sagittarius; Pisces
MOON	Cancer	Capricorn

Fig. 11 Planets and Rulership: Domicile Signs and Signs of Detriment

*Fig. 12 Thema Mundi and the
First Level of Essential Dignity:
Rulership or Domicile Signs*

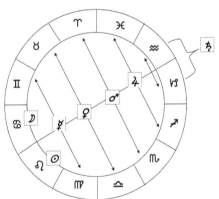

*Fig. 12a The Shared Rulerships
of Thema Mundi*

"When a Planet is in its own domicile or in the sign of its own exaltation, it is like a man who is in his own house; and his decree and his own will is carried out – what he wishes to be done is done."[29]

Rulership benefits Jupiter when it is moving through Pisces or Sagittarius by providing it with the best opportunity to reach its potential as a dignified planet, and to bring success to anything it signifies through its essential qualities.

Rulership is the first of five levels of Essential Dignity – Rulership (or Domicile), Exaltation, Triplicity, Terms and Face – and although they are judged differently, each dignity allows a planet to express its essence, or to gain advantage through placement in a sign, and in the case of Terms and Face, through a grouping of degrees in a specified sign.

The ease or difficulty for any of the seven original planets to express or materialise their essence is described by the sign through which they are travelling in the heavens, and the more dignified the planet, the more likely it is to be able to achieve its purpose.

Traditional texts use the different levels of Essential Dignity for specific purposes, but all acknowledge the importance of Rulership and Exaltation and it is worth noting that these are the only two levels of Dignity, whereby the opposing signs of Rulership or Exaltation earn a mark against them and are described in terms of their debility.

The sign where a planet is considered to be in Detriment is opposite to Rulership or Domicile, and a planet in the sign of its Fall opposes the sign of its Exaltation.

There is no such debility for oppositions to the dignities of Triplicity, Term or Face.

"A planet in a place where it has no dominion is like a person who is not in his own country."[30]

If a planet is not in dignity, it is called peregrine, and this includes planets in detriment or fall.

This term is derived from the same word as 'pilgrim' and describes a planet wandering through a sign which is foreign to its nature.

The planet cannot exercise influence or gain power, in much the same way as a wandering pilgrim or an impoverished stranger is treated with suspicion when they enter a tightly insulated community.

If something goes amiss whilst the stranger is in the location, they are vulnerable to accusations or punishment purely from the fact that they are different or an unknown quantity to the local people of the district.

There are different opinions as to whether the individual with dignified planets in their chart will directly benefit, or gain happiness or success, from their elevated planets.

Robert Hand has played a major role in the translations from the texts of the old masters in astrology and he has been at the forefront of the resurrection of traditional techniques.

His involvement in Project Hindsight with Robert Zoller and Robert Schmidt in the early 1990's allowed so many current astrologers access to astrological teachings from Greek, Latin and Arabic sources which had previously been accessible to scholars outside of our field.

Robert has continued his passion for traditional astrology by lecturing across the globe and through his ARHAT (Archive for the Retrieval of Historical Astrological Texts) Media website.

Robert offers the opinion that the impact on planets when they become essentially dignified can be better understood if the medieval term *"intensive magnitude"* is reintroduced to best describe a sliding scale which places a planet's essence at its maximum level of intensity when it is dignified, or to see its essence at its lowest level of intensity when it is debilitated in detriment or fall.[31]

"Intensive magnitude" means that the planet is best able to act with authenticity, to be genuine or true to its own nature.

Pukka is originally a Hindu cooking term which has entered the English language meaning cooked, ripe, or mature.

If something is *pukka* it means that it is solid, reliable, perfectly or properly constructed to be exactly what it was meant to be.

Pukka means that the food being described is in its peak form and anyone consuming the food can be confident that what they are eating is guaranteed to be authentic, that is, legitimate, credible and original in flavour, texture and taste.

This term *pukka* is an excellent word to describe a planet when it has dignity.

It is as rich and as robust and as bona fides (meaning good faith) as it is going to be according to Essential Dignities.

However, a planet in debility has poor *pukka* quality.

It struggles to be solid or to achieve its maximum capabilities, its intensity is watered down or spoiled by being in a sign which least describes its essence, so the planet's ability to be competent or consistent is compromised by its poor situation.

Robert Hand makes the comment that a dignified planet in the chart is not an automatic guarantee of good fortune or benefit for the chart's owner, and that it is not a matter of judgement over whether it is good or bad for a planet to be essentially dignified, it is merely a difference in the style of a planet's energy.

For instance, you may eat a food which, to all intents and purposes, qualifies as *pukka,* but if you are allergic to it then the genuine nature of the food makes little difference to your body's reaction to it.

In fact sometimes, its richness makes the impact of your allergy even worse than it would have been if the food had not been so pure in essence.

Another leading medieval astrologer and translator, Benjamin Dykes, agrees that dignity shows competence and consistency in whatever the planet signifies by its essential nature[32] and although he does not use the same terms to describe dignity he is basically saying that the planet has maximum intensive magnitude and is therefore confident of its own strength and its ability to manifest its energy.

For instance, Mars in Aries or Scorpio is a fearsome competitor, whilst Venus in Libra or Taurus shows great potential to bring forth beauty, grace, artistry and ease in social relations.

Ben Dykes has a strong opinion on debility, stating that a planet in detriment conforms to the word's core meaning "corruption" and signifies a planet in discord with its own essence, suffering disintegration, lack of control and capable of impropriety or misconduct.

The affairs which this planet has control over are in disarray, or are obscure or uncertain in some way.

The debility of fall (opposite exaltation) brings disrespect or disrepute to the individual and generally indicates a difficulty that the native is trying to overcome.

The other term for fall is descension, and is used to describe someone who is rejected in some way, by being ignored, ostracised, downtrodden or despised by others.[33]

Twelfth century Hebrew astrologer Avraham Ibn-Ezra, has this to say on the two states of debility, which seems to support Ben Dykes' opinion on detriment and fall:

"A planet in its house of detriment is like a person fighting with himself."[34]

"A planet in its house of fall is like a person who has fallen from his great position."[35]

Exaltation: The Second Level of Essential Dignity

Firmicus gives an insight into the second level of Essential Dignities when he says that a planet in exaltation rejoices in its sign, as it is raised up to a maximum of its own natural force, and when it is in fall, it suffers the loss of that force.

According to Firmicus, natives who are born with exalted planets are fortunate and successful but debilitated planets in either detriment or fall make men wretched, poor, and plagued by bad luck.

Firmicus says that the Babylonians called the exalted signs their "houses", but says:

"In the doctrine we use, we maintain that all the planets are more favourable in their exaltations than in their own signs." [36]

A number of traditional authors agree with Firmicus that a planet in exaltation is more majestic than a planet in rulership, that it gains benefit as an honoured guest to whom all courtesies are extended, but is free from the responsibilities which burden a house owner.

The twelfth century Jewish scholar Avraham Ibn Ezra says:

"When a planet is in its domicile (rulership), *it is like a person in his home, but a planet in its exaltation is like a person at his greatest rank."* [37]

Whilst this statement may be true, an exalted planet is only as powerful as the planet which backs it up.

A planet in exaltation borrows a sign from its rightful owner, and the owner (called the dispositor of a sign) can greatly affect the height

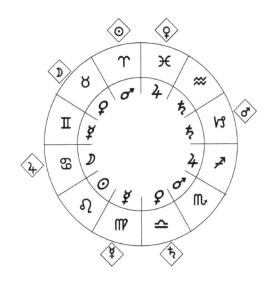

Fig. 13 Level One and Two of Essential Dignities: Rulership and Exaltation

to which an elevated planet can rise, and for how long it will remain in its lofty position.

For instance, Jupiter in Cancer is exalted so presumably it has the capacity to gain great power and influence on the native's behalf.

However, Jupiter is not the ruler of Cancer, and if the Moon is in a poor state, then Jupiter will suffer for it.

Jupiter in Cancer is limited by how high it can rise because the Moon, the owner of Cancer, is limited itself by its own poor condition.

The tenuous nature of exaltation becomes evident when one step further is taken to explore the planet behind the sign, as a Scorpio Moon in fall or a Capricorn Moon in detriment will ultimately ruin Jupiter's chances of success.

The concept of ownership or dispositorship as it was known comes into play, and although Jupiter may be an honoured guest, if he is living in a house of thieves or disreputable villains rather than temporarily residing in the mayor's house, then he will suffer by association.

"Each of the planets has powers in the signs. Some of them are by nature; some by accident. Those by nature are: house (domicile or rulership), exaltation, triplicity, term and face." [38]

Two distinct categories of Dignity exist in order to illustrate two different, but often complementary, planetary circumstances which Guido Bonatti (1210-1296) describes as being by nature or by accident.

Essential Dignity describes the natural affinity between a planet and particular signs, whilst Accidental Dignity describes a planet's situation according to certain environmental factors surrounding the planet.

The distinction between the two categories is quite specific. However, there are times when one type of dignity will affect the other, and the choice a planet makes for its exaltation is one example of cross-pollination between nature and accident.

Exaltation is the second level of Essential Dignity, but the connection between a planet's rulership sign, and its exalted sign, is determined by the Accidental Dignity known as Sect.

Planetary Sect divides a chart into two distinct sections, the hemisphere above the ascendant and descendant line, and the hemisphere below the ascendant and descendant line also known as the chart's horizon.

The Sun's position relative to the horizon in a chart reflects its physical presence in the world. In the day-time, the sun is above the horizon and we experience the light and warmth of the sun for approximately twelve hours in a day. Astrologically the chart reflects this phenomenon by placing the symbolic Sun above the chart's horizon line in a position from the seventh house to the end of the twelfth house.

The chart is called diurnal because it occurred during the hours of daylight.

In contrast, if the sun has physically set below the horizon and we are experiencing the darkness of night, the symbolic Sun in the chart will be situated in any of the houses from the first to the sixth house and it is deemed to be a nocturnal (night-time) chart.

Under the rules of Sect, some planets prefer a diurnal chart, and some prefer a nocturnal chart and this will affect how the signs of exaltation are chosen from the list of zodiac signs.

The day-time or diurnal planets – Sun, Saturn and Jupiter – choose their exalted signs by a trine aspect to one of their preferred rulership signs.

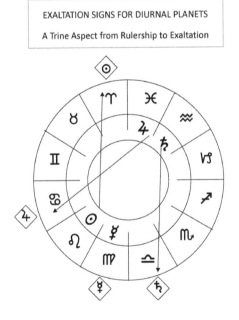

EXALTATION SIGNS FOR DIURNAL PLANETS

A Trine Aspect from Rulership to Exaltation

The night-time or nocturnal planets – Moon, Venus and Mars – cast 'weaker rays' by sextile from a rulership sign to find their exalted sign.

Mercury is the only one with the same sign, Virgo, for both rulership and exaltation, because 'he is tired from his constant risings and settings.' [39]

Fig. 14 Exaltation Signs for the Diurnal Planets

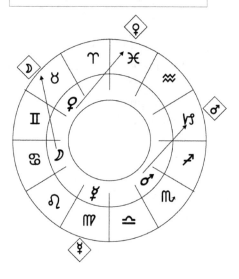

EXALTATION SIGNS FOR NOCTURNAL PLANETS

A Sextile Aspect from Rulership to Exaltation

Fig. 15 Exaltation Signs for the Nocturnal Planets

PLANET	SECT IDENTITY	RULERSHIP SIGN	ASPECT BETWEEN SIGNS	EXALTATION SIGN	FALL (Sign Opposite Exaltation Sign)
☉	Diurnal	Leo	Trine	Aries	Libra
♃	Diurnal	Pisces	Trine	Cancer	Capricorn
♄	Diurnal	Aquarius	Trine	Libra	Aries
☽	Nocturnal	Cancer	Sextile	Taurus	Scorpio
♀	Nocturnal	Taurus	Sextile	Pisces	Virgo
♂	Nocturnal	Scorpio	Sextile	Capricorn	Cancer
☿	Diurnal or Nocturnal	Virgo	Same Sign	Virgo	Pisces

Fig . 16 Table of the Aspects connecting Rulership
to Exaltation via the rules of Sect

Triplicity: The Third Level of Essential Dignity

"Jupiter in a night-time chart in a fire sign - Aries, Leo or Sagittarius - is essentially dignified."

The third level of Essential Dignity is Triplicity, a reference to the connection between three signs and their element – a triad of signs which have the same lord according to whether they belong to the fire, earth, air or water element.

The elements are broken into masculine or feminine gender, and once more the accidental dignity of Sect is involved in determining which of the planets will be the triplicity lord for a particular element.

The masculine signs of fire and air are deemed to be diurnal, so it is only fitting that the diurnal planets – Sun, Jupiter and Saturn – should rule the fiery signs, and also include Mercury, which can belong to either sect, to replace the Sun and to rule the air signs with Jupiter and Saturn.

The earth and water elements are feminine in gender and belong to the nocturnal planets, Moon, Venus and Mars under the rules of Triplicity.

The third level of Essential Dignity appears to diverge from the first two categories in that it was used for a different purpose apart from the elevation of a planet through its Essential Dignities.

This level is used for guidance in the prediction of future events and the planets became time lords who presided over the native's life for different periods of time.

Thirteenth century astrologer Guido Bonatti says the rulers of triplicity were noted because of their involvement in the native's 'nutrition', an odd expression presumably describing the nature and quality of nurturing that a planet might provide during a lifespan.

In this method, the life was split into three distinct time periods, with each period belonging to one planet from the list of triplicities.

The ascendant determined the choice in planets as the rising sign's element, plus the sect of the chart, gave clues as to which planet was in control of one-third of life.

To demonstrate this method Bonatti uses the example of a diurnal chart with Taurus on the ascendant.[40]

The lord of the ascendant's sign, Venus, gave the overall ruler of life, but the triplicity lords each ruled one period, roughly thirty years in duration, and depending on their condition, indicated the level of a native's nutrition.

As Taurus is an earth sign, the order of planets would be Venus for the first three decades, the Moon as the second triplicity lord for the middle years, and Mars for the remaining thirty years of life.

As each triplicity lord changed, so too did the fortunes take a different turn as the condition of each designated planet affected the period of time over which the planet ruled.

Bonatti says that if any time lord was in mediocre condition, then that mediocre condition would correspond to that particular time of life.

Earlier writers such as Vettius Valens from the first century, looked at the three periods of life through the eyes of the luminaries.

If the chart was diurnal the three triplicity lords of the Sun's sign were to be examined, but if it was a nocturnal chart, the Moon's sign was examined and life was divided and ruled according to the night luminary's sign.[41]

Not all ancient writers used the last category of Participating lord.

Ptolemy, for instance, uses only the first two categories in his examples on the triplicities, so presumably he was unaware of the use of triplicity rulers to determine the three periods of life.

Element	Diurnal Lord	Nocturnal Lord	Participating Lord
Fire	☉	♃	♄
Earth	♀	☽	♂
Air	♄	☿	♃
Water	♀	♂	☽

Fig. 17 The Triplicities

The Table (*Fig. 17*) is the generally accepted form for drawing up the various divisions of Triplicity.

The information is correct, but it does not always provide a clear account of how a planet receives dignity through this third level of Dignity.

Generally speaking, the search for either Rulership or Exaltation involves looking for the sign in which a planet is situated, and the process for Triplicity should be no more difficult to determine through a planet's sign.

For instance, Jupiter rules the mutable fire sign of Sagittarius so when it is found here it is easily identified as dignified and can therefore express its essential qualities.

However, it is afforded the same courtesy in the other two fire signs, but only if the Sun is below the horizon in the chart.

In the eleventh century textbook *The Book of Instruction In the Elements of the Art of Astrology* by Arabic astrologer al-Biruni, the Triplicities Table is set out differently, and perhaps it is a more direct way in which to determine if a planet has dignity through the third level of Triplicity.

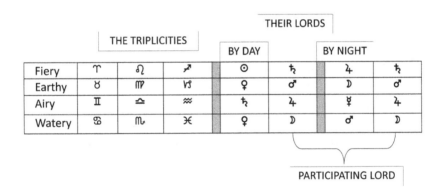

Fig. 18 The Table for Triplicities from al-Biruni

Al-Biruni's text reads :

"Each triplicity (element) *has a lord by day and another by night, also a third which shares this responsibility both by day and night. Thus the fiery triplicity has as lord the sun by day, and Jupiter by night, while Saturn is a partner both by day and night.*

The earthly triplicity has Venus by day, the moon by night, Mars being in this case the partner.

The airy triplicity has Saturn by day, Mercury by night and Jupiter as the partner, while the watery triplicity has Venus by day, Mars by night and the moon as partner." [42]

It is worth noting that al-Biruni recommends the correct ruler for sect division plus the participating lord and discards the ruler of the opposite sect.

However, other authors will keep all three Triplicity lords, and rather than discard the nocturnal lord in a diurnal chart, or reject the diurnal lord in a nocturnal chart, will instead change the order of the planets to complement the chart's sect.

The difference between day or night gains greater weight when the Triplicity lords are examined and each of the twelve houses are divided into three separate categories, often with very different lords in various states of good or bad condition.

In his later section on the houses, Bonatti once more uses all three Triplicity lords as minor or sub-rulers of a house, so that not only can these time lords be applied to deduce the three periods of life using the ascendant's sign for fortunate times, but all twelve houses can also be examined using the third level of Essential Dignity.

In this older technique Bonatti divides a house into three segments under the umbrella of its general signification and judges each one separately in order to find specific information which relates to the house's topic of interest.

For instance, when Bonatti describes the tenth house he says that it is a kingly house and that it signifies rule, professions, dignities and offices, and every skill which one may exercise and be called a "master".

He then says: *"Alezdegoz said that the first ruler of the triplicity of the kingly house rules work, exaltation, and the elevation to a higher seat of authority, and to the highest dwelling. The second lord signifies the voice of command and audacity in the same. The third signifies its stability and durability."* [43]

In an example of Bonatti's text, if Virgo was shown to be the chart's tenth sign, Mercury would be the principle lord of the house and according to its condition in the chart, it would describe the type of office, profession or elevation the native might enjoy from the house's ruler.

However, if the astrologer of the day wanted to ascertain whether the native would rise to higher levels of success they would consult earth's first Triplicity lord, then if they wanted to know if others would listen to the commands of the native, follow and support them, or respect their increased authority, then they may consult earth's second Triplicity lord.

Lastly, if they wanted to know if the rise was long-term and would not be challenged in the future, they would look to earth's third Triplicity lord for stability or the durability and longevity of the native's advancement.

In other words, there was little point in getting a promotion if others did not think it was deserved, if you were likely to be ignored or ridiculed, or if you did not have the power to hang on to a higher rank in society or within an organisation.

In the example of Virgo on the tenth house cusp, the Triplicity lords of the earth element would require examination, but the order of the three ruling planets will differ according to whether it is a diurnal or nocturnal chart.

If the native is born during the day, the Sun is above the horizon, and the order of the three Triplicity lords will be Venus, followed by the Moon and finally, by Mars.

As the diurnal lord, Venus is the advancement, the Moon is the level of power, and Mars determines if control and success can be maintained by the native.

However, if the Sun is below the horizon, then the first two rulers are reversed, and the Moon as the primary lord will now direct the native's elevation in the first place.

Venus will follow and its condition in the nocturnal chart will determine how seriously others will take the promotion, and whether they will support or undermine the new authority.

The participating lord is always last, regardless of whether the chart is diurnal or nocturnal, and again, Mars will be the decider over the promotion's stability.

The nature of the planetary lord also affected the outcome of the affairs of a particular house, whether Venus (day) or the Moon (night), as each will use very different techniques to achieve promotion.

Although both planets will subtly use popularity and an emotional appeal to gain attention, Venus is more likely to call on friendships and networking to advance, whilst the Moon uses service and practical experience as its 'ace in the hole'.

The change in the second triplicity lord will also display two different methods in getting others on side and the Moon works for the day chart to emotionally bond with others, whilst Venus works for the night chart using charm, favours or negotiation to encourage alliances, and dissuade or deflect any resistance to its authority.

In either chart, Mars as the participating lord will fight to maintain the native's power, so if sweetness and self-inflicted sacrifice fail for the first two lords, Mars had better be in good condition so that it can take on any challengers to its authority.

Weighting The Dignities

Triplicity's application to find information on the present and for direction in future times is an excellent tool for astrologers which is explored in detail in Chapter Seven on the Houses.

However, there are times when the third level of Essential Dignity creates confusion over the true state of a planet in particular signs.

Debilities from the two previous levels are created as a result of the planet being in opposite signs from their dignities, detriment is the sign opposing rulership or domicile, and fall is the sign opposite the dignity of exaltation.

For instance, Saturn in Leo is in its sign of detriment, yet in the Triplicities Saturn is the fire element's Participating lord and therefore gains some dignity in Leo.

Likewise, Mars in Cancer is in a state of fall, yet it is the dignified lord of water signs in a nocturnal chart.

Taken at face value it seems that a planet can be debilitated by one rule, yet dignified by another.

Presumably the various writers were aware of this contradiction, but many things are left unsaid or have been lost in translation, and it may have been that it was assumed that the reader would automatically know how to deal with any discrepancies in Dignity.

Nor is it helped by the later system of removing points, numbers or 'fortitudes' (Bonatti's term) from the planets when they are in debility.

Bonatti lists the various points in the weighting system used for each of the dignities:

"the lord of the house (rulership) has five fortitudes, the lord of the exaltation has four, the lord of the triplicity has three, the lord of the term has two, and the lord of the face has one fortitude."[44]

This text refers to an earlier system of judging the 'Almuten'(used for determining length of life) or the overall ruler of a house and the weighting system gave true measure as to which planet was in control of a particular house.

In his *Christian Astrology* William Lilly (1602 – 1681 CE) followed the same practice using a numbering system to rate the various dignities.

However, Lilly went one step further and devised a system of negative rating (by removing points) for debilities and included both the Essential and the Accidental Dignities.

The original list is quite long, so for the point made here, it has been abbreviated to include just the Essential Dignities and their debilities.

A READY TABLE WHEREBY TO EXAMINE THE FORTITUDES AND DEBILITIES OF THE PLANETS*

Essential Dignities (Identical to Bonatti's Point System)	Point System — Positives	Debilities (Lilly's System)	Point System — Negatives
A Planet in His Own House, or in Mutual Reception by House, Shall Have Dignities	PLUS 5	In His Detriment	MINUS 5
In His Exaltation, or Reception by Exaltation	PLUS 4	In His Fall	MINUS 4
In His Own Triplicity	PLUS 3	Peregrine (no dignity)	MINUS 5
In His Own Term	PLUS 2	—	—
Decanate of Face	PLUS 1	—	—

*Fig. 19 William Lilly's Point System for Essential Dignities and Debilities[45] *Lilly's Title*

Lilly allotted a (+3) reading for Triplicity in the same manner as the traditionalists, but when he added a negative reading for Detriment or Peregrine (-5), and Fall (-4), it became more confusing to decide how these two Dignities could work side by side to determine a correct reading of the planet's condition.

Under Lilly's system Saturn in Leo would rate as a dignity (+3) but would lose (-5) for detriment, giving it a negative score (-2) in total which is somewhat half way between the two initial scores.

Under Lilly's system Triplicity appears to be almost a 'consolation prize' to comfort the planet and mitigate the harsh reality of debility in certain signs and to ward off the disadvantage of peregrination (no dignity).

Perhaps Robert Hand's interpretation mentioned earlier holds some truth, that a debilitated planet has limited power, or a lesser intensive magnitude, by which to express its natural qualities, but gains a reprieve in some signs which is born from an elemental advantage.

Rather than acting from a point of weakness or a constant dispersal of its energy, it gains focus or strength from a particular sign which demonstrates affinity between element and planet.

However, if Triplicity is solely available to direct the astrologer to the appropriate sub-lord of one of the houses, rather than using it as a judgement of a planet's strength, then the conflict of dignity verses debility can be avoided.

Planet	Element	Triplicity Position	Triplicity Sign In Debility
♄	Fire	Participating lord	Aries (♄ in ♈ is in Fall) Leo (♄ in ♌ is in Detriment)
♃	Air	Participating lord	Gemini (♃ in ♊ is in Detriment)
♂	Earth Water	Participating lord Nocturnal lord	Taurus (♂ in ♉ is in Detriment) Cancer (♂ in ♋ is in Fall)
☉	Fire	Diurnal lord	No Debility for ☉ in Fire Signs
♀	Earth Water	Diurnal lord Diurnal lord	Virgo (♀ in ♍ is in Fall) Scorpio (♀ in ♏ is in Detriment)
☿	Air	Nocturnal lord	No Debility for ☿ in Air Signs
☽	Earth Water	Nocturnal lord Participating lord	Capricorn (☽ in ♑ is in Detriment) Scorpio (☽ in ♏ is in Fall)

Fig. 20 Table of the contradictions between a planet's dignity by triplicity and its debility by the two higher levels of Essential Dignity (Rulership and Exaltation).

The Egyptian Terms: The Fourth Level of Essential Dignity

"The five planets, Saturn, Jupiter, Mars, Venus and Mercury are said to have defined and designated terms in each of the signs. They are called terms or limits because, while the planets are within these degrees, they are said to have a certain power which is called a fortitude." [46]

It should be noted that there are five divisions in the Terms, and that whilst the planets are mostly rotated through the degrees, the luminaries are not featured as Term rulers.

In Bonatti's introduction to the Terms, the Latin word for 'boundary' is also used for the fourth level of dignity. For this reason, the Terms are also called the Bounds by some authors.

Bonatti takes the term 'boundary' literally and explains that just as boundaries in an agricultural context limit the size of land and divide one field from another, so too do the degrees assigned to a planet limit it to its term division, and in this manner divide the virtue of one planet from the virtue of another.

This description provides an interesting view into the mindset which created this fourth Dignity through imitating everyday experiences.

For instance, there is purpose and advantage in livestock being placed in particular paddocks which benefit both the animal and the pasture.

The animal has the opportunity to thrive in the paddock which best suits its needs for food, shelter and movement.

The outlook from the paddock, the amount of shade or wind protection it provides, the proximity to roads or the house paddock, the type of feed planted on the pasture, all of these factors must be taken into account when choosing the best paddock which suits an animal's needs.

In the Terms there are five categories with a different lord.

One sign (farm) divided into five Terms or Bounds (fields) with one planet (very different animal).

Each planet (animal) has a different requirement, a different outlook and personality, and each one becomes the Term ruler over its particular number of degrees in a sign. In the farm analogy, when you enter a particular paddock you expect to see a certain type of animal and the jobs you need to perform are dependent on the animal's specific requirements.

A horse needs different care to a cow, a goat, a pig, or the property's prize bull.

Seen from this perspective, the descriptions provided by Vettius Valens (1st century CE) for each of the sixty Bounds or Terms *(Figs. 23-25)* indicate the difference between the Terms being ruled by benefic or malefic planets.

Venus and Jupiter are friendly and gentle creatures who wish you no harm and will eagerly approach with a greeting when you enter their territory.

However, when you are required to engage with the two malefic planets, Mars and Saturn at the end of a sign, you are likely to receive a hostile reception from an animal that may be worth a great deal of money at the markets, but has a meaner temperament than the other paddocks' occupants.

Valens' description of the Term Rulers for Aries has been lifted from the Table at the end of this section to demonstrate the differences between one Term Ruler and the next.

ARIES		DEGREES	TERM LORD	VETTIUS VALENS' INTERPRETATION
	1st Term	0—6	♃	Temperate, robust, prolific, beneficent
	2nd Term	6—12	♀	Cheerful, clever, radiant, even, pure, handsome
	3rd Term	12—20	☿	Changeable, clever, idle, windy, stormy
	4th Term	20—25	♂	Baneful, fiery, unsteady, rash, wicked
	5th Term	25—30	♄	Cold, barren, malicious, injured

Fig. 21 Term Rulers – Aries Example

Aries' first two Term Rulers are Jupiter (0-6 degrees) and Venus (6-12 degrees); these are paddocks into which you can take visitors to the farm to feed and pet the animals and everyone enjoys the experience.

The third Term Ruler of Aries is Mercury (12-20), and you may have to pay a little more attention to this animal as it changes in mood constantly, making its behaviour unpredictable from one day to the next, so visitors should steer clear of this field or only go in with the farmer.

The final two fields are definitely no-go zones for visitors, and even the farmer is wary of entering the field where Mars lives (20-25 degrees) because this animal has a wicked temperament and is looking for trouble.

The same caution with even more care applies to entering the last field to tend the pasture or fix the boundary where the most valuable, and sometimes the most vicious animal calls home (Saturn ruling 25-30 degrees of Aries).

The Terms as Time Keepers:
A Predictive Model for The Egyptian Term Rulers

Similar to the Triplicity lords, the Term rulers can also be used for predictive purposes.

Ibn-Ezra refers to the Terms of the Egyptian astrologers saying that a man's life is divided according to the Terms and that sometimes (like the different occupants of the fields), a change in boundaries can mean that a man can go from one situation to another from bad to good or vice versa according to the nature of the Term rulers.[47]

In Bonatti's *Liber Astronomiae* (Chapter 37) he gives an example on how the planets ruling different degrees of the Terms can become time lords by owning years which parallel to number of degrees in a sign (i.e. 6 degrees = 6 years of life).

Bonatti's list of degrees is supposedly identical to Ptolemy's list which differs from the Egyptian Terms, but it is believed that translation errors have caused some discrepancies in the degree boundaries.

It should be noted that planetary sect does not affect the order of the Term Rulers in the same way as the three Triplicity lords (which reverse diurnal and nocturnal lords) as the five Term rulers will maintain the same sequence, regardless of whether the native is born during the daytime or in the night-time hours.

For example, a Gemini ascendant will create the five term rulers in the order of Mercury, Jupiter, Venus, Mars, and Saturn.

In accordance with the Term degrees Mercury will rule the native's life from birth to the sixth birthday, as these are the number of degrees (0-6) which Mercury rules in the Terms of Gemini.

At the age of six Jupiter, the second term ruler, will take over and guide the next six years of life (6-12 degrees of Gemini).

At the twelfth birthday, Venus becomes the time lord and will be in charge from twelve to seventeen years of age, after which Mars rules from seventeen to twenty four, and the last term ruler, Saturn, will determine the following six years up until the thirtieth birthday when Gemini's five term rulers have fulfilled their Geminian obligations.

Presumably, the term rulers of the following sign, Cancer take over in their order, when Bonatti says after the terms of Saturn:

"And understand the same with regard to all the terms and all the rulers of the terms."[48]

Ibn-Ezra also gave significant importance to Terms (bounds) inferring with his statement that a Term ruler may not own the entire house (a Domicile lord), but he does have complete confidence in the fact that he owns the chair in which he sits, and that it is the chair which gives him status and an honourable place at the table:

"A planet in its bound (terms) is like a person in his seat."[49]

The breakdown of the signs into five term rulers is an interesting interpretation of how the same sign can react differently to the virtues of a different planet *(Fig. 21).*

First century astrologer Vettius Valens goes to great lengths to describe the differences and this list features at the very beginning of Book I in his *Anthologies,* so presumably he thought the dignity of Term had great merit, as it is the only dignity which is broken down into so much detail in order to analyse the five divisions of a sign.

The order of preference in Term rulers appears to be random, but only up to a point, as either of the two malefic planets are the final Term ruler at the end of all twelve signs.

Saturn is Libra's first Term ruler and Mars is the first term ruler for Scorpio and this seems fitting as both planets gain previous honours in these signs by exaltation and rulership respectively.

However, Mars claims line honours as Cancer's initial Term ruler but Mars dislikes this sign as it is in fall in Cancer. Just one example of the difficulty in understanding the reasoning behind Term Ruler allocation.

Sign	1st Term Lord	2nd Term Lord	3rd Term Lord	4th Term Lord	5th Term Lord
♈	0 - 6 ♃	6 -12 ♀	12 - 20 ☿	20 - 25 ♂	25 - 30 ♄
♉	0 - 8 ♀	8 -14 ☿	14 - 22 ♃	22 - 27 ♄	27 - 30 ♂
♊	0 - 6 ☿	6 -12 ♃	12 - 17 ♀	17 - 24 ♂	24 - 30 ♄
♋	0 - 7 ♂	7 -13 ♀	13 - 19 ☿	19 - 26 ♃	26 - 30 ♄
♌	0 - 6 ♃	6 -11 ♀	11 - 18 ♄	18 - 24 ☿	24 - 30 ♂
♍	0 - 7 ☿	7 -17 ♀	17 - 21 ♃	21 - 28 ♂	28 - 30 ♄
♎	0 - 6 ♄	6 -14 ☿	14 - 21 ♃	21 - 28 ♀	28 - 30 ♂
♏	0 - 7 ♂	7 -11 ♀	11 - 19 ☿	19 - 24 ♃	24 - 30 ♄
♐	0 -12 ♃	12-17 ♀	17 - 21 ☿	21 - 26 ♄	26 - 30 ♂
♑	0 - 7 ☿	7 -14 ♃	14 - 22 ♀	22 - 26 ♄	26 - 30 ♂
♒	0 - 7 ☿	7 -13 ♀	13 - 20 ♃	20 - 25 ♂	25 - 30 ♄
♓	0 -12 ♀	12-16 ♃	16 - 19 ☿	19 - 28 ♂	28 - 30 ♄

Fig. 22 The Egyptian Terms

♈	1st	0 - 6	♃	Temperate, robust, prolific, beneficent
	2nd	6 - 12	♀	Cheerful, clever, radiant, even, pure, handsome
	3rd	12 - 20	☿	Changeable, clever, idle, windy, stormy
	4th	20 - 25	♂	Baneful, fiery, unsteady, rash, wicked
	5th	25 - 30	♄	Cold, barren, malicious, injured
♉	1st	0 - 8	♀	Prolific, moist, downward-trending, convicted
	2nd	8 - 14	☿	Intelligent, sensible, criminal, sinister, fatal
	3rd	14 - 22	♃	Great-hearted, bold, lucky, ruling and beneficent, magnanimous, temperate
	4th	22 - 27	♄	Barren, a vagabond, censorious, theatrical, gloomy, toilsome
	5th	27 - 30	♂	Masculine, tyrannical, fiery, harsh, destructive
♊	1st	0 - 6	☿	Temperate, intelligent, versatile, skilled, active, poetic
	2nd	6 - 12	♃	Competitive, temperate, luxuriant, beneficent
	3rd	12 - 17	♀	Blossoming, artistic, poetic, popular, prolific
	4th	17 - 24	♂	Much-burdened, a wanderer, destructive, inquisitive
	5th	24 - 30	♄	Temperate, having possessions, intellectual, wide knowledge, distinguished
♋	1st	0 - 7	♂	Uneven, contradictory, manic, poor, destructive, base
	2nd	7 - 13	♀	Censorious, changeable, skilled, popular,, promiscuous
	3rd	13 - 19	☿	Precise, leader in public matters, rich, a robber
	4th	19 - 26	♃	Kingly, imperious, glorious, judging, great-hearted
	5th	26 - 30	♄	Everything is water, poor in personal property, needy

Fig. 23 Valens' interpretations of the Planets' virtues
as Term Rulers – Aries to Cancer

♌	1st	0 - 6	♃	Experienced, masculine, leadership qualities, eminent
	2nd	6 - 11	♀	Very temperate, yielding, talented, luxurious
	3rd	11 - 18	♄	Much-experienced, fearful, scientific, clever, narrow
	4th	18 - 24	☿	Popular, scholastic, guiding, prescribing, intelligent
	5th	24 - 30	♂	Base, destructive, injured, torpid, censured, unlucky
♍	1st	0 - 7	☿	Lofty, an arranger, handsome, most intelligent, noble
	2nd	7 - 17	♀	Censured, poor choices in love and marriage
	3rd	17 - 21	♃	Agricultural, proper, fruitful, reclusive but not ignorant
	4th	21 - 28	♂	Masculine, harsh, public, demagogues, imposters
	5th	28 - 30	♄	Chilled, destructive, the term of deluded men
♎	1st	0 – 6	♄	Kingly, lofty, effective (day births), disturbed (night)
	2nd	6 – 14	☿	Businesslike, marketing, just and intelligent
	3rd	14 - 21	♃	Wealth-producing but unlucky men, hoarders
	4th	21 - 28	♀	Loving beauty and crafts, rhythmic, pious, lucky
	5th	28 - 30	♂	Ruling, optimistic, spirited, steady, successful
♏	1st	0 - 7	♂	Easily upset, disturbed, unsteady, arrogant, frank
	2nd	7 - 11	♀	Lucky in marriage, pious, loved, wealthy, fortunate
	3rd	11 - 19	☿	Competitive, bitter, contentious, mischief making
	4th	19 - 24	♃	Talented, lucky, high-priestly, glorified
	5th	24 - 30	♄	Punitive, melancholic, resist their superiors, despised by inferiors, cursers of fate

Fig. 24 Valens' interpretations of the Planets'
virtues as Term Rulers – Leo to Scorpio

♐	1st	0 - 12	♃	Active, dabbling in crafts & skills, prolific but poor
	2nd	12 - 17	♀	Prominent, victorious, pious, honoured and blessed
	3rd	17 - 21	☿	Philosophical, prominent in science and wisdom
	4th	21 - 26	♄	Baneful, cold, harmful, completely unlucky
	5th	26 - 30	♂	Hot, rash, violent, shameless, destructive, restless
♑	1st	0 - 7	☿	Theatrical, comic, seducing, talented, blessed
	2nd	7 - 14	♃	Glory & infamy, wealth & poverty, public ridicule
	3rd	14 - 22	♀	Lecherous, thoughtless, censured, unsteady
	4th	22 - 26	♄	Severe, cheerless, alien, destructive, malicious
	5th	26 - 30	♂	Lofty, prosperous, dictatorial, solitary, aims to rule
♒	1st	0 - 7	☿	Rich but miserly, intelligent, learned in law, petty
	2nd	7 - 13	♀	Loving well, pious, prosperous, advantaged by the old
	3rd	13 - 20	♃	Lucky, petty, careless of reputation, unsociable
	4th	20 - 25	♂	Diseased, troubled by lawsuits, wicked and incapable
	5th	25 - 30	♄	Enfeebled, afflicted in health, poor, envious
♓	1st	0 - 12	♀	Cheery, luxurious, living graciously, loving, friendly
	2nd	12 - 16	♃	Literary, learned, pre-eminent, victorious in words
	3rd	16 - 19	☿	Ruling, highly ranked, many friends, charitable
	4th	19 - 28	♂	Active, bold warriors, success in mystical lore
	5th	28 - 30	♄	Enfeebled, poor health, entirely unlucky

Fig. 25 Valens' interpretations of the Planets' virtues
as Term Rulers – Sagittarius toPisces

The Faces or Decans: The Fifth Level of Essential Dignity

"A planet in its face is like a person with fine ornaments and clothing."[50]
The final level of Essential Dignity divides the signs into three equal parts, each of which is called a face or decan.

Each face consists of ten degrees and the planets follow one another in the Chaldean Order.

The list of decans always begins at zero Aries with Mars, the domicile ruler, as the ruler of the first ten degrees of this sign.

The luminaries are included as lords of the Faces and the Sun follows Mars for the middle ten degrees of Aries, with the planets continuing in their correct order as the lords of the Decan degrees.

The diagram below gives a clearer picture of the planets' procession through the ten degree allotment of the signs.

The decans are believed to be of pre-Ptolemaic Egyptian origin and were personified by the Egyptians, being described in various terms such as 'thrones', or as taking protective mundane roles such as 'soldiers', or 'guardians', or as supernatural protectors in the term *'daimons'*.

Sign	First 10 degrees (0 – 10)	Second 10 degrees (10 – 20)	Third 10 degrees (20 – 30)
Aries	♂	☉	♀
Taurus	☿	☽	♄
Gemini	♃	♂	☉
Cancer	♀	☿	☽
Leo	♄	♃	♂
Virgo	☉	♀	☿
Libra	☽	♄	♃
Scorpio	♂	☉	♀
Sagittarius	☿	☽	♄
Capricorn	♃	♂	☉
Aquarius	♀	☿	☽
Pisces	♄	♃	♂

Fig. 26 Table of the Faces or Decans

Fig. 27 Diagram of the Chaldean Order of the Faces

A Final Word on Essential Dignities From Guido Bonatti

Guido Bonatti (1210-1296 CE) begins his introduction to the Essential Dignities in the Second Tractate Part Two of his *Liber Astronomiae* with the Chaldean Order of the planets (Chapter 25), and then proceeds to discuss the five levels of Dignity which he calls powers by nature (Essential Dignities), as opposed to the powers by accident (Accidental Dignities).

Bonatti continues for fifteen chapters detailing each of the five categories of Essential Dignity and finalises at Chapter 40 with a summary on the differences between the five levels. Bonatti precedes Triplicity with Term and the following text has been swapped to maintain consistency in the order of the Essential Dignities.

"Concerning this subject there is a kind of analogy, that while a planet is in its house (RULERSHIP), it is like a man who is in his own home, who is all the stronger in his own home, even legally than in another's, and in fact so much more than another who elsewhere would be stronger than he.

Whence Trutanus, "Every serf is a cock in front of his own gate."

And while a planet is in its EXALTATION it is like a man who is in his own kingdom, and in his own glory like a kingship, dukedom, or podesta (chief magistrate) *and are as other lay dignities which can be lost to him sooner than that which is properly his own (house).*

While a planet is in its own TRIPLICITY, it is like a man among his allies, his people, his ministers, and followers who obey him and follow him, but are not related to him by kinship.

And while a planet is in its own TERM it is like a man who is among his relatives and blood relations, kin, kith, neighbours, and those related to him by kinship.

While the planet is in its FACE, it is like a man who is among unknown peoples such as happens with foreigners and the like, but he lives among them by art and skill, or by service, or by any other craftsmanlike or lay art."

Five Kinds of Accidental Dignity

If we wanted more information about Socrates we might add:
"Socrates is an ugly man with a brilliant mind who is well-skilled in the use of spear and sword."

This statement describes the nature of Socrates' matter as well as some of the traits which are contributing factors to the essential qualities of this man called Socrates.

The changing circumstances of life will affect when and where his attributes will stand him in good stead, or with an alteration in his environment, will be of little use to him or those with whom he comes in contact.

If a beautiful countenance, good manners or even cleanliness are required to impress society or to gain an invitation as an honoured guest at my daughter's wedding, then Socrates is not my man.

In these surroundings he would be accidentally debilitated, by making himself appear awkward and those around him uncomfortable by his presence, and therefore more likely to cause upheaval or distress to myself, the wedding party or the gathering in general.

However, if I take him on a military campaign or stand by his side on the battlefield, his skill as a cunning and resourceful strategist, his courage in the face of danger, and his mastery of weapons places Socrates in fantastic accidental dignity in this environment, and both he and I are likely to survive the battle.

The same rule applies in the case of the planets.

The more suitable or appropriate the circumstances which are compatible with a planet's nature, the more likely that planet can achieve maximum advantage in order to perform the tasks expected of it within the confines of a horoscope.

Socrates knows full well that he is an unsuitable candidate to be well-behaved at the wedding, but he flourishes in warfare because he understands the rules of combat, and he can apply his military skills with confidence and proficiency.

Solar Phasing: The Planets' Relationship to The Sun

*"The Sun signifies light, splendour, beauty, intellect, and faith.. .the Sun himself is placed in the middle of the other planets as a king, and the others stand near him, some on one side, others on the other side, **namely the superiors on the right, the inferiors on his left**. And he himself has power over all of the planets because he burns them all."*[51]

Guido Bonatti, *Liber Astronomiae*

In the Chaldean Order the Sun takes pride of place in central position with three planets situated above (Saturn, Jupiter, Mars) and three planets placed below it (Venus, Mercury, Moon).

The Sun is the all-important 'light-bringer' and early astrologers such as Vettius Valens (1st century C.E.) praised its qualities and recognised its powers.

Valens lauded the Sun as being *"all-seeing; Nature's fire and intellectual light; ruler of man's spiritual faculties and the purveyor of the ordinance of the gods"*[52], and whilst the geocentric or earth-orientated schema is best suited to represent the astrological model, the Chaldean Order acknowledges the importance of the Sun as the source of light and heat when placed as the life-giving nucleus of the seven planets.

The Sun created a marked division between the planets, so much so that Saturn, Jupiter and Mars were named as 'superior' planets, being placed higher in the heavens than the Sun and therefore closer to '*first cause*' or *Primum Mobile* (Prime Mover).

Venus, Mercury and the Moon, with their spheres or heavens situated beneath the Sun's own sphere and closer to Earth, were considered to be the three 'inferior' planets.

There is a list of terms which are born from this concept of a planet's relationship in regard to the Sun.

Not only does it divide the remaining six planets into two groups according to placement above or below the Sun's position in the Order, it also creates a division according to the positions right or left of the Sun.

The Latin word *dexter* is used to describe the direction on the right-hand side but it also means *skilful*, the derivative for dexterity, meaning mental or physical agility, which enables special expertise or artistry.

The opposite direction to right is left, or *sinister* in Latin, meaning wrong-handed, and the word became synonymous with misfortune, bad luck or evil intent.

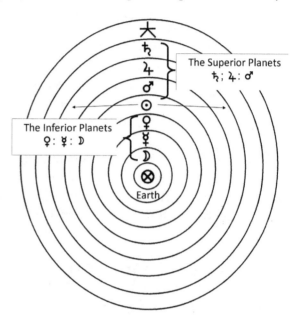

Therefore, when superior is linked to *dexter* (good) and inferior becomes *sinister* (bad), the division between desirous and undesirous becomes clear so far as the planets are concerned.

Fig.28 The Superior planets Above the Sun and the Inferior planets Below the Sun in the Chaldean Order

From outside of the circle and looking inwards at the Sun, on first appearance the text seems to have the directions reversed as sinister is often assumed as the Sun's left-side (above the Sun) and dexter is assumed to mean to the Sun's right side (below the Sun).

The same misunderstanding occurs when aspects, especially squares, are referred to as dexter or sinister quartile aspects (quarter of a circle = 90 degrees).

However, imagine that you are standing at the centre of a chart and looking outwards at a planet.

Then the directions are reversed, and a dexter square describes a planet which is to the right of the focal planet and in fact, has risen before it in earlier degrees of the zodiac.

A sinister square is below the focal planet and the planet making the aspect will rise after it because it is situated in later degrees of the zodiac.

The same rule applied to the planets in the Chaldean Order.

If you were standing inside the circle and looking back at the Sun, Mars, Jupiter and Saturn would be placed to the Sun's right-side (dexter) and take their place as superior planets, whilst Venus, Mercury and the Moon would be situated on the left-side of the Sun in the sinister position and thereby take their place as inferior planets.

The relationship between the other planets and the Sun is also taken into account when all seven planets are placed within the framework of the ecliptic belt.

For instance, if a planet rises before the Sun it will be in an earlier degree of the zodiac than the Sun and the planet is identified as being oriental to the Sun.

In astrological terms, oriental means 'east of the Sun', and the term *'matutine'*, or morning star, is used to describe a planet which rises in the East and is visible until the Sun itself rises and its light obliterates the planet in the day-time sky.

A planet which is in a later zodiacal degree than the Sun will follow the Sun through the day sky, and will only be visible once the Sun has set over the western horizon.

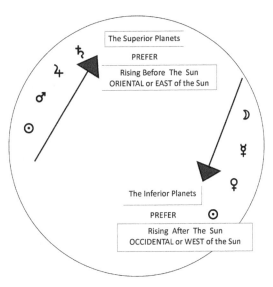

Fig.29 Planets Preference to be Oriental or Occidental to the Sun

The Superior planets prefer to be oriental to the Sun (rise before the Sun, or to the East of the Sun).

The Inferior planets prefer to be occidental to the Sun (rise after the Sun, or to the west of the Sun).

The term occidental is used to describe a planet's position when it is 'west of the Sun', and the term *'vespertine'*, or evening star, denotes a planet which suddenly becomes visible after the Sun sets in the West.

The planets were considered to be in a minor level of accidental dignity if they occupied a post reminiscent to their position in the Chaldean Order *(Fig 29)*.

Ideally, if a superior planet was oriental to the Sun and visible in the morning before the Sun rose it gained dignity, or if an inferior planet was occidental to the Sun and visible in the evening after the Sun had set, then it was considered to have benefitted from its position.

Ptolemy's *Tetrabiblos* contains a footnote by Placidus stating that

> *"...the three superiors are supposed to be stronger, if they are found to be matutine, or eastern from the Sun; (and too if) the three inferiors, vespertine, or western; for then they have a greater degree of light, in which consists their virtual influence, and then they are called oriental; but occidental if otherwise".*[53]

Every planet is constantly in motion, and every planet moves at a different speed. This means that a planet is in a state of perpetual motion and its position in relation to the Sun is forever changing.

This rule on position in regard to the Sun may seem archaic but the visual impact in the sky cannot be overlooked.

Simply put, the superior planets prefer to have their own shining period (devoid of the Sun's overpowering light) in the morning before the Sun rises, illuminates the sky, and diminishes visibility of Saturn, Jupiter or Mars.

In contrast, the inferior planets prefer the evening sky as their backdrop, when the Sun has set and they begin to appear on the western horizon.

Mercury does not get a great deal of opportunity to savour this experience as the maximum angle between the Sun and Mercury is 28 degrees so the natural curve of the horizon often hides Mercury's appearance.

Venus fares a little better and she is truly beautiful as the Evening Star, but even then her maximum angle of separation is only 47 degrees from the Sun.

The Sun has a completely different relationship with the Moon from its two other inferior planets which cannot move from its side, as the Moon travels independently from the Sun and this movement is demonstrated through the waxing and waning phases of the Moon *(Figs. 31 and 32)*.

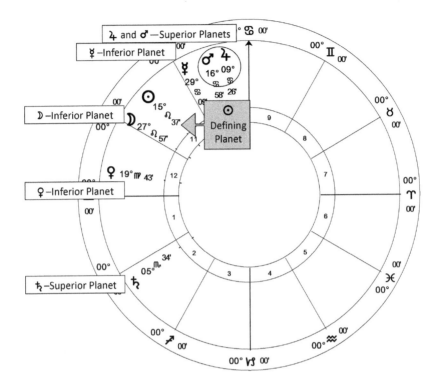

Fig. 30 Example Chart for Oriental and Occidental Planets

The chart *(Fig. 30)* shows Mercury, Mars and Jupiter in oriental position to the Sun, having risen earlier than the Sun whilst the Moon, Venus and Saturn will rise after the Sun, and follow the Sun in occidental position.

According to Placidus' rule, two superior planets, Jupiter and Mars, will benefit from their position in the chart, as do the two inferior planets, Moon and Venus, by being in correct Chaldean relationship to the Sun.

However, Mercury, an inferior planet, is placed ahead of the Sun, and Saturn, a superior planet, will rise after the Sun, and therefore both are in a weaker position due to their counter-Chaldean placement in the chart.

The terms (superior and inferior) which distinguished one set of planets from another, also divided their power, and ultimately impacted on the planets' delineations according to their superior and inferior status.

The three superiors carried more weight than the inferiors, so much so that when Saturn, Jupiter or Mars formed an aspect to Venus, Mercury or the Moon the three planets with higher elevation and venerable position had a marked influence on the circumstances of the three lower-set planets.

In practical terms, the movement of the three inferior planets is much faster than the planets placed above them in the Chaldean Order, so in most cases (retrograde movement can alter this rule) it is the inferiors themselves who bring about the exact application of an aspect to a superior and who then activate the subsequent separation, as the inferiors are the swifter of the two planets.

We might conclude from this natural occurrence that differences in speed between superior and inferior means that whilst the inferiors are the ones who bring this event into being, they are also the ones who bear the brunt of the impact when aspects manifest.

However, their faster speed also provides them with the capacity to move past the powerful influence of one superior planet in order to create the next aspect with another planet placed deeper in the zodiacal degrees.

At a maximum speed of fifteen degrees a day, the Moon's movement through the zodiac is more rapid than Mercury and Venus and when she passes through a sign every two days the Moon has perpetual contact with the other planets and experiences a variety of aspects to the superior planets within a short period of time.

Given that the Moon is highly susceptible to external influence it follows that she has very little breathing space to absorb, adapt, and recover from one hard aspect to Saturn, Jupiter, or Mars, before moving on to the next entanglement with a superior planet.

In one month alone the Moon will activate all five Ptolemaic aspects (conjunction, sextile, square, trine and opposition) to each of the three superior planets, and whilst some aspects are friendlier than others, all three superiors have the ability to affect the Moon's significations, that is, the general condition of the native's physical health and their emotional well-being.

Hellenistic astrologers viewed two of the superior planets, Saturn and Mars, as 'malefic' in nature due to the extreme coldness of Saturn and the excessive dryness of Mars.[54]

Therefore the condition of the inferiors was damaged by difficult aspects to these harsh superiors, as opposed to Jupiter, the more temperate 'benefic' planet who bestowed benefit and largesse on the inferior planets.

However, Jupiter can create its own style of havoc if the conditions are right, so the inferiors are just as much at its mercy as they are to the more maligned planets.

Modern texts are inclined to group Mercury, Venus and Mars together, referring to them collectively as the *personal planets* [55] and similarly classifying them in strength.

But when the concept of a division caused by the Sun is considered important, then Mars gains power over Mercury and Venus, and its malefic nature impacts hugely on the two inferior planets.

Venus in particular struggles with Mars for a number of reasons as they respectively represent the female and male archetype and therefore carry patterns and images which reflect the dichotomy of the two sexes.

Tension always exists between these two planets and their conflict is reflected astrologically on two occasions in their conflicting rulerships over signs within the Thema Mundi chart when Libra opposes Aries and Scorpio opposes Taurus in the archetypal chart.

Venus is the inferior planet and the faster of the two, so that when she approaches an aspect to Mars, she is the one who is susceptible to his influence and who experiences the innate distrust which exists between them, creating anxiety and stress for a sensitive Venus.

The type of aspect will indicate the extent of Mars' intention to harm Venus as well as her speed in recovering from his impact, and the signs in which they are both placed are significant in interpreting how both planets will react to their liaison.

The best case scenario finds Mars in a sign of its own dignity, as whilst strong in essence, it is more likely to behave in a straightforward manner, making it easier for Venus to pacify him and protect herself.

However, if Venus is forced to deal with Mars when it is in a sign of debility, when this malefic's intention and behaviour is less obvious and more harmful, it is difficult for Venus.

She can struggle to understand the superior planet's trickier nature, and when he displays destructive tendencies, Venus is often left in tatters by the resultant carnage.

The Moon's relationship differs from the other two inferior planets in that it is a satellite of the Earth, not a planet like Mercury or Venus both of whom are found in close proximity to the Sun.

In astrological lore the Moon is considered to be a luminary in its own right and therefore conforms to a different set of rules regarding its relationship with the other luminary, the Sun.

The Sun's light is projected onto the Moon, and whilst its light is actually consistent and permanent, from Earth's perspective our experience of the Moon's cycle is one of constant change.

On a monthly basis, we view the Moon's light increasing each evening until it achieves maximum light at full moon when it opposes the Sun.

Its light then begins to gradually fade as it returns to the dark phase in preparation for a new cycle once it has perfected a conjunction with the Sun.

In the example chart *(Fig 30)* the Moon is in a later degree of Leo than the Sun which indicates that the two luminaries have recently experienced a conjunction, but as the Moon has moved away from the Sun a new lunar cycle has already begun.

In terms of direction to the Sun, the Moon in the chart is situated to the west of, or behind the Sun, and has therefore risen after the Sun.

For this reason, the Moon would be judged as being in an occidental position which suits this inferior planet perfectly.

There is a correlation between the Moon's eight phases and its oriental and occidental position in relation to the Sun, as the Moon will stay in occidental position until it achieves an exact opposition to the Sun at full moon, but will move to oriental position once it has reached full moon.

All four of the Moon's waxing phases (new moon, crescent, first quarter, and gibbous) occur when the Moon's light is increasing, so to also find optimum advantage through its occidental position strengthens the Moon and helps to explain why so many traditional texts prefer a waxing Moon over a waning Moon in their lunar interpretations.

The moment the exact opposition aspect has passed, the Moon becomes weakened on two accounts.

Although it takes a few nights after full moon to visibly show, the Moon has already begun to lose strength as it enters the first of its four waning phases (full moon, disseminating, third quarter and balsamic).

As the Moon travels back towards the Sun it will begin to register as an earlier degree of the zodiac, and therefore it will visually occupy an oriental position to the Sun. A waning Moon is not only losing light but it is now placed in a position which is contrary to the one it inhabits in the Chaldean Order.

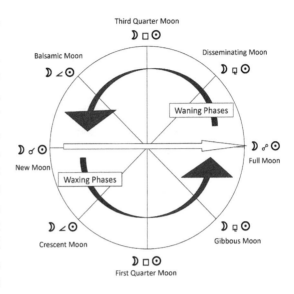

Fig.31 Moon's Phases: Waxing and Waning

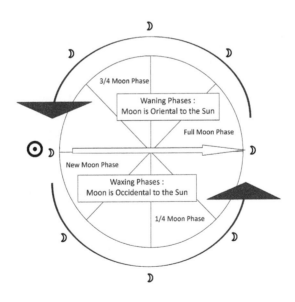

Fig. 32 Moon's Phases and its Occidental/Oriental Positions

Solar Phasing: Conjunctions With The Sun

"A combust planet is like a dying person."[56]

Whilst the Sun is seen as the Light-Bringer too much light and heat is destructive for the planets and if a planet is standing within a certain range of the Sun, it will be invisible to the naked eye and will also be burnt by the Sun's rays.

This is called combustion, from the Latin *comburere,* meaning to 'burn up', and a planet is most likely to be in danger if it is anywhere between a range of zero degrees seventeen minutes and eight degrees thirty minutes from the Sun.

Even after the conjunction has widened, there is further threat from the Sun, as the planet is still under the Sun's rays (Ln.*absconsae,* 'hidden') from eight degrees thirty minutes up to seventeen degrees away from the Sun.

"A planet under the light of the Sun is like a person in prison."[57]

In traditional practice the concept of a planet's orb differed from modern ideas as each planet possessed its own orb of influence in varying sizes of degrees. This was known as a planet's 'moiety' and was believed to be an imaginary sphere of light surrounding each of the planets.

Aspects between planets occurred when the light from one planet in motion interacted with the light from another planet moving at a different speed.

Naturally, the Sun possessed the strongest light and therefore owned the largest orb of influence, so its moiety was generally seen as being between fifteen and seventeen degrees from one side to the other, like the diameter of a circle.

The outer range of the degrees of combustion (8.5 degrees) were created through the concept of moiety meaning 'half-measure', or the radius of the circle of light which surrounds the Sun.

Part of the importance of working with solar phasing was an awareness of the two critical aspects, conjunction and opposition, which a planet could make to the Sun.

The conjunction damaged a planet by its proximity to the Sun and the immediate threat of combustion, whilst an opposition to the Sun meant that it was dangerously appearing as retrograde in motion when viewed from Earth.

Firmicus' translator Jean Rhys Bram adds in her Footnote on a planet's position to the Sun:

"The planet was not regarded as being either matutine or vespertine whilst it was in orb of conjunction; some held the opposition to be merely the point of transition between being oriental or occidental, but others considered the planet to be neither whilst it was retrograde."[58]

In terms of the conjunction, it became critical to know whether the danger zone was approaching either from the Sun moving toward the slower moving superior planets, or if the quicker inferior planets were about to conjunct the Sun in their smaller circles around the luminary.

Moiety also meant that the conjunction's degree was dependent on the planet, not on the aspect itself, and was affected by a number of variables such as the brightness of the planet, its longitude and latitude, and the latitude of the observer.

Firmicus uses the following degrees to define when a planet moves out from the Sun's rays and into their desired position.

When Saturn rises fifteen degrees ahead of the Sun, it is considered to be matutine as the Sun had separated far enough away from Saturn to put it out of harm's way. Likewise, Jupiter is matutine when it precedes the rising of the Sun by twelve degrees, and ideally Mars is eight degrees ahead of the Sun when it is a matutine planet.

Venus is vespertine when it rises eight degrees after the Sun, and Mercury has escaped the Sun's burning rays and classified as vespertine when it rises eighteen degrees after the Sun.

Firmicus does not mention the Moon, however, as the Sun's orb is between fifteen and seventeen degrees, presumably the Moon's cycle completing an old cycle or commencing a fresh one at New Moon is in a better position when the Moon has moved this far from the Sun. The general practice was that a planet was matutine or vespertine when further from the Sun than the Sun's orb – usually 15 degrees.[59]

As the Moon is the fastest moving planet at fifteen degrees of movement in one day, it takes

PLANET	FIRMICUS	PTOLEMY
MOON	(15°)	—
SATURN	15°	14°
JUPITER	12°	12°
VENUS	8°	6°
MARS	8°	15°
MERCURY	18°	12°

Fig. 33 The orb of conjunction to the Sun.

the Moon a little over twenty four hours to be safely separated from its light source.

The preceding Table *(Fig. 33)* shows the orbs of conjunction to the Sun provided by Firmicus in Book II, Ch. IX, and Ptolemy's figures for heliacal risings of planets in Cancer at Alexandria are listed above alongside Firmicus' orbs.

In the example chart shown earlier *(Fig. 30)* the two planets closest to the Sun are Mercury in oriental position, and the Moon in occidental position.

Mercury is sixteen degrees ahead of the Sun and is just short of Firmicus' moiety orb (18 degrees), but fits within Ptolemy's given orb of twelve degrees for Mercury.

The Moon has recently separated from the Sun (both are in Leo) and there is twelve degrees between them so technically she will be properly classified as vespertine in a few more hours when she reaches the separation of fifteen degrees away from the Sun.

"A planet joined with the Sun (cazemi) *is like a person sitting with the king in one chair."*[60]

Paradoxically, if any planet is closer to the Sun than zero degrees seventeen minutes it passes into a powerful position known as *cazemi* meaning in the heart of the Sun. Figuratively speaking the Sun is eclipsed by the planet and the Sun is required to pass its power and life force to the interloper.

This was an 'eye of the storm' situation or the calm nucleus of an otherwise treacherous experience. Not the end of the problem, merely a respite for the planet at the centre of the proceedings.

A Planet's Speed and Direction

"A planet swift in motion is like a young man running."
"A planet slowing down is like a person who is exhausted and has no strength to walk."[61]

The speed of a planet was also significant and speed equated to energy expended and proper purpose or productivity so a planet was accidentally dignified if it was moving quickly relative to its own range of movement.

As soon as a planet began to slow down or it became stationary it was a sign that change was about to occur and this meant the planet was either about to go retrograde or it had been retrograde and was recovering from the experience of moving backwards.

Firmicus mentions earlier that retrogradation can occur at the opposition with the change from oriental to occidental position, but this rule applies only to the three superior planets.

The Moon can oppose the Sun at full moon but it never goes retrograde, and Mercury and Venus cannot move far away from the Sun and therefore can never form an opposition to the Sun.

The apparent backwards movement of Saturn, Jupiter or Mars can also occur at several other periods in their solar phasing, such as at conjunction when the synodic cycle between the Sun and another planet begins, or at a square, or trine or quincunx aspect to the Sun.

Both inferior planets, Mercury and Venus, orbit the Sun in shorter periods than the Earth as Mercury takes 88 days to orbit the Sun and Venus goes around the Sun every 225 days.

When viewed from Earth, the planet appears to be travelling backwards in retrograde motion and when a conjunction occurs the planet is between Earth and the Sun. This is known as an inferior conjunction.

For Mercury this retrograde motion occurs three times in approximately every thirteen months, whilst Venus appears to be retrograde approximately once every eighteen months.

So far as movement is concerned, to the ancients a planet going backwards was an abomination of the Prime Mover's perfect order, a planet gone rogue and an omen of disaster about to occur, with the planet's signature marked strongly on the advancing event.

We now understand that it is impossible for a planet to reverse its movement, and retrograde motion is simply an illusion caused by the moving Earth passing the outer planets in their orbit, but to our ancestors the sight of a planet moving unnaturally and contradictory to the laws of nature was an insult to the gods, and therefore a warning of their displeasure and the advent of impending doom.

The backwards movement of a planet indicated a decline or deterioration in the planet's essence and was therefore deemed to be an accidental debility for the planet as well as an environmental disaster instigated by the retrograde planet.

"A planet about to turn retrograde is like a frightened person, fearing adversities that are coming to him."[62]

Ibn-Ezra offers two different Aphorisms for retrograde planets, stating

> *"A retrograde planet is like a rebellious and defiant person"* in one version, and,

> *"You should know that when Planets are retrograde, they are like a man who is weak, stunned, and worried."*[63]

At first sight it appears as if the two statements are contradictory – one is negatively proactive whilst the other appears disadvantaged and incapable of action – but in both examples they make a similar point.

The planet is distressed to find itself in such terrifying circumstances, and like someone who has lost their bearings, the planet/person does not cope well when they no longer have control of the situation.

Ibn-Ezra's Aphorisms on the speed and direction of a planet emphasizes two significant points:

> firstly, the impact of movement on a planet's behaviour and the importance of its celestial environment, given that movement which was fast and direct bestowed accidental dignity on a planet,

> and secondly, a slowing down in movement was indicative of weakness, and going retrograde was a definite debility for the planet.

The second point to Ibn-Ezra's statements are his constant comparisons between the macrocosm and the microcosm as he deliberately uses analogies between the workings of nature, and those of human experience, to make his point about the connection between the heavens and life on Earth.

Aspects: Good Relationships With Beneficial Planets

"The Planets do the same thing by trine as they do by sextile, but the sextile aspect produces less good or evil than the trine."[64]

From the principles behind solar phasing involving movement and aspects in relation to the Sun, the Accidental Dignities move on to describe other types of aspects between planets of good intent, called benefics, and planets with extreme qualities, called the malefic planets.

The aspect known as a sextile occurs at a distance of two signs, or sixty degrees, between planets and links them through the genders; either the masculine fire to air or vice versa, or the feminine elements of earth and water.

A trine aspect has an angle of one hundred and twenty degrees and links two planets through the same element.

A sextile or trine to Jupiter, Venus, the Moon, or the Sun produced a favourable environment for a planet to become accidentally dignified, and even a conjunction to a well-situated Jupiter, Venus or a Moon in good condition meant that a planet could benefit from the union.

The ancients believed no planet created by the Unmoved Mover (God) could contain any corrupted, impure or unholy essence, therefore malefic planets, Saturn and Mars, are not evil by nature.

However, both planets have natures with extreme qualities – excess cold and dry for Saturn and excess hot and dry for Mars – and the ability for humankind to experience them in a purely positive manner is limited, as the environment surrounding these planets is likely to reflect their qualities and to produce situations which were inclined to be extreme or unpleasant in nature.

"Saturn produces evil with slowness, but Mars produces it suddenly; and therefore Mars is reputed to be worse in harming."[65]

It was not so much a matter of wickedness that brought about misery for mortals, it was more that the uncomfortable environment created occasions marked by separation, loss or conflict, and the reactions of mankind were subsequently acute or destructive in their outcomes.

The aspects which appeared to create the greatest level of mayhem were a conjunction, a square of ninety degrees, or an opposition of one hundred and eighty degrees.

The planet connected to a malefic in this way was accidentally debilitated as the environment surrounding it was made tense or hostile because of the malefic's extreme qualities.

"Caput (Moon's North Node) with the malefic produces terrible evils, for it will increase their malice. But it produces many good things with the benefics, for their goodness is augmented by it. But when Cauda (Moon's South Node) is located in just the same way, it reverses the significations of Caput."[66]

A planet can have varying degrees of good fortune when it is placed alongside the Moon's North Node, *Caput Draconis* or the Dragon's Head, as rather than being a direct conduit for accidental dignity, it can bring mixed blessings by exaggerating the statement made by the adjoining planet.

If condition is good, then even a malefic can bring success to the native, but not without the usual trials and tribulations attributed to the malefic.

However, if the malefic's condition is terrible then this can be exacerbated by a conjunction to the North Node.

The Moon's South Node, *Cauda Draconis* or the Dragon's Tail, had a minimising or shrinking effect so that a benefic lost its power for good, but a malefic's menace could be lessened by a conjunction with the South Node.

Good Placement: The Priority of Houses

"A planet in the pole (angular house) *is like a person staying in his place."*

"A planet in the adjacent (succedent house) *is like a person who is hoping."*

"When a planet is cadent, it is like a man who is troubled and timid."

The chart serves as a scale model for our experience of the heavens and the circumstances which surround a planet are critical to its efficient operation. The more comfortable a planet is through the various classifications of accidental dignity, the better it will be able to express its essential qualities.

For instance, if I know that Socrates is a skilled general then I will deliberately locate him at an advantageous vantage point and give him as many soldiers as he needs to produce victory on the battlefield.

If I want to learn his philosophy I will engage him in a meaningful discussion on politics or moral virtues and the result will be insightful and I will gain knowledge from the encounter.

However, if I take him to the temple or the courthouse then I can expect that his outspokenness, his scorn for authority, and his lack of remorse will land us both in trouble, and will eventually lead to his conviction, imprisonment and a lethal dose of poison.

My fate may be different, but my association with Socrates is likely to do me more harm than good in the eyes of the Athenian Senate.

Similarly, good house placement in a chart greatly assists a planet and provides it with the necessary dignity to produce beneficial or successful outcomes for the chart's owner.

The ascendant in a chart is constantly moving at a rate which is far in advance of any planet and this gives the appearance that the planets are rising in the opposite direction to the zodiacal degrees, or in contradiction to the order of the twelve houses.

This optical illusion makes it appear as if the planets themselves are moving in a clockwise direction by rising in the east at the ascendant, reaching their peak at the Midheaven and setting twelve hours later in the west of the chart at the descendant (hence the term 'diurnal motion', the apparent daily motion of stars around Earth).

But as we are placed on a swiftly moving planet it is the chart's ascendant which keeps dropping through the degrees of the zodiac in an anti-clockwise motion and Earth's movement against the backdrop of 'fixed stars' gives the false impression of a stationary horizon and planets rising and setting over the horizon.

Most computer generated charts can be sped through a twenty four hour time period to demonstrate the planets' positions in the chart at any given moment of the day.

Rather than watching the change in the planets' position, try focusing instead on the rapid movement of the ascendant's degree through the zodiac.

If this is done, then the rise and fall of the planets makes sense as they are propelled forward in diurnal motion by the surge in speed at the ascendant.

The ascendant can be likened to a mouse running in a wheel.

The mouse looks as though it maintains a stationary position on the wheel, and yet by its ability to keep constant motion going, the mouse stays still and the wheel spins out behind it.

If a piece of string is tied to the wheel then we would see it 'rising and setting' by moving back behind the mouse and then returning to face it again when it has spun through the 360 degree circle.

The mouse is the ascendant and the piece of string is the planet over a period of a day.

The most significant alteration will be in the Moon's degree as it is capable of moving a maximum of fifteen degrees over the twenty four hour period.

Even at this speed when the Moon moves in the same direction as the ascendant's degree, the Moon still gets caught up in the momentum in much the same way as if the string were to be moved along the mouse's wheel.

Chapter Seven discusses the houses in detail but, it is worth knowing that poor placement in a house can mean a potentially good planet with essential dignity and good aspects to a benefic can suffer from its location.

A planet in a passive house – with no light from the ascendant – is disadvantaged by being left in the dark and struggling to produce from a bad vantage point.

A planet in a debilitated house – cadent and dark – as the sixth and twelfth houses are described, is a planet imprisoned within a house and frustrated by the debility which infringes on its abilities.

Effectively it is a waste of the planet's essence, but this is part of the accident of birth which turns a chart quickly and changes the planet's possibilities over a period of twenty four hours.

Anyone observing a young child in an international airport after twelve hours of being in transit, tired, irritable, confined to alien spaces and surrounded by equally frazzled and short-tempered adults, will understand the analogy that this child represents a planet in the wrong place at the wrong time.

Under favourable circumstances the child is likely to be delightful and a pleasure to its loved ones.

But not in the early hours of the morning, and certainly not, during the next long flight on the way to their final destination.

As fellow passengers, we can be hugely sympathetic to the child's current plight, but that does not mean we want to sit in the seat alongside them for the entire journey.

The Planetary Joys: Placement in Houses With Kinship

The next classification of accidental dignity also involves a planet's house placement.

Certain houses will benefit certain planets and a planet placed within an environment which is compatible to their basic nature often bodes well for the individual whose chart coincides with a planet's joy.

For instance, four of the houses below the horizon have planets which enjoy the benefit of house to planet association.

Mercury is accidentally dignified when it is found in the first house as this is the house of its joy.

The Moon has a natural affinity for the third house and is subsequently in its joy here.

Venus rejoices in the fifth house of play, leisure and children.

Mars is somewhat at home in the turbulent sixth house where it has ample opportunity to express its nature in a house where unexpected illness, accidents or work commitments are the agenda of the sixth house.

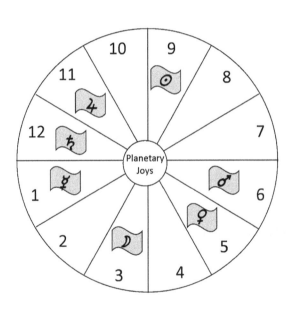

Fig. 34 The Houses of Planetary Joys

In the houses above the horizon, the Sun is in its joy in the ninth house, a house which receives ample light from the ascendant, and although cadent in position, is still considered to be a beneficial house for the native (the individual who owns the chart).

Jupiter is in its joy in the eleventh house which has several advantages in the chart.

The eleventh house aspects the ascendant by the beneficial sextile aspect and is an elevated house, but not too elevated to stress or expose the native.

It is the house where a planet reaches on its last stop before heading to the apex of the chart and describes an individual's hopes and aspirations, a resting place before the planet begins the commitment and hard work necessary for the success of an angular tenth house.

It also signifies relief for the planet which has been ejected from the dark twelfth house and is visually appearing to begin its ascent in a clockwise direction ('diurnal motion').

In the order of the houses, the planet in the eleventh house has expectations of being in a place of enjoyment, entertainment and friendship, often feeling that the respite is well-earned when wedged between the rigours of the tenth house and the debilitated twelfth house.

For all of these reasons, Jupiter finds its accidental dignity through its joy in placement in the eleventh house.

Finally, Saturn is accidentally dignified in the twelfth house, not because it brings success to the affairs of this dark house, but because there is an affinity between a difficult planet, Saturn, and a difficult place, the twelfth house.

Bonatti writes that Saturn rejoices in the twelfth house because the house signifies *"labour, lamentation, and weeping"*[67] and this would appear to be the perfect environmental conditions for Saturn's dour energy in the assembly of planets.

It is unclear whether a dignified Saturn in the twelfth describes the power of the hidden enemy, the type of sorrow experienced, or the nature of one's antagonist or gaoler, but the condition of Saturn's essential qualities are worth detailed examination when Saturn is found in the house of its joy, considering that it is worth remembering that a planet's rejoicing does not necessarily translate as happiness for the chart owner.

The joys of the planets is also compatible with Sect as the diurnal planets – Sun, Jupiter and Saturn – are all situated above the horizon in a diurnal position, whilst the nocturnal planets – Moon, Venus and Mars - each chooses for themselves a house which is below the horizon.

Mercury chooses the ascendant or first house as its house of joy for a number of reasons.

The first house is the strongest house in the chart and is extremely changeable considering that its movement determines the chart's layout and focal points.

First house suits Mercury's nature as a volatile planet subjected to the influence of other planets which learns to adapt to constant changes in the environment triggered by external forces.

Mercury's fluidity in changing from diurnal to nocturnal sect also reflects its position in the neutrality of the first house, but perhaps the most compelling argument for Mercury's choice is the fact that the first house is one of constant activity, and Mercury loves the stimulation and energy of a house with so much natural light.

It should be remembered that one of the reasons behind the accidental dignity of the joys is the fact that it matches planet with like-minded house, and Bonatti says of Mercury in its joy in the first, that

> "Mercury rejoices in it (first house) because he signifies knowledge, and that is a matter more adapted to the person of the native than any other, for knowledge alone can ennoble man, which no other accident can do."[68]

Planetary Sect: A Planet's Affinity With Day or Night

If environmental compatibility is the key phrase best describing accidental dignity, then the final classification has the greatest relevance so far as the seven original planets are concerned.

"A planet in its similitude (in sect) is like a person dealing in a proper matter."

"A planet in its dissimilitude (out of sect) is like a person dealing in an improper matter."[69]

The translator for Ibn-Ezra chooses the term 'similitude' to describe a planet linked to its correct planetary sect.

It is a word not commonly used in the English language but basically it means affinity, correspondence, community, kinship or uniformity.

Planet in sect affinity means that the planet is in agreement with certain features in the chart, and when this occurs the planet feels supported and comfortable and has a genuine desire to act like a person *"dealing in a proper matter"* and even Mars and Saturn is willing to be generally well-behaved under their appropriate sect divisions.

The exhausted and irritable child from the airport lounge is now recovered, well-rested and released from confinement and is now ready to play the part of the loving, well-behaved and cheerful progeny that its parents know it to be most of the time.

This is the child in similitude with its environment.

Sect begins with the idea that human behaviour changes in accordance with the opposition of light and darkness, or more correctly, the presence of light verses the absence of light.

During the light-time hours humans become more active and most business practices are at their peak during the day.

The hours of darkness are more likely to be used for rest and recreation as the frenetic activity of the day has passed and food is consumed at a more leisurely pace.

During the hours of darkness time is allocated to entertainment, social or romantic pursuits or spent in relaxation or for sleep.

The Sun is the celestial donor of natural light and the horizon which cuts the chart from east to west is the intangible junction between earth and sky. This line dictates whether the world is warm and bright in the day-time, or cold and dim during the night's hours of darkness.

Under the rules of sect, a term derived from the Latin *"seco"* meaning 'to cut' or 'divide', the most significant diameter of a chart occurs at the horizontal line beginning at the ascendant, where we witness a planet rising, and after a period of approximately twelve hours, where the same planet sets over the descendant.

The Sun above the horizon indicates day-time, or a diurnal chart.

The Sun below the horizon, placed anywhere from below the ascendant to the degree of the descendant, signals that the Sun has set and the birth has occurred in the night-time hours, creating a nocturnal chart for the individual.

Naturally the Sun prefers the twelve hours above the horizon when it is visible and its light and warmth can illuminate the atmosphere.

Jupiter and Saturn also prefer a diurnal chart and work to their best advantage in their preferred day-time environment.

A hint as to the reasoning behind the Sun's choice in planets comes from first century astrologer Vettius Valens who says :

"The Sun attached to himself Zeus and Kronos as co-workers in his own sect and as guardians of what is accomplished by him – Zeus as the imitator and proxy of the king himself, the chooser of good things, the bestower of reputation and life; Kronos as the promoter of ills and oppositions and as the depriver of time."[70]

There is a kinship between the Sun and these two superior planets as the Sun has a drive for reputation and honours and the diurnal native wants the attention and respect that they believe only success or an imagined goal can deliver.

Jupiter aids the Sun in its quest as Jupiter resembles the Sun's ambitious thirst for the trappings which accompany any victory in life.

The Sun only has to ask and Jupiter will show it a glorious vision of adventure, knowledge, achievement and self-government.

Saturn provides the balance of reality, and asks for timelines and spread sheets to see if the dreams of its two other sect members are possible, or if there is any way that Saturn can make the dream materialize into solid form.

Alternatively, the nocturnal chart with the Sun below the horizon appoints the Moon as its major luminary and the world through the eyes of a nocturnal native is seen in a different light from its counter-part.

The Sun's energy and warmth originates from its own light source but the Moon gains its varying shape from the Sun's reflected light.

Similarly, the individual with a nocturnal chart will search for ways in which it gains pleasure from others' comfort, happiness or safety, and are at their most content in their role as service-provider.

This role is not subservient because the native is not submissive or down-trodden, nor are the opportunities provided by the Moon forced onto the nocturnal chart.

Rather, it is a role chosen with joy, and any self-sacrifice made by the individual is brushed aside as a minor incidental, and not as the main focus of the nocturnal chart.

The public face of the Moon in the night sky is one of constant change and variances in light and dark are characteristic of her twenty nine day cycle with the Sun.

Nocturnal individuals often reflect the Moon in cycles of commitment and withdrawal within their own lives and will speak of life as progressing through waves of retreat or resignation only to come back with renewed energy or a devotion to a new purpose or goal.

External success will not hold a lunar chart for long if the passion is gone or the service is no longer warranted or holds little meaning for the individual, and nocturnal charts are known to walk away when others would have stayed to reap the benefits of all their hard work.

Valens says on the Moon's choice of nocturnal planets:

"She has Aphrodite and Ares as co-sectarians – Aphrodite, suitable enough, for benefaction and to distribute reputation and time; Ares for looking askance at nativities."[71]

Venus and Mars join the Moon in rejoicing in the lunar light and are accidentally dignified in a nocturnal chart.

Valens' statement implies that Venus aids the Moon by bringing good fortune and the opportunities for beneficial social connections, and good timing by meeting the right person at the right time.

Mars plays the role of the Moon's protector in the nocturnal chart, constantly on the guard and is fiercely loyal to the beliefs and ideals held by the nocturnal native.

If Saturn is the time-keeper in a diurnal chart, then Mars takes the position of bodyguard in the nocturnal chart and its weapons are a passion to uphold the Moon's cause of choice, and a long memory for slights suffered by the chart's owner.

In keeping with the nature of these three planets' nocturnal sect, imagination, intuition and 'a gut feeling' are the mainstay of a night-time chart.

Feelings of "*kismet*", the Turkish term for "*fate* or *destiny*", best describes two random and totally unrelated incidents coming together at exactly the right moment to create an outcome which was previously unforeseen by the individual.

All charts, regardless of sect, can experience "*kismet*" moments, but whilst a solar chart questions and analyses the moment against its perception of reality (the Sun's lieutenant, Saturn), a nocturnal chart offers no resistance and accepts *kismet* as a gift whilst moving forward with Grace to meet Fate at the next junction.

Mercury hedges its bets and can be rated as either a diurnal or a nocturnal planet, depending on where it sits in relation to the Sun.

If Mercury rises ahead of the Sun it is accidentally dignified in a diurnal chart, but should it follow the Sun in its preferred occidental position, it receives a double dose of accidental dignity if the Sun is below the horizon, considering that Mercury is dignified according to its correct solar phasing position, and as a nocturnal planet, is also compatible with a night-time chart.

My intention to show the difference between one sect type and the other is not to present the diurnal chart as self-seeking or the nocturnal chart as a consolation prize or inferior to the Sun-orientated chart.

Nor is the nocturnal individual a saintly person who gives everything to others and takes no reward for themselves.

In truth, both sect divisions *do* serve the native's best interests, purely because the Sun and the Moon are luminaries of equal strength according to their own sect and they are duty-bound to serve the chart and its owner.

Even the end results can look very similar as nocturnal births can rise just as high in prestige, power and position as charts with the Sun in elevation at the top of the chart.

But this is achieved through variances in either sect's guidelines whether it is diurnal motivation or nocturnal resolution, success depends on how the luminaries in charge of the chart are situated, and the nature and condition of each sect's two accompanying lieutenants.

The Williams sisters from the United States are both tennis players who have maintained long careers at the top of their profession when most other players of their age have fallen by the wayside.

Venus Williams, the elder sister by fifteen months, was born in the afternoon and has a diurnal chart, whilst Serena Williams was born at 8:30pm when the Sun was situated in her nocturnal chart's sixth house.

Each of the sisters works beautifully within the framework of their own sect division and have achieved phenomenal success by understanding what drives them and how they can best achieve their goals within the set perimeters of their diurnal or nocturnal chart.

This is a summary of Sect as one of the Accidental Dignities, and as such it is a factor which plays a huge part in a planet's condition and comfort, but sadly sect has been by and large discarded or ignored over the past few centuries.

The topic of Planetary Sect features in the sequel to this book entitled *A Tiny Universe's Companion* whereby the rules of sect are examined and their effect on each of the planets is discussed in further detail.

Summary of Dignities

This chapter began with a logical argument so it is only fitting that it ends in the same manner.

The exploration of a planet's dignity, both Essential and Accidental, extends much further beyond whether the planet behaves well or badly, according to its essential qualities.

The rulership of the signs by the planets has a flow-on effect which impacts on the entire chart, depending on the difference between a planet's location in the chart, and the houses that a planet rules via its sign on a house cusp.

The relationship between a house and its ruling planet is intimate, binding, and critical to the house's affairs, but sadly the practice has been somewhat neglected in modern times.

An awareness of a planet's condition is vital in understanding the working mechanics of a chart, not only through the planet's position but also in its power as the ruling lord (or lady) of one or two houses in the horoscope.

	Deductive Reasoning applied to House Rulership by the Planets	
MAJOR PREMISE	*All Men are Mortal*	*All Signs are Ruled by a Planet*
MINOR PREMISE	*Socrates is a Man*	*A Sign is on the Cusp of Each House*
CONCLUSION	*Therefore, Socrates is Mortal (due to the Major Premise)*	*Therefore, A Planet Will Rule Each of the Houses (due to Major Premise)*

Fig. 35 Conclusion Planets and Houses

The rulership of the houses by a planet is the conclusion to the astrological premises stated above. The following chapters on the intimate relationships of the planets themselves deeply impacts on the houses that they rule, as does the sign in which they reside and which particular house axis for which they are responsible.

The ability for a planet to successfully manage its house is dependent on its condition.

Therefore, it is necessary to take each of the steps listed above to judge the condition of each planet, and also to be aware of the condition of the lord of the signs in which each planet appears as the dispositor of the sign (its owner) will greatly affect the ability of a planet to perform well in that particular sign.

The process of judging a planet and determining its condition may seem time-consuming at the beginning of the reader's learning process, but it does get quicker as the astrologer becomes more familiar with the techniques and more confident in understanding the type of information they are looking to extract from the chart.

CHAPTER FOUR

Friends and Enemies

"An astrologer cannot make a combination of the significations of the stars before he knows their friendships and enmities, of which there are three kinds – one indeed according to their nature, another according to their domiciles, and the third according to their aspects".

Fifth Aphorism, *Centiloquy of Hermes Trismegistus*[72]

The *Centiloquy of Hermes Trigmegistus,* attributed to the legendary figure Hermes Trismegistus *(thrice-greatest),* is a collection of one hundred aphorisms, or astute observations on astrology's most important principles, found in an extant translation by Stephen of Messina in 1262 C.E. from earlier Arabic sources.

The fifth principle cited in *Centiloquy* states three conditions whereby a planet may be judged.

> Firstly, knowledge of the nature and characteristics peculiar to each planet is crucial to judgement.
> Secondly, a planet's essential dignity is vitally important.
> And thirdly, the aspects recorded in the Thema Mundi chart need to be acknowledged and complied with, in order to successfully judge a planet's condition.

Hermes supports this premise with examples in the following aphorism, citing the nature of the relationship between Venus and Mercury, and then between Jupiter and Mars.

The sixth Aphorism states: *"Venus is the opposite of Mercury, who rules speech and learning, but she embraces pleasures and delights. Similarly also, Jupiter is the opposite of Mars, the former indeed wishes for mercy and justice, but the latter, impiety and cruelty".*[73]

All *'three kinds of friendships and enmities'* are covered in these examples by mention of the incompatibility of their natures, the planets' dignity through exaltation, and the opposition which exists between their exalted signs.

It is general practice to address the conflict which is inherent in the planets' signs of rulership, that is Jupiter's Pisces opposing Mercury's Virgo, but instead Hermes' text identifies Pisces as Venus' exalted sign, in opposition to Mercury's exaltation sign of Virgo.

Likewise, Hermes concentrates on Jupiter's opposition to Mars through their exalted signs of Cancer and Capricorn, whereby Jupiter's exalted sign of Cancer is hostile towards Mars' exalted sign of Capricorn.

This rule would also extend towards the Sun and Saturn through the opposition of their exalted signs, Aries and Libra, but perhaps no mention is made as tension already exists through the antagonism of their rulership signs' opposition of Leo and Aquarius.

The signs of exaltation are extremely old in origin and were first assigned by the Babylonians who called them *"the secret houses of the planets".*[74]

They were based on a version which differed from Firmicus' Thema Mundi whereby a substitute World Chart placed the seven planets not in their signs of rulership, but instead in the degree and sign of their

Fig. 36 Hermes' Sixth Aphorism Planets' Exaltations

exaltations, supposedly to honour the planets' positions at the moment of the world's creation.[75]

Whilst Firmicus Maternus prefers the Hermetic horoscope for the Birth of the Universe,[76] he acknowledges the importance of exaltation, saying that a planet is raised up to a maximum of its own natural force, and when in the sign of its fall the planet suffers the loss of that force.[77]

Deborah Houlding has added the words of Antiochus of Athens (2nd century) to her annotations on Hermes' sixth aphorism, with Antiochus remarking:

"Mercury is the master of arguments, while Venus is the overseer of desire and intercourse, so when the intellect increases, the desire and pleasure in intercourse decreases. And where the appetitive and pleasurable is exalted, there the intellect is depressed".[78]

Animosity between planets, Jupiter and Mars, occurs for the same three reasons as it does for Venus and Mercury.

Their inherent natures are discordant, the placement and order of exaltation is at odds in Thema Mundi, and the hostile aspect of opposition is a result of this second-level dignity in the World Chart.

Cancer (Jupiter's exalted sign) lies at the eastern boundary and Capricorn (Mars' exalted sign) is the western boundary of Thema Mundi, leading to the chart's ascendant and descendant axis being representative of the archetypal battle between life and death.

Antiochus states that Jupiter is the overseer of the life-breath and abundance, whilst Mars is the overseer of death, and that where the life-breath increases (at the ascendant), there the bringer of death is depressed; and likewise, where death increases (at the descendant), there life is depressed.[79]

The writings of both Hermes and Antiochus indicate that oppositions between domicile rulership are not the only signs which cause antagonism between planets, but that the second classification of Essential Dignity, namely exaltation, can also create bad feeling between two planets.

In the case of sign rulership, the opposition of Capricorn to Cancer naturally disposes Saturn to be an enemy of the Moon.

However, when Mars borrows Saturn's sign for its own exaltation, and Jupiter borrows Cancer from the Moon, both planets inherit the adverse relationship that exists between the domicile rulers of opposing signs.

The same principle of sharing signs applies to the remaining cardinal signs as Aries is the domicile sign of Mars and the exalted sign of the Sun, whilst Libra belongs to Venus, but is also Saturn's sign of exaltation.

Thus the animosity between Mars and Venus is repeated by the Sun and Saturn when they share the cardinal signs through the second level of dignity.

The Sun already opposes Saturn through their domicile rulerships of Leo and Aquarius, so when their signs of exaltation also oppose one another via Aries and Libra, there are twice as many reasons for these two planets to experience an acrimonious relationship.

Hermes cites Mercury's opposition to Venus through their signs of exaltation, but Mercury is also the exception in the two levels of essential dignity as Virgo is both its rulership and its sign of exaltation.

For this reason, Mercury dislikes Jupiter as much as it dislikes Venus, as Jupiter and Venus share the sign of Pisces.

Seven is an uneven number so there must be one planet which is excluded from an opposition via exaltation, and it is the Moon in Taurus which gains the benefit of no further agitation, purely because Scorpio is not an exalted sign for the planets.

Antiochus says there is a reason why the Moon is relieved from interference by another planet, and this is because the Moon is directly connected to Fate *(Fortuna)*, and that when Fate chooses to exalt the native there can be no opposing force to hamper or infringe on the native's good fortune.

Likewise, if Fate chooses to strike the individual down in order to teach humility, then no other significator can be permitted to intervene and save them, except by the hand of Fate herself.[80]

Al-Biruni's Table of Friendship and Enmity: Notation 447

Abu Rayhan al-Biruni (973-1052 CE) was a Persian scholar and scientist who is still today considered to be one of science's greatest pioneers.

He was an astronomer, mathematician, ethnographer, anthropologist, historian, and geographer, and although his body of work on astrology was produced more than ten centuries after the times of Hermes and Antiochus, al-Biruni cites many of the Hellenistic techniques practiced by his predecessors.

His *Book of Instruction in the Elements of the Art of Astrology* was written in 1029 C.E. and al-Biruni repeats Hermes' fifth and sixth aphorisms on the three conditions for judgement in his Notation 447 titled *"Friendship and Enmity of the Planets"*.[81]

Al-Biruni begins his notation by stating that the temperament and the basic nature of the planets will determine their attraction or repulsion towards one another.

He gives Saturn and Jupiter as an example of incompatibility, saying that they are regarded as being inimical (harmful) because Saturn is dark, maleficent and extremely distant, whilst Jupiter is shining, beneficent and only moderately distant from Earth.

He mentions the planets' elementary qualities and that those planets judged as fiery, i.e. the Sun and Mars, will be inimical to watery planets such as the Moon, and that those who are of an airy nature, presumably Jupiter, will reject those planets of an earthy nature, again, a reference to Saturn.

Notation 447 continues with the statement that the situation of a planet's domiciles and exaltations will also reveal the basis of the relationships between the planets, and al-Biruni completes his introduction by saying:

"The views of Abu al-Qasim, the philosopher, based on the foregoing considerations are shown in the columns of the subjoined table".[82]

We have no way of knowing who al-Biruni is referring to by name as Abu al-Qasim as it is an honorary title meaning *"son of Muhammad"*, but the table from al-Biruni's text is reproduced below *(Fig. 37)* and lists the various relationships of the planets.

The planets are organized in the Chaldean Order, with the two columns on the left listing antagonistic relations since al-Biruni describes them as *'hurtful'* and *'injurious'*, whilst the two columns on the right of al-Biruni's Table list alliances and bonds of friendship between the planets.

Planet	Mutually Hurtful With	Injurious To	Offering Friendship To	Asking Friendship From
♄	Sun and Moon	Jupiter	Mars	Venus
♃	Mars; Mercury	Mercury	Venus	Moon
♂	Jupiter; Venus	Moon	Sun	Saturn
☉	Saturn	Venus	—	Mars
♀	Mars; Mercury	—	Saturn	Jupiter
☿	Jupiter; Venus	Venus	Neither Offers Friendship	Nor Asks for Friendship
☽	Saturn	Mars	Jupiter	Venus

Fig. 37 al-Biruni's Table of Friendship and Enmity of
Planets in the Chaldean Order (Notation 447)

The last two columns on the right of al-Biruni's Table show the kinship shared between planets when the signs belong to both Domicile and Exalted ruler.

For instance, Saturn offers friendship to Mars through his sign of Capricorn, but asks Venus for friendship so that he might borrow her sign of Libra for his own exaltation.

Likewise, Jupiter offers up his rulership sign of Pisces to Venus, and approaches the Moon to ask for Cancer as his exalted sign.

Mars offers Aries to the Sun, but asks permission from Saturn, the Sun's enemy, for his sign of Capricorn.

The Sun does not share Leo with another planet, but asks Mars for his fire sign to become the Sun's exaltation.

Venus offers Saturn Libra and asks Jupiter for Pisces as her exaltation.

However Mercury uses his own sign of Virgo for exaltation so he does not need another planet's blessing, and neither does he offer Virgo or Gemini to his fellow planets for their exaltation.

Lastly, the Moon offers Cancer to Jupiter, but needs to ask Venus for her consent to borrow Taurus for her own exaltation.

Dispositors: Planets Who Lend Out Their Signs

*"Everybody you fight is not your enemy and everybody that helps
you is not your friend."*

Mike Tyson (1966 -)

In his Table of Friendship and Enmity, al-Biruni demonstrates that
the planet at the highest level of essential dignity, the domicile ruler, is
the one which is the fundamental owner of a sign.

This ruler – Saturn offering its sign to Mars, or Mars offering its
sign to the Sun – is like a monarch who legally has the right to offer
something as a temporary loan, usually because it is confident of its
ownership in the first place.

The term *'dispositor'* is used to describe the ruling planet, derived
from the French *'disposer'* meaning to arrange, set in order, regulate, or
distribute, and if we activate the word as a verb, it is assumed we have
the authority to place it into the hands of another person, and that we
remain its rightful owner.

The same rule applies in astrology, when a planet is the dispositor of
a sign, it owns that sign, and any other planet found in the sign, must
look to its owner for support.

No matter how strong a position the exalted planet may believe itself
to be in, if the ruler of the sign is weak or damaged in some way, then
the exaltation will fall in a heap.

For instance, Mars may be more than willing to offer friendship to
the Sun by loaning the sign of Aries but if Mars' own condition in the
chart is poor, then the Sun in Aries will not rise as high in exaltation as
it might have, had Mars (the owner of Aries) been in better condition.

An allegory for the relationship between a dispositor and the lender
is to imagine that I borrow a friend's beautiful red Ferrari to impress
my new girlfriend, but my friend has failed to tell me that the brakes
on the car are faulty. When I speed and take the corner too quickly I
crash because my brakes have not held and I have lost all the dignity I
may have built up from the use of the car.

Mars, the owner of the car, has been negligent in not fixing the
breaks before lending the car, and has also failed to tell me of the

problem, and I, the Sun as an exalted planet, perhaps showing off and driving too fast, have been unable to control the vehicle.

My actions have impacted on both myself and the car's dispositor.

I have ended up in hospital and am now without a girlfriend, and Mars has a hefty repair bill and is without transport in the future.

A dispositor's lack of viability has a direct impact on any planet which 'borrows' its sign and exaltation is an excellent example of how a planet can start at the top and somersault to the depths of despair if the owner of its exalted sign is itself in a terrible condition.

Each time a planet finds placement in anything other than its own rulership sign, it takes the risk of being disposited by a planet in poor condition.

However, a planet which is peregrine, that is, in a sign which has no essential dignity, its situation can be improved if the ruler of that sign is essentially dignified in some way.

If I am bullied at school, it would make sense to take my scarily strong older brother with me one day to show that I have powerful back-up, and that by association I am protected by my brother from future harm.

The same situation occurs within a chart. The nature and condition of a sign's dispositor will indicate two things; how a planet in the sign reacts, and how the planet that owns the sign will help or hinder the planet borrowing its sign.

It soon becomes apparent that a planet which is located in its rulership sign has power for two reasons. One, the planet has the best advantage and opportunity to express its essential qualities when it is found in its domicile sign. Two, when placed in its domicile sign it does not borrow from another planet and therefore it is **never** dependent on another planet's situation.

If Mars takes his own car out and the breaks fail, it is his fault and his problem. But it is likely that Mars will handle the situation far better than the Sun simply because he knows and understand his car better than someone who has merely borrowed it for the day.

"Mutually Hurtful With" –
The Problem With Debility

The Table of Friendship and Enmity reflects information found within the Thema Mundi chart, especially where the first column, the animosities of the planets, is concerned.

For example, the Thema Mundi chart begins with the first sign of Cancer followed by Leo.

These two signs are owned respectively by the Moon (Cancer) and by the Sun (Leo).

Opposite these two signs are Capricorn and Aquarius, both owned by Saturn, the terminator of the physical Life (Moon) and the destroyer of Light (Sun).

So harmful are these two oppositions that we use the term *'detriment'* to describe a Moon found in Capricorn or a Sun situated in Aquarius.

The detriment occurs for two reasons, one because the luminary is cast as far away as possible from their domicile sign so there is a sense of alienation from home territory, and two, because the territory is not only foreign to them, but it is the residence of their arch enemy.

A Moon in Capricorn or a Sun in Aquarius are not only restricted in their ability to perform according to their true nature, but their signs are both owned by Saturn.

In reverse, if Saturn is placed in either Cancer or Leo, the dispositor (owner) of its sign is respectively, the Moon or the Sun.

This is the idea behind al-Biruni's *"mutually hurtful with"* because the planet in detriment has borrowed it sign from an enemy and both parties, the lender and the borrower, are unlikely to be happy about the situation.

Robert Zoller was one of the instigators behind Project Hindsight, the 1990's retrieval of traditional astrology and in his opinion, dispositorship was a type of service, inasmuch as one planet lent its sign but it expected service from the planet which was using the sign.

In other words, the borrower is required to serve the lender.

In the example of the Moon in Capricorn or the Sun in Aquarius, the rule of dispositorship means that Saturn holds power over them and that they are obligated to serve Saturn, as well as seeing to their own needs.

The condition of Saturn in the chart will determine how much is expected from the luminary in detriment, and of course, Saturn may have its own problems seeing to the needs of its sign's dispositor if not fortunate enough to be in rulership.

Likewise, if Saturn is found in detriment in either Leo or Cancer it will be duty-bound to serve either the Sun (Leo) or the Moon (Cancer).

The first column in al-Biruni's Table is fairly straight forward as there are clear reversals of power when it comes to an exchange of the first level of dignity, but it becomes more complicated when the second column is dissected for the purposes of interpretation.

The second column also deals with dispositorship (ownership) but addresses exaltation, the second level of essential dignity – or rather the opposite of exaltation through the debility of fall – and looks at the level of damage a planet might incur at the hands of its dispositor.

For instance, Jupiter experiences two calamities when it is in the sign of Capricorn, it is in a state of fall (opposite its exalted sign of Cancer), and it is disposited by Saturn who is the rightful owner of Capricorn.

Jupiter's brief in its role as the greater benefic is supposedly to produce benefit for the native, but it must now do so through a difficult and restrictive sign, at the same time being bound to serve Saturn, its natural enemy.

The stress Jupiter encounters in trying to fulfil both assignments shows in the chart and also through the two houses that Jupiter rules via its own signs of Sagittarius and Pisces.

If Jupiter is in Aquarius it is still disposited by Saturn, but it does not suffer the debility of fall and therefore is not as damaged as when it lies in Capricorn.

Saturn's own relationship with Mars is complicated as it is in fall in Aries, but is disposited by a planet which, in other circumstances, is trying to buy favour from Saturn by borrowing Capricorn for its own exaltation.

It is easy to see how al-Biruni's Table starts to imitate the delicacy of diplomatic trade agreements between countries, as they borrow, share and swap favours from one country/planet to another.

The most successful trade agreements are the ones where there is reciprocity, in other words, both parties benefit from the agreement and neither one is deemed to be more powerful than the other.

The same idea applies in terms of dispositorship and is called 'generosity' whereby two planets are placed in each other's sign and therefore become each other's dispositor.

Ibn-Ezra (1089-1164 CE) defines 'generosity' in the following manner.

"Generosity is when two planets are in each other's domicile, or exaltation, or some other rulership; even though they do not join or aspect one another, there is still reception between them."[83]

Similar to the idea of house-swapping with another party for an agreed period of time, both parties agree with mutual trust and understanding that each will be responsible for the other's property using the same care as if it were their own dwelling.

Generosity becomes *Mutual Reception* when there is a Ptolemaic aspect (sextile, square, trine) between the two dispositors, as not only do they swap houses, but they stay in contact with one another and this is added security for both parties.

Sending photos back and forth or having Skype chats means that the owner of each property feels as though they are still in control, even though they are no longer physically present at their property.

With aspect they can acknowledge each other's presence and share conversation, thereby creating a strong alliance between them.

Without aspect they are still each other's dispositor (generosity), but they are blind to one another's presence and are unlikely to gain a direct advantage from the connection.

An opposition is also a Ptolemaic aspect, and if two planets are situated in opposition in each other's signs then technically, this too is mutual reception.

However, both planets will be in their signs of detriment if they face one another across the chart and rather than being mutually beneficial to one another, are likely to remain hostile or demand something impossible from the relationship.

If these two parties are living in each other's homes they are not happy with the situation, and if one party damages the property, the other will reciprocate by doing the same thing in its borrowed location.

The situation can soon escalate so that damage is done to both homes and this is exactly what can happen in a chart.

If the Sun in Aquarius opposes Saturn in Leo there is a hostile state of mutual reception because the Sun is acting out in the house owned by Saturn and vice versa.

Both planets are struggling and this will be obvious in the affairs of the two houses which form an axis across the chart.

Each of the six axes works to a similar theme but from different sides of the chart, some are intimately connected to the native and some have outside interference from others.

The first house shows my actions and the opposing seventh house is the actions of others towards me, both with favourable and antagonistic intentions.

The second and eighth house axis is concerned with money, mine (2nd) and others (8th).

The third and ninth axis has a common theme of learning and education.

The skills I can perform with the greatest ease are third house and the skills I grapple with because they are foreign to me or I need outside expertise to learn them, are indicated by the ninth house.

The fourth and tenth axis (and their lords) will show the relationship between father and mother, the beginnings of life and the native's aspirations throughout adulthood, and the private life as opposed to the public life and social status.

The fifth and eleventh house axis is my children and my leisure (5th) as opposed to other people's children and joint leisure pursuits with friends and groups.

The final axis involves the troubled sixth and twelfth house axis and again one side (6th) is concerned with my woes, ill health and the servitude I inflict on myself, whilst the opposite house (12th) is what is inflicted on me, or where I look to alleviate or to compound the suffering of others through my fears or misgivings.

When planets in detriment are in mutual reception through an opposition they will reside in each other's houses and the axis involved will be a constant trial for the individual.

The astrologer's recommendation would be for the native to refrain from using the detrimental planets to trash each other's house as neither party (planet) will win the battle in the end.

As for the improved relations of planets, al-Biruni's Table shows that Saturn has a better alliance with Venus who disposits (owns) the sign of Saturn's exaltation (Libra), and even though Saturn serves Venus it does so with some good will.

Sometimes if there is genuine friendship between two planets through their generic rulerships, then the expected outcome may not be as bleak for the native as it first appears when the Table is not taken into account in the planets' delineation.

For instance, an astrologer presenting a modern interpretation of Saturn in aspect to Venus may choose to highlight a breakdown in close relationships, or a poor attitude towards women, or possible intimacy issues.

However, given the two planets' mutual friendship over their joint ownership of Libra, the combination of Saturn with Venus may not be as harsh or as negative as anticipated, especially when both planets are in good condition in the chart.

Ptolemy says for moral fibre, Saturn with Venus denotes a man who is *"solicitous of the priesthood, studious of wisdom, faithful in friendship, reflective, and scrupulous in regard to female virtue"*.[84]

However, if Saturn or Venus is in terrible condition then it will bring moral weakness, but this is dealing with how the two planets are situated according to essential dignity, rather than any damage Saturn might be assumed to inflict on Venus, simply because it is a malefic and it is presumed to act badly towards the planet of relationships and women.

Applying al-Biruni's Table to the Modalities

"The unalike is joined together, and from differences results the most beautiful harmony."

Heraclitus (535 – 475 BCE), Greek Philosopher

The Table of Friendship and Enmity of Planets can be viewed from a different perspective, namely through the three levels of quadruplicities or the modalities of cardinal, fixed and mutable, in order to see how the planets' relationships will impact on the three crosses.

These poles are the backbone of the chart, and the modalities' rulerships will directly impact on an axis which shares a common thread.

The relationship between planets according to al-Biruni's Table will automatically create an underlying dialogue between certain planets, and this dialogue, whether friendly, co-operative, hostile, or merely tolerated will affect houses simply because astrological logic works.

All planets rule signs.

A house has a sign on its cusp.

Therefore, planets rule houses.

The Cardinal Cross

The cardinal cross involves a number of possibilities regarding the rulership of its signs by the first rule of Essential Dignity, domicile rulership, and by the second rule of exaltation (circled in diagram).

The two malefic planets appear to have the highest number of hostile relationships as they feature in both cardinal axes.

Saturn opposes the Moon through rulership and the Sun through exaltation.

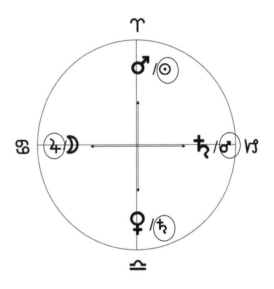

Fig. 38 Rulership and Exaltations of the Cardinal Signs

Mars opposes Venus through rulership and Jupiter through exaltation.

We are reminded of Hermes' sixth aphorism:

"Jupiter is the opposite of Mars, the former indeed wishes for mercy and justice, but the latter, impiety and cruelty".

When dispositorship is taken into account we find Saturn dislikes Mars, and Mars dislikes the Moon, because they are the planets who own the malefics' fall signs.

The power of the four cardinal signs – called *tropical* or *movable* signs – lies in them being the mainspring of action, or the *'fount of energy'*,[85] in whose placement the Sun turns from one season to the next.

These four initiating signs all have a domicile lord and an exalted lord so the combinations for the cardinal cross is more complicated than the fixed or mutable crosses.

The Fixed Cross

The fixed cross contains only one planet's exaltation – that of the Moon in Taurus.

Once more, Saturn's hostile relationship with the Sun is evident, but in the fixed Cross of Matter it is an animosity born of domicile rulership, rather than the exaltation problem of the cardinal signs of Aries and Libra.

It is noteworthy that in both cardinal and fixed modalities Mars and Venus are mutually harmful as they own signs in both quadruplicities.

In the cardinal cross Mars dislikes Cancer's owner, the Moon, and the Moon reciprocates by

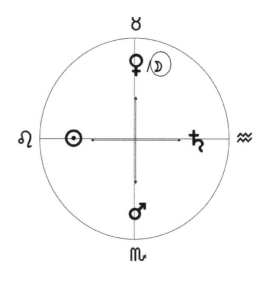

Fig. 39 Rulership and Exaltations of the Fixed Signs

disliking Mars who owns her fall sign of Scorpio in the fixed modality.

The Mutable Cross

The mutable cross differs from the other modalities in that Mercury and Jupiter's signs are in square aspect and only two planets share domicile rulership of the four mutable signs.

For this reason Mercury and Jupiter are mutually harmful to one another as they twice own opposing signs.

Venus is the only other planet which claims a mutable sign, having asked Jupiter for Pisces as its exalted sign.

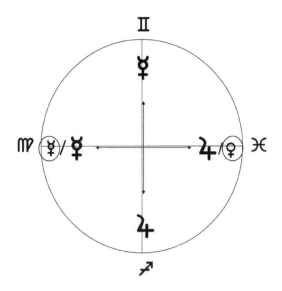

Fig. 40 Rulership and Exaltations of the Mutable Signs

Venus' state of exaltation puts it at odds with Mercury as Hermes' *Centiloquy* explains earlier:

"Venus is the opposite of Mercury, who rules speech and learning, but she embraces pleasures and delights."

Mercury breaks the pattern of asking another planet for favours when it retains Virgo for its own exaltation.

This could be the result of Mercury being shrewd and observing the virtue of prudence as it does not want to pay service to another, nor be honour-bound to do another planet's biding.

In Shakespeare's *Hamlet* the character Polonius counsels his son Laertes saying:

> *"Neither a borrower nor a lender be;*
> *For loan oft loses both itself and friend*
> *And borrowing dulls the edge of husbandry (thrift)."*

Act-I, Scene-III, *Hamlet*

Mercury seems to have taken this advice to heart when it keeps Virgo for itself and does not lend out Gemini to another planet.

This is the one time that Mercury becomes self-sufficient and this is important for a planet which is greatly influenced by the other planets.

Mercury's autonomy is often compromised for several reasons.

It is often in a state of combustion due to its proximity to the Sun and from Earth's perspective Mercury appears retrograde more often than any other planet.

Mercury often mimics other planets' personalities rather than retaining its own, and it changes its sect preference constantly according to its relation to the Sun.

Perhaps ownership of its own signs is one way for Mercury to retain some level of stability in the midst of all the surrounding chaos.

Mercury is also the planet with the least number of predestined relationships to other planets.

Mercury is mutually harmful to just two planets, Jupiter and Venus, whilst the Sun follows next by sharing relations with three planets, Saturn, Venus and Mars. Both benefic planets, Jupiter and Venus, share relations with four other planets.

Saturn and Mars have the greatest number of relations with other planets, with five planets apiece being affected by the malefics through both the cardinal and the fixed modalities.

A naturally good relationship with a malefic can ease all kinds of tension and improve the state of a planet which may otherwise have experienced difficulty.

In the case of Saturn, both Venus and Mars can benefit from a benevolent relationship, whilst Mars reciprocates the favour with Saturn and offers friendship to the Sun.

However, when it comes to animosity Saturn is innately harmful to both luminaries and Jupiter, whilst the other malefic Mars harms Jupiter, Venus and the Moon.

An Example of al-Biruni's Table in Practice

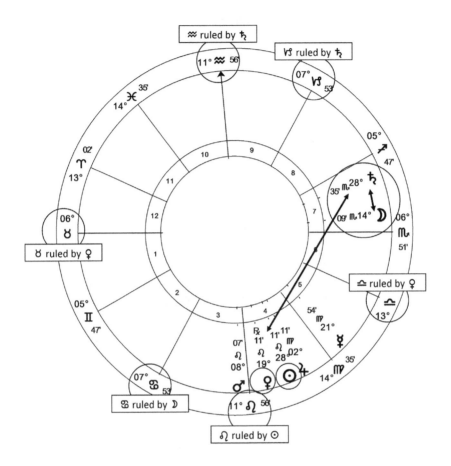

Fig.41 Example Chart for al-Biruni's Table

The example chart *(Fig. 41)* demonstrates a practical side to al-Biruni's Table by merely following Saturn's alliances and animosities.

The fast-moving Moon is in its sign of fall and is approaching a conjunction to its natural enemy Saturn in the seventh house of relationships.

This approaching conjunction will affect the third and ninth axis through the houses ruled by the Moon (Cancer on the 3rd house cusp) and Saturn (Capricorn on the 9th house cusp).

Both planets are disposited by Mars who owns the sign of Scorpio, but Mars is more likely to harm the Moon, as the Moon is in fall in Scorpio and there is also a separating square between Mars (the lender) and the Moon (the reluctant borrower).

Some of the Moon's discomfort may be alleviated by its approaching square to Venus as although they do not share a link through their signs in this chart, the Moon has a one-sided friendship with Venus since she asks for Venus' sign (Taurus) for her exaltation.

Venus does not have to aid the Moon but the square may not be as stressful for the Moon as it may have been without al-Biruni's Table.

Also, by the agreement of exaltation (see al-Biruni's Table) Saturn is inclined to offer friendship to Mars, and even though there is no direct connection between the two planets in this chart, Mars is less likely to want to harm Saturn because it borrows Capricorn for its own exaltation.

The only problem Saturn is likely to have with Mars is when it is placed in the sign of Aries, which is Saturn's fall sign and Mars is the dispositor of Aries. However, this is not the case in this chart as Saturn is situated in Mars' other sign of Scorpio.

The Sun is in its own sign of Leo so it has no requirement to serve another planet.

However, the *partile* (same degree) square to Saturn means there is tension between Saturn and the Sun which is likely to display itself through their placement in the angular fourth (Sun) and seventh (Saturn) houses.

Whatever tension the Sun square Saturn creates will reverberate through their opposing signs of rulership so that the axis of the fourth (Leo on the cusp), and tenth (Aquarius on the cusp) will be affected by a hostile square aspect between two planets whose intentions toward each other are potentially harmful, purely because they face off against each other in Thema Mundi chart.

Jupiter, who is naturally injured by Saturn (Saturn owns Capricorn, the sign of Jupiter's fall) has no contact with Saturn in this chart, either through aspect or dispositorship, so is unharmed by Saturn.

The square between the two friends, Saturn and Venus, is close enough to connect them at nine degrees and the sixth house with Libra on the cusp may reflect a possible health concern considering that this house is jointly ruled by Venus through domicile rulership, and Saturn by the dignity of exaltation. Venus is also the ruler of the Ascendant with Taurus on the first house cusp and the connection between Venus' rulership of the house of the physical body and the sixth house, the destruction of health and the weakening of the body, is likely to mean that Saturn's connection to Venus is ultimately damaging to the native's health, in spite of the underlying friendship which exists between the two planets.

Venus is the major sponsor for the prevention of poor health and Saturn plays a secondary role in matters of the sixth house.

As *Fig. 41* demonstrates the impact of al-Biruni's Table goes far beyond mere theory as it affects the way in which the relationship of the planets are viewed, and ultimately, how the chart is delineated with al-Biruni's Table as a constant reminder of what is going on behind the scenes.

An awareness of this Table is similar to being forewarned of the underlying alliances and tensions which exist in a new work situation.

If someone prepares you beforehand as to who gets along with whom in the office, then as the newest recruit, you can avoid the pitfalls of upsetting the delicate balance of friendships or inadvertently agitating a pre-existing problem, of which you would otherwise have been totally unaware.

By reviewing the first two classes of essential dignity and applying it in practice the impact of Saturn's relationship with five of the planets – Sun, Moon and Jupiter through animosity, and Mars and Venus through alliance, we can see that this leaves Mercury as the sole planet which has no preordained relationship with Saturn.

The following tables present a rearrangement of al-Biruni's Table in order to isolate each of the seven planets and to focus independently on their connection with one other by providing an explanation as to the reasoning behind their complex associations.

In the same manner as al-Biruni lists his planets in the Chaldean Order, the following tables begin with Saturn and end with the Moon's relationships.

The seven Tables listed below individualize each planet's circumstances in relation to the exchange of dignities and those readers who are interested in applying al-Biruni's *Table of Friendships and Enmities* to their own chart analyses would be well advised to spend time studying the various relationships encountered by each of the seven original planets.

Seven Tables of the Planets' Relationships

SATURN's Relationship with Five Planets

Saturn / Moon cardinal cross	mutually harmful	♄'s domicile is ☽'s detriment (♑) ☽'s domicile is ♄'s detriment (♋)
Saturn / Sun fixed cross cardinal cross	mutually harmful	♄'s domicile is ☉'s detriment (♒) ☉'s domicile is ♄'s detriment (♌) ♄'s exaltation is ☉'s fall (♎) ☉'s exaltation is ♄'s fall (♈)
Saturn / Jupiter cardinal cross	♄ injures ♃	♄'s domicile is ♃'s fall (♑)
Saturn / Mars cardinal cross	♄ offers friendship to ♂	♄'s domicile is ♂'s exaltation (♑)
Saturn / Venus cardinal cross	♄ asks friendship from ♀	♀'s domicile is ♄'s exaltation (♎)

Fig. 42 Breakdown of Saturn's Friendships and Enmities

JUPITER's Relationship with Four Planets

Jupiter / Mars cardinal cross	mutually harmful	♃'s exaltation is ♂'s fall (♋) ♂'s exaltation is ♃'s fall (♑)
Jupiter / Mercury mutable cross	mutually harmful	♃'s domiciles are ☿'s detriments (♐, ♓) ☿'s domiciles are ♃'s detriments (♊, ♍)
Jupiter / Mercury mutable cross	♃ injures ☿	♃'s domicile is ☿'s fall (♓)
Jupiter / Venus mutable cross	♃ offers friendship to ♀	♃'s domicile is ♀'s exaltation (♓)
Jupiter / Moon cardinal cross	♃ asks friendship from ☽	☽'s domicile is ♃'s exaltation (♋)

Fig. 43 Breakdown of Jupiter's Friendships and Enmities

MARS' Relationship with Five Planets		
Mars / Jupiter *cardinal cross*	mutually harmful	♂'s exaltation is ♃'s fall (♑) ♃'s exaltation is ♂'s fall (♋)
Mars / Venus *cardinal cross* *fixed cross*	mutually harmful	♂'s domiciles are ♀'s detriments (♈, ♏) ♀'s domiciles are ♂'s detriments (♎, ♉)
Mars / Moon *fixed cross*	♂ injures ☽	♂'s domicile is ☽'s fall (♏)
Mars / Sun *cardinal cross*	♂ offers friendship to ☉	♂'s domicile is ☉'s exaltation (♈)
Mars / Saturn *cardinal cross*	♂ asks friendship from ♄	♄'s domicile is ♂'s exaltation (♑)

Fig. 44 Breakdown of Mars' Friendships and Enmities

The SUN's Relationship with Three Planets		
Sun / Saturn *fixed cross*	mutually harmful	☉'s domicile is ♄'s detriment (♌) ♄'s domicile is ☉'s detriment (♒)
Sun / Venus *cardinal cross*	☉ injures ♀	☉'s exaltation is ♀'s detriment (♈)
Sun / Mars *cardinal cross*	☉ asks friendship from ♂	♂'s domicile is ☉'s exaltation (♈)

Fig. 45 Breakdown of The Sun's Friendships and Enmities

VENUS' Relationship with Four Planets		
Venus / Mars *cardinal cross* *fixed cross*	mutually harmful	♀'s domiciles are ♂'s detriments (♎, ♉) ♂'s domiciles are ♀'s detriments (♈, ♏)
Venus / Mercury *mutable cross*	mutually harmful	♀'s exaltation is ☿'s fall (♓) ☿'s exaltation is ♀'s fall (♍)
Venus / Saturn *cardinal cross*	♀ offers friendship to ♄	♀'s domicile is ♄'s exaltation (♎)
Venus / Jupiter *mutable cross*	♀ asks friendship from ♃	♃'s domicile is ♀'s exaltation (♓)

Fig. 46 Breakdown of Venus' Friendships and Enmities

MERCURY's Relationship with Two Planets		
Mercury / Jupiter *mutable cross*	mutually harmful	☿'s domiciles are ♃'s detriments (Ⅱ, ♍) ♃'s domiciles are ☿'s detriments (♐, ♓)
Mercury / Venus *mutable cross*	mutually harmful	☿'s exaltation is ♀'s fall (♍) ♀'s exaltation is ☿'s fall (♓)
Mercury / Venus *mutable cross*	☿ injures ♀	☿'s domicile is ♀'s fall (♍)

Fig. 47 Breakdown of Mercury's Friendships and Enmities

The MOON's Relationship with Four Planets		
Moon / Saturn *cardinal cross*	mutually harmful	☽'s domicile is ♄'s detriment (♋) ♄'s domicile is ☽'s detriment (♑)
Moon / Mars *cardinal cross*	☽ injures ♂	☽'s domicile is ♂'s fall (♋)
Moon / Jupiter *cardinal cross*	☽ offers friendship to ♃	☽'s domicile is ♃'s exaltation (♋)
Moon / Venus *fixed cross*	☽ asks friendship from ♀	♀'s domicile is ☽'s exaltation (♉)

Fig. 48 Breakdown of The Moon's Friendships and Enmities

CHAPTER FIVE

Qualities, Elements and Aspects

"The death of earth is to become water, and the death of water is to become air, and the death of air is to become fire, and reversely." [86]

Heraclitus (535-475 BC), *Fragment 126*

Four Primitive Qualities : Hot, Cold, Dry, Wet

When Aristotle wrote on cosmological theory in his *On The Heavens* (350 BC) he claimed there were five elements in existence which followed a particular order in the universe.

The first element was ether or 'quintessence' which was a pure, clean substance breathed by the gods and surrounding the planets in the realms of heaven.

Ether was an imperishable substance, unchangeable, with no beginning and no end and therefore totally indestructible like the planets themselves.[87]

The lower regions contained the remaining elements, namely fire, air, water and earth, which Aristotle claimed were inferior to ether as they displayed very different characteristics.

These inferior elements changed their state constantly, coming together and separating almost at will, as the four qualities of which they were composed, namely hot, cold, wet and dry, swelled and shrank the elements according to conditions in the natural world.

Aristotle identified the elements according to the principle of weight and lightness, saying weight is motion pulled towards the centre, and lightness is motion pulling away from the centre of the world.

Fire was the lightest of these four elements and pulled away from the centre of earth, preferring to rest instead at the circumference of the subliminal realm. In contrast, earth carried the maximum amount of weight amongst the elements, and therefore, it pulled towards the centre of the globe.

Together fire and earth marked the boundaries of the mundane world, and as such they were the two extremes of the four inferior elements.

The element of air was found in the quarter immediately below fire, and water belonged to the quarter immediately above the earth element.

Fire and earth were considered to be the absolute extremes of light and heavy respectively, air and water only relatively so, and for this reason were called the two intermediate elements.

Aristotle further split the elements into a separate category containing two pairs, one member from the boundaries and one from the intermediate elements, calling them the light pair (fire and air) and the heavy pair (water and earth).[88]

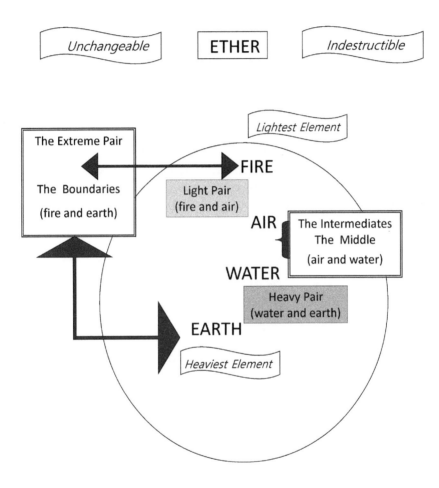

Fig. 49 Aristotle's Elemental Model of the World

The Four Qualities: Hot and Cold; Wet and Dry

"It is cold things that become warm, and what is warm that cools; what is wet dries, and the parched is moistened." [89]

Heraclitus, *Fragment 76*

Aristotle's *Model of the Universe* breaks the inferior elements into four qualities (hot, cold, dry, wet) which are further divided into two pairs of contrarieties – hot/cold and dry/wet.

The first pairing of hot and cold is called the Active Contrary because both qualities are capable of initiating change through a range of different temperatures.

Humankind has always been acutely aware of the changes that occur within the span of a year and although common experience tricks the eye into believing that the sun is moving, it is the movement of Earth which alters the average temperatures of the four seasons.

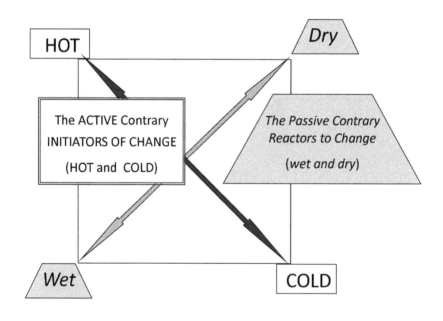

Fig. 50 The Four Qualities : Active Contrary and Passive Contrary

The Active Contrary: Hot and Cold

A summer sun heats and dries the other elements; it warms the air above and the earth below, it ripens the harvest and through evaporation the sun's heat reduces the water levels during summer.

Energy created by the sun alters our physical environment and Earth's constant movement means that nothing material stays the same from one month to the next as matter changes form with every passing season.

When the sun no longer warms in the months following summer we learn to create our own heat source by burning combustibles to create warmth and energy (fire) during the colder winter period.

The change from hot to cold in the seasons also brings constant change in the other three elements as summer's cooling breezes become swirling air currents that blow in from the seas to bring storms and rain, the dry earth becomes a sodden landscape and in extreme temperatures, water solidifies to became snow and ice.

The oppositions in gender also played a part in the concept of the Active Contrary as the masculine gender became associated with heat, and the feminine gender was believed to share an affinity with the cold quality.

It may seem to be an odd relationship to link gender with temperature but it was born from the mythical and philosophical pathway which then led to astrological associations between the two classifications.

Aristotle refers to Pythagorus' Table of Opposites, a set of ten pairs or contrary conditions which list Light and Darkness as one pair and Male and Female as another pair of contradictory oppositions.[90]

Although the two qualities belonging to the active contrariety, Hot and Cold, did not appear in Pythagorus' Table, the Sun's combined characteristics of light and warmth meant that Hot belonged to the Sun and to the column listing Light and Male together, whilst the opposing conditions of Dark (cold) and Female were assigned to the right-hand column of the Table.

In Greek mythology the sun gods were male (Apollo, Helios, Zeus, Hyperion) and the Sun's astrological qualities of hot and dry linked the masculine gender with heat and energy.

Likewise, the moon was deemed to be feminine and the Greek goddesses of the moon, often changing to represent the moon's different phases – Phoebe, Selene, Artemis and Hecate – were worshipped at different times of the moon's cycle when the sun was removed from the atmosphere and the night became dark.

The moon receives reflected light from the sun and so possesses no light or heat source of its own, and the temperature drops at night with the sun's absence creating coolness and moisture during the night-time hours.

For these reasons feminine and cold became linked together and created a relationship which continues to affect astrological principle through the four elements and the twelve signs of the zodiac circle.

The Masculine Gender: Heat in Action = REACT

The sword in mythic tales is a symbol of power, protection, courage and authority.

The sword's magical correspondent is the wand and whilst the wand is less threatening in appearance it symbolises much the same as the sword, yet still adds the properties of wisdom and magic to the sword's list of virtues.

Both sword and wand are represented in the Tarot deck of cards. Interestingly their roles are almost reversed in the Tarot as the sword (normally associated with fire) stands for ideas and the air element, whilst the wand symbolises ambition and the element of fire.

Metaphorically speaking, together the sword and the wand represent the qualities of Heat as they constantly seek challenge by keeping alive the allure of 'A Quest' or awakening the hero's desire to defend truth, beauty or justice.

This urge to squander endless amounts of energy on pursuing quests and searching for things of perceived value may be traced back to earlier times when banding together in a tribal structure was paramount to humankind's survival as a species.

Each tribe member played a specific role and usually it was the younger males who possessed the physical strength, the agility, and the foolhardiness to go forth each day in search of an animal large enough to feed the entire tribe.

Tracking and killing prey, sometimes up to three times a man's size, requires an enormous amount of heat in the form of energy which needs to gather quickly under extreme or frightening circumstances.

A surge of adrenaline allows the hunter to make the kill to provide meat to sustain and replenish not only their own energy, but enough to generate energy for the entire tribe in the form of meat so that the tribe can keep on the move to the next hunting grounds.

In times of confrontation these same younger men became the warriors urging the tribe to respond in one of two ways, either to stand and fight an adversary judged as lesser or equal in size and strength, or to take evasive action through swift flight in order to avoid a more powerful enemy.

The tribe's survival relied on either of these 'hot' responses and both strategies required a high level of 'in motion' activity to stimulate the tribe's decision, as the speedier the response, the greater their chances of success.

Heat, motion and energy are all essential for survival, and although today's tribe appears more sedate than its ancestors, the reaction to danger remains much the same as hot energy can be restored relatively easily and is necessary if the threat is prolonged or continuous in nature.

Our language is peppered with terms that support the 'hot' principle's ability to regenerate, words such as re-vitalized, re-energise, and re-activate are 'hot' words meant to imply that once the original spurt of energy is spent, the possibility of rejuvenation, or replenishment of energy, is easily attainable.

Heat equals vitality, therefore speed and renewable energy is possible, but likewise, the same high level of expendable energy cannot be sustained over an extended period of time.

The two elements at the top of Aristotle's model of the universe are described as the light pair (fire and air) as their components have the greatest ability for motion with the least amount of effort spent.

These same qualities and gender placements of hot and masculine, or cold and feminine, are echoed within the zodiac circle through the association between quality, element and sign.

For this reason, the astrology signs which affiliate with the active quality of heat are the six masculine signs from the fire and the air element.

The hot signs from the fire and air element instinctively react to danger or external physical stimuli and, like the tribe's young warriors, will want to evaluate situations quickly and act swiftly and confidently on those evaluations.

The fire element accelerates the production of energy so that it can confront the challenge or perceived threat, and the three astrological fire signs of Aries, Leo and Sagittarius share the common denominator of swift access to the heat quality to react, protect or attack anything which threatens their safety or environment.

The ruling planet of Aries (Mars), Leo (Sun) and Sagittarius (Jupiter) will approach the threat within the parameters of their own inherent natures, but the initial increase in energy will allow all three fire signs to instinctively act to contain any visible sign of danger.

The air element will use its hot quality in a different manner to fire in that air gathers momentum and speed when it needs to identify and classify the nature of the challenge or threat. Energy then processes the information to enable the air element, that is, the signs of Libra, Aquarius and Gemini, to find a workable solution as quickly as possible.

The ruling planet of Libra (Venus), Aquarius (Saturn) and Gemini (Mercury) will apply their natural talents to decide which of the fight or flight modes to activate and will assemble the necessary data to gain the greatest advantage over the situation.

The air signs will also stockpile a few options so that if Plan A fails, they can quickly activate Plan B or Plan C.

In this manner, they believe they have used the active hot quality to the best of their ability, whilst still keeping their options open when circumstances change, expected outcomes fail, and plans unravel.

The Feminine Gender: Cold at Rest = RETRACT

Cups, chalices, urns and cauldrons are containers which represent feminine symbols in mythology.

These are containers of differing shapes and sizes, inactive in form, but all created to hold precious or magical contents.

In mythology these containers often appear lifeless, worthless or empty of content.

However, the void is deceptive as they are neither abandoned nor barren and their continued safety lies in the fact that they appear to hold nothing at all.

Within the magical container dormant energy lies invisible to the naked eye and the inert vessel is merely waiting for the right circumstances to release its power.

In the tribe the cauldron waits for the hunter to return with the prize. It warms slowly but retains its heat and feeds and nourishes all who gather around it.

The cauldron creates a central point for the tribe and becomes a symbol for unity as members gather to eat the food, celebrate important spiritual ceremonies, rejoice as a new birth swells the tribe's number, or mourn those who have been left behind.

The cauldron is carried from place to place as it represents the life-force of the community. When the tribe meets to communicate any important news, it gathers at the cauldron.

If the hunter is unsuccessful and comes home empty-handed, the cauldron is still heated and ready to receive the gifts of its secondary providers, the gatherers, who fill it with a collection of fruit, grain or legumes to provide necessary, but less appealing sustenance, for the tribe's survival.

These secondary providers are often the tribal women with a back-up plan, and in lean times they bend their backs to scrounge from the earth in order to feed the tribe.

The female members fulfil a special role in the tribe, not only through providing physical comforts of food preparation and domestication, but also through offering the most sacred of chalices, the womb, so that the tribe can remain in existence.

This perpetuation of the species is the reason the hunters go out to hunt and is the impetus for the warriors to initiate their active response to protect those to whom they are emotionally and physically bound in the tribe.

If the hot response of fight or flight fails, there is a third option to fortify and similar to the disaster of a lean hunt, the quality of coldness initiates its own plan for survival.

In terms of confrontation, a cold response involves the choice of retreat and hide, in order to remain alive.

Survival through passive behaviour involves the art of fortification, camouflage, disguise or adaptation – all techniques designed to wait out the danger until it has passed or circumstances have changed for the better.

The skill to 'cold' survival lies in being able to weather the storm, to delay an unpleasant outcome, or to keep strengthening the fortifications that already exist and to use patience, resolve and cunning to outwit the enemy.

With some good luck and perseverance, the opponent might exhaust their own resources, or be destroyed in 'hot' mode as they grow tired, weak, lose momentum or interest, and ultimately move on to agitate another less resourceful tribe.

The cold quality's survival depends on careful planning and fore-thought and when cold rises to action it is like watching mist rise from the earth, it is alarming, other-worldly and designed to confuse the enemy.

Cold combat is not loud and chaotic like the hot battlefield.

Silence is its weapon as a cold response to danger is rarely visible to others but it has a calculated and deliberate outcome in mind.

Its power lies in survival under the most extreme or difficult circumstances, weaving and binding its strengths together quietly and unobtrusively, observing the enemy's greatest weakness, and then driving home the final blow with deadly precision.

The tool of warfare best described by the cold quality would be victory through besiegement.

The invading army surrounds the enemy's home territory thereby cutting off food and water supplies to the city and simply waiting for hunger, a plague, death or despair to overtake the city's inhabitants.

On the other side of the wall the city's occupants are waging their own cold war of attrition by refusing to surrender, by fortifying from the inside, and by physically adapting to ever diminishing levels in their provisions.

The city's inhabitants wait with hope for an active solution that will bring about the destruction of their enemies, perhaps an ally's forces to attack on their behalf, or for the enemy to fight amongst themselves and self-destruct outside the city's walls.

Besiegement was a horrific and inglorious way to end a conflict. It stripped the victors of the honour of battle and it took the lives of the aged, the women and the children as the first victims in a pitiless and cowardly conquest.

Perhaps for this reason, passive energy and non-violent survival techniques have been branded with negative connotations and words such as guile, deceit, duplicity and manipulation have crept into a vocabulary leaning towards the cold principle of the active qualities.

The fact that these words have been linked to the female gender is not accidental, and hiding one's motives or playing down resourcefulness became known as a woman's cunning.

In earlier times, a woman's desire to protect herself from a hostile world somehow became deceitfulness or passive aggressiveness and her motives were questionable.

Worse still, any desire for solitude or a need to maintain her personal space was treated suspiciously as laziness, anti-social behaviour or insanity.

Apparently her behaviour became a threat to society and was a valid reason to either equate her strangeness with witchery, or to lock the unwanted and inconvenient female away from her loved ones and throw away the key.

According to Aristotle the elements of water and earth are both heavier and denser in matter than the masculine fire and air element and for this reason the water signs, Cancer, Scorpio and Pisces are feminine in gender and carry the cold quality in the active contrarieties.

The ruling planet of Cancer (the Moon), Scorpio (Mars) and Pisces (Jupiter) will alter how each of the water signs will protect themselves and will describe the type of 'cauldron' which will contain and active the cold energy of the water signs.

The earth signs of Capricorn, Taurus and Virgo join the water signs in being both feminine and cold in quality. Their rulers are respectively Saturn, Venus and Mercury and these three planets will choose how their own sign will withdraw to collect its energy in order to act with precision and calculated risk as the time for attack approaches.

Whichever planet rules either the water or earth sign the binding factor will be their similar response to threat or external stimuli in that they retract in order to protect themselves, rather than surging forward, as is the response of the hot masculine signs.

Adaptation and fortification is their modus operandi, and the feminine signs preference for quiet withdrawal or stoicism means that the endurance of pain or hardship is conducted without the outward expression of feelings. These are two vital components in their self-protection models.

Some modern interpretations equate the water signs with displays of dramatic or excessive emotional outbursts but this description is somewhat misleading as water is far too private and self-protective to give away secrets as to its emotional well-being.

In general principle, the quieter water becomes, the more dangerous its response to threat or negativity.

Rather than losing the battle, its opponent would do well to keep in mind that the water sign is merely retreating to fight in another moment of time when its defences are prepared, its efficiency is maximised and victory (whatever that may be) is a certainty rather than a mere possibility.

The Passive Contrary: Wet and Dry

In order to expand on the twelve signs in the following chapter, it is necessary to examine the concept behind the other side of the qualities of Wet and Dry identified in *Fig. 50* as the Passive Contrary of the four qualities.

The contrast between the two groupings of active qualities and passive qualities lies in the fact that it is the two actives (hot and cold) which initiate change through the mechanics of temperature.

The two passives qualities describe the form of the physical matter or the material which is affected by the changes wrought by the hot or cold quality.

When Heraclitus says *"what is wet dries, and the parched is moistened"* he is referring to the fact that heat is the initiating force behind the conversion of moisture to dryness, and that cold is the main contributing factor for condensation when something which is dry begins to accumulate moisture when there is a considerable drop in temperature.

These two passive qualities can help to describe much of the physical world as this pairing is not simply about the presence of liquid, or the absence of it, but can be used to describe form and matter according to various gradients of these same two qualities.

The term 'squishy' describes something which is soft, yielding and easy to change form and would be considered to be wet, not because it contains moisture, but because its form is pliable and external pressure (my hand) alters its shape.

Squishy is also a term which describes something that instigates a feeling of emotional attachment because it has a cute, soft or endearing form.

If a material is described as 'rigid' the implication gained from this adjective is that there is stiffness in the form and that it supports, divides or forms a barrier between one object and another. Similarly, the terms of 'dryness' such as hard or firm (a lesser degree of hard) in the material's form can also apply to behaviour when rigidity can mean inflexibility in opinion, attitude or methodology.

There are terms we use for varying degrees of temperature which describe extreme heat such as scalding, boiling or sweltering hot to lower levels of heat where the opposite quality of coolness has been applied.

Weather terms such as balmy or mild, or terms such as tepid or lukewarm to describe liquids or even a person's temperament or reaction to an event, are all varying levels of heat, or the absence of heat.

Likewise, the polarity in the passive contrariety is not set to extremes as there is a sliding scale of the level of wetness or dryness of an object, depending on its circumstances or its composition.

The ability for a material to yield (or to resist yielding) is often its level of wet or dry quality and sometimes time and heat can change its matter from one quality to another.

Fruit which is unripe has a dry quality but given a few days in the sun, it ripens and becomes sweeter, softer and more inviting, that is until it becomes over-ripe and disintegrates into a mushy pulp of spoiled plant material.

Water in a glass has wetness until it is frozen and becomes 'less wet' in the form of ice, but when coldness is no longer applied and the ice is removed from refrigeration, it returns once more to its original wet state.

It was easy for Aristotle to explain the difference between the active and passive qualities because there were so many examples which could be drawn from the mundane world around him and therefore he could always use a practical example to explain the philosophy behind his Model of the Universe.

For instance, the quality of dryness is evident within a handful of sand as each grain of sand, under 250x1 magnification, becomes individualized as a delicate, colourful structure which is as unique as a snowflake.

To the human eye sand particles look identical but each grain is a miniature particle of fragmented crystals, spiral fragments of shells, and crumbs of volcanic rock which can be hundreds of years old.

In order for these grains to stay together when they are in a state of extreme dryness they require a temporary vessel, such as my hand, for containment.

The quality of dryness means that the walls of their structure separates one grain of sand from the next so that when the vessel is removed they do not automatically hold together, but instead, trickle through my fingers with each grain's movement independent of the others.

Their outside coating looks similar but the microscope shows that they are all individual in size, shape and composition and that each grain maintains its rigid outer coating in order to be discrete and separated from the next.

If I want to create a permanent structure, or even a semi-permanent one, I need to add the other contrary of wetness so that I have a chance of getting these grains to meld together to form a different and larger structure, i.e. a sand castle.

As soon as I moisten the sand, the liquid saturates the outer barrier and provides the medium through the surface tension of the water, to keep the grains together as a joined structure.

Now I can hold the wet sand in my hand more easily, as it is the water itself, and not the grains, that through the process of surface tension, moves from one 'more wet' grain to another 'less wet' grain, so that eventually the grains will stick together.

The form in my hand has now changed, becoming compliant, movable, and fluid in its attempt to purchase a new shape.

The grains are bound together, they now have a common 'mind', a common purpose and design, as once I have added moisture, I can no longer separate or distinguish one grain from the one alongside it.

Wetness brings connection, flexibility, softness, and a form which has the potential to become anything, and to hold that shape until I re-form it into something else, provided I add the right amount of fluid.

If I keep adding fluid after I have reached maximum saturation point, the shape will not hold, and I will have to wait for the sand to dry out, which it will do if I add the quality of heat.

To relate Aristotle's passive qualities to human behaviour is not as simple as the exercise of changing sand particles from one physical form to another with the use of water.

Previously, the idea was suggested that the active qualities (hot and cold) could be viewed as an individual's physical reaction to danger or external stimuli.

A hot response was an immediate reaction whilst a colder response involved taking a step back to review and consider the consequences of acting rashly.

In the same way as temperature corresponds with temperament, so too the passive qualities which are defined by physical matter can be assimilated with the idea that the body's most advanced physical matter, i.e. the human brain, can retain information via the differences between 'dry thinking' and 'wet thinking'.

The idea of left and right thinking was developed as a result of Roger Sperry's research in the 1960's into the different hemispheres of the brain.

In his research Sperry recorded experiments on epilepsy patients whose symptoms had been treated by having the bridge between the right and left hemisphere of the brain surgically severed in order to control the disease.

Sperry discovered there were specific differences between the abilities of the two hemispheres and when the bridge had been severed, one side of the brain was completely unaware of the other.

This research led to the idea that the left-sided hemisphere of the brain was better at tasks that involve logic, language and critical thinking, whilst the right-sided hemisphere was better able to assimilate information by identifying similarities and grouping thoughts, images and emotions together.

The following Table *(Fig. 51)* demonstrates the thinking patterns of the left and right hemispheres.

If 'dry thinking' existed as a valid term then it would function in a similar way to the left side of the brain by strictly adhering to the facts and separating thoughts to retain a perceived 'correct memory' of events as they happen or as they have occurred in the past.

Similarly, the concept of 'wet thinking' would naturally align itself with the right side of the brain as this best describes the desire to group images and thoughts together in order to form an abstract idea or to reach a hypothesis which may change at a later time when viewed from a different perspective.

LEFT-BRAINED : Dry Thinking *Best at tasks that involve logic, language and analytical thinking*	RIGHT-BRAINED : Wet Thinking *Best at expressive and creative tasks*
Thinking in words	Feelings visualisation – context and tone
Sequencing	Imagination
Linear thinking	Holistic thinking
Mathematics	Rhythm and Music
Retrieval of Facts	Intuition
Logic	Arts
Language processing	Expression in Images and Creativity

Fig. 51 The similarities between the hemispheres of the brain and Dry and Wet Thinking

If the passive quality of dryness is separation and division, then dry thinking involves being able to separate facts so that they remain special, unique and different.

A problem can then be solved through the rearrangement of these discrete facts in a different order so that a new solution eventuates in the left-sided brain.

The elevated level of focus which a dry thinker can apply to a particular problem can create scientific, medical or technological breakthroughs when able to isolate data to look for new pathways into old problems.

However, dry thinking can have its weaknesses.

Matter which is exceedingly dry can suffer from the problem of brittleness whereby the lack in flexibility can ultimately break the object's form when put under excessive stress.

The association between a dry substance and dry thinking can create a similar problem if thinking patterns become obsessive or so rigid that a different perspective is no longer possible or acceptable for the individual.

Brittle thinking patterns create a fragile mind if its owner is unwilling or incapable of being supple or resilient – both of which are terms that are linked to moisture and wetness.

Wet thinking rummages through the mind's treasure trove of memories to find experiences from the past which will connect old information with the new, and rather than looking for uniqueness, this method finds comfort in consistency and commonality.

Wet thinking pulls thoughts together and searches for patterns, hence the link to intuition or imagination to find the key which ties all loose ends together.

The wet thinker is a hoarder of ideas, images and useless scraps of information because like all hoarders of physical paraphernalia, 'you never know when it may come in handy'.

Training the mind to be more disciplined is the challenge for the wet thinker and learning to place barriers between thoughts is essential for their clarity of mind.

In terms of astrology, fire possesses the passive dry quality so that when Aries, Leo and Sagittarius are enthusiastic about a new project or idea their dry thinking pattern has forgotten what may have failed the last time they tried something similar.

In short, they simply do not remember or do not equate the past with the present because they are focussed on what is different, rather than what is being repeated.

Their optimism and child-like wonder is endearing but also frustrating for those who do remember the fire element's previous attempt which ended badly.

There is little point in drawing fire's attention to similarities as they will look past the pattern and instead stress the unique elements of the new plan.

Likewise, the memory of past victory is soon forgotten as fire is not prone to reminiscing and would prefer instead to focus on the future than to dwell in the past.

The earth signs of Capricorn, Taurus and Virgo also belong to the dry quality and these signs focus their patterns on separating information for the purpose of using it for practical application.

The ability to divide and concentrate on the small particles of facts and figures not only creates dedicated scientists, researchers and mathematicians, but also bestows comedic brilliance and timing.

Many comedians are observers of human nature and the dry quality is capable of retaining the smallest of incidents (like grains of sand) and playing with language to bring forward astute comments borne from these observations.

Similar to the dry quality which unites a masculine element (fire) with a feminine element (earth), the passive wet quality also borrows from each of the genders to combine the masculine (air) with the feminine (water).

The wet thinking model is perfect for air signs, Libra, Aquarius and Gemini, all of whom belong to an element which relishes the flow of connected sound, sight, rhythm and intuition that collectively creates the holistic thinking patterns of wetness.

Cancer, Scorpio and Pisces are the feminine signs which form the water triplicity and their patterns of thought, communication and memory are as fluid as their element suggests.

Containment of ideas and discrimination between fact and fantasy is a challenge for an element whose form can change rapidly with the vessel in which it is held.

It is important for water to consciously place barriers between its thoughts otherwise a lack of dryness is reminiscent of less positive terms such as 'water-logged' and 'brain-washing' where the mind has reached saturation point and can no longer discern what marks the boundaries of reality.

Aristotle's (Part) Model of the Elements

The earlier version of Aristotle's Model of the Universe *(Fig, 49)* was drawn as a circle in keeping with the shape of Earth and our familiar view on how the elements are rated in order of Aristotle's perception of their weight and density.

However, Aristotle's Model usually appears in the shape of a diamond with Fire at the apex and Water at the opposite tip of the diamond.

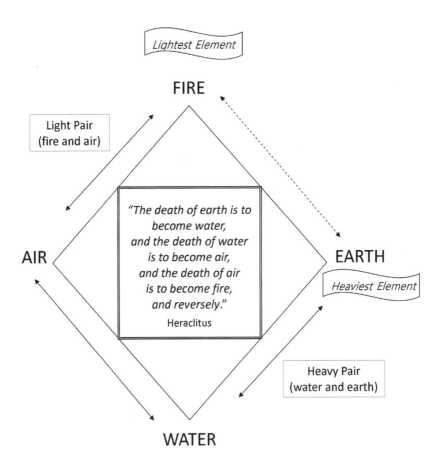

Fig. 52 Aristotle's Model of the Elements in Diamond Form

Heraclitus' quote in the centre of the diamond shaped diagram *(Fig 52)*, illustrates one element flowing into the next through the change in qualities, and he begins at the heaviest element (earth) and moves from the centre in an upwards direction to explain the changes from earth to water, from water to air, and from air to the lightest element (fire).

The last two words *"and reversely"* indicate that the flow also occurs in the reverse as well, moving from the destruction of fire to become air (smoke) to the transformation of air to become water (condensation) to the end of water's clarity to become intermingled with earth in the creation of mud or wood (contains water).

Even though Heraclitus does not specifically mention a link between the heaviest element (earth) and the lightest (fire), earth and matter are destroyed by fire, and likewise fire becomes ash once matter has burned so a link between the two extremes obviously exists in the natural world.

Aristotle's (Full) Model of the Qualities Which Create the Elements

The common version of Aristotle's model *(Fig. 52)* seems deceptively simple as it ties all the factors previously discussed into one neatly drawn diagram.

However, similar to his philosophies, Aristotle's Elements are neither simple nor neat.

Each element draws from the halfway point of qualities – taking them either one direction or the other to show the individual classifications which contribute to the construction of an element.

In this manner the two masculine elements of fire and air break into separate categories according to the passive qualities. The element of Fire becomes a volatile combination of Hot *(active)* and Dry *(passive)* and the element of Air unites Hot *(active)* with Wet *(passive)* to stimulate the constant flow of ideas and conversation.

The two feminine elements of water and earth also possess an opposing passive quality. The element of Water binds Cold *(active)* to

Wet *(passive)* to express its nature, and lastly, Earth amalgamates Cold *(active)* with Dry *(passive)* to manifest its characteristics.

Aristotle's complete Model of the Elements *(Fig. 53)* demonstrates the qualities which connect the elements as well as those elements which share nothing in common. The apex element shows fire's combination of qualities (hot and dry) which shares no commonality with water's qualities (cold and wet).

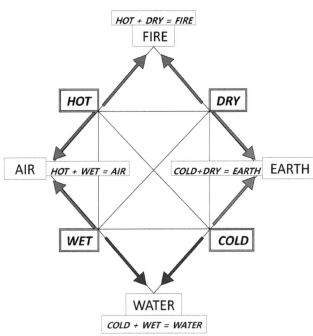

The same scenario exists between air (on the extreme left) and earth on the right-hand side of the diagram. Air's combined qualities are hot and wet and earth's are cold and dry. Aristotle's square diagram is pictorially correct when it comes to the opposition of qualities inherent in the four elements

Fig. 53 The usual depiction of Aristotle's combination of qualities and elements

which describe the nature of Earth's physical matter.

Humours and Temperaments

"As to the nature and temperament of the signs if they are written down in two rows, upper and lower, the first sign above and the second below it, and so on to the last, all those of the upper row are hot and those of the lower are cold, while the pairs so arranged are alternately dry and moist."[91]

	DRY	MOIST	DRY	MOIST	DRY	MOIST	GENDER
HOT	Aries *FIRE*	Gemini *AIR*	Leo *FIRE*	Libra *AIR*	Sagittarius *FIRE*	Aquarius *AIR*	MASCULINE SIGNS
COLD	Taurus *EARTH*	Cancer *WATER*	Virgo *EARTH*	Scorpio *WATER*	Capricorn *EARTH*	Pisces *WATER*	FEMININE SIGNS

Fig 54. al-Biruni's Table of Qualities and Signs[92]
(The Elements and Gender are an addition to original Table)

The Arabic polymath al-Biruni (973-1048 CE) begins his work on the principles of astrology with instructions for the table above *(Fig. 54)*.

The top row of al-Biruni's Table shows the six masculine signs which share the quality of heat and alternate between a fire sign (dry) and an air sign (moist).

The second row contains the six signs of feminine gender which alternate between the earth signs (dry) and the water signs (wet).

Immediately after the table the text continues:

"When therefore you know the active virtues of a sign whether heat or cold, and the passive virtues, whether dryness or moisture, it will not be concealed from you what particular element of the world and what particular humour of the body each sign resembles. Each sign that is hot and dry is related to fire and yellow bile, each that is cold and dry, to earth and black bile, each that is hot and moist to air and blood and each that is cold and moist to water and phlegm."[93]

ELEMENT	QUALITIES	HUMOUR	TEMPERAMENT
FIRE	HOT : DRY	YELLOW BILE: Fluid produced by the liver and stored in the gall bladder. Bile has a hot caustic nature that digests and consumes, metabolizes and transforms.	CHOLERIC: Yellow bile provokes, excites and emboldens the passions. It provokes anger, irritability, envy, ambition, courage and jealousy.
AIR	HOT : WET	BLOOD: The essence of vitality and health, nutrition and growth.	SANGUINE: Blood brings feelings of joy, optimism, enthusiasm, affection and well-being.
WATER	COLD : WET	PHLEGM: Clear fluids of the body: mucus, saliva, plasma and lymph fluids. Together these fluids cool, moisten, nourish, lubricate, protect and purify the body.	PHLEGMATIC: Phlegm induces passivity, lethargy, subjectivity, sensitivity, devotion and sentimentality.
EARTH	COLD : DRY	BLACK BILE: Healthy black bile is a normal sediment of the blood. It has a cooling, drying and solidifying effect on metabolism and is necessary for building bones and teeth.	MELANCHOLIC: Black bile makes one pensive, melancholy and withdrawn. It encourages prudence, caution, realism, pragmatism but can create pessimism.

Fig. 55 Table on Elements, Qualities, Humours and Temperament[94]

In ancient times, the approach to health was holistically based so that mind and body were connected through the qualities, elements, humours and temperament.

Poor health or illness was believed to relate to an element's imbalance, and if an excess existed in one element, then the physician would recommend exercise and diet to address the excess, and to rebalance the patient.

If the body was overheated, then gentle exercise in tepid water and cooling foods was recommended, but if the patient suffered from a cold complaint and an excess in either phlegm or black bile, then regular exercise, preferably of a strenuous nature was prescribed by the physician and warming, spicy foods were included in the diet.

Thema Mundi and the Qualities

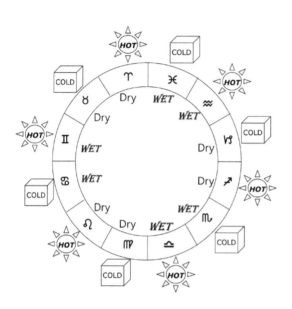

Fig. 56 The Qualities and Signs

The order of the signs creates a pattern which immediately separates the signs according to their gender.

In the diagram *(Fig. 56)* the active qualities of hot and cold are listed alternately on the outside of the circle of signs.

The change in gender identifies with the change in qualities as the hot signs are masculine and the cold signs are feminine.

The inner circle inside the ring of sign lists the passive qualities of wet and dry.

As the diagram shows the passive quality is repeated once before changing, and creates a pairing of the two wet signs followed by two dry signs.

This doubling up of the passive quality results in the aspect of an opposition between one element which is like, but not identical, to the one which is directly placed across the circle from it.

Directly opposite Cancer is Capricorn and whilst they share the active cold quality they are unlike in element as Cancer is wet whilst Capricorn is dry.

Therefore, water (cold and wet) has a kinship with earth (cold and dry) as they are both feminine signs, with the same cold response to danger, but there is also tension when one sign is wet and the other is dry and when it comes to problem-solving or perspective, each sign will see things differently from the other.

Six oppositions across the chart share the same dilemma. They will have similar hot or cold responses to danger or external stimuli, but will differ in how and what they see, and how they choose to absorb the information through the model of either dry or wet thinking.

The planets are added into the picture because they rule the signs and the order of the qualities creates a pattern wherein each of the planets experiences the four qualities through the signs they rule.

The luminaries rule one sign each so between them they cover the four qualities; the Moon owns the cold/wet sign of Cancer, and the Sun rules the hot/dry sign of Leo.

The luminaries have taken possession of two elements which are diametrically opposed, and Aristotle's diamond-shaped model of fire at the top and water at the bottom is recreated by the Sun and the Moon.

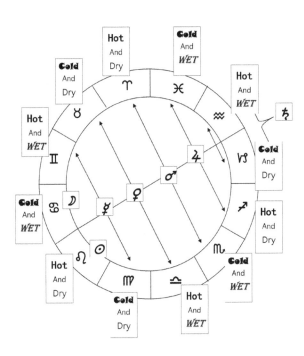

Fig. 57 The Ruling Planets and the Qualities

The five planets each have rulership over one masculine (hot) sign and one feminine (cold) sign.

Saturn owns the consecutive signs of Capricorn and Aquarius which together cover the four qualities of cold and dry to produce an earth sign (Capricorn) and hot and wet to meet the requirements of an air sign (Aquarius).

At first glance this would seem natural given that Saturn's two signs oppose those of the Sun and Moon and that, if the combined luminaries represent all four qualities, then logically the signs of Saturn which opposes them should follow the same rules.

However, the remaining four planets also combine all four qualities in the signs which they own through essential dignity.

Like the Sun and the Moon which rules a fire and water sign respectively, Jupiter and Mars both rule a fire sign (hot/dry) and a water sign (cold/wet) in Sagittarius and Pisces (Jupiter), and Aries and Scorpio (Mars).

Saturn sets the precedent for Venus and Mercury, who both rule an earth sign (cold/dry) and an air sign (hot/wet) in the signs of Taurus and Libra (Venus), and Virgo and Gemini (Mercury).

Set out in this manner sign rulership by the planets makes perfect sense as an even dispersal of qualities allows the planets to experience each of the four qualities.

All five planets can initiate the hot response through their masculine sign or exercise caution and restraint through their feminine sign. Each planet can gather information little by little using the dry thinking model learnt from the fire and earth signs but can just as easily garner impressions and store experiences through the wet thinking model characterized by the air and water signs.

Aspects and the Qualities

"The universe stands continually open to our gaze, but it cannot be understood unless one first learns to comprehend the language and interpret the characters in which it was written. It is written in the language of mathematics, and its characters are triangles, circles, and other geometrical figures, without which it is humanly impossible to understand a single word of it."

Galileo Galilei (1564-1642 CE)

The division of the three hundred and sixty degree circle by significant spiritual numbers such as two, three, four and six, creates angles and points where one zodiac sign is situated in relationship to another.

These mathematical points provide the language of the universe and are created through the links of the number two (gender), the number three (elements) the number four (modality) and the number six (qualities).

The Ptolemaic aspects are the sixty degree angle of a sextile, the ninety degree angle of a square, the one hundred and twenty degree angle of the trine, and the opposition, the diameter aspect which cuts across the circle at one hundred and eighty degrees.

The ancients did not consider the conjunction to be an aspect, rather it was a critical position of power because the circle was undivided (and unharmed) by the conjunction, and Hermes reinforces this notion with his statement:

"An aspect cannot diminish the signification of a conjunction. But a conjunction diminishes the signification of an aspect, for a conjunction is stronger than an aspect."[5]

indicating that a conjunction was more powerful than any aspect which broke the circle's perfection.

This concept of the conjunction as a position rather than an aspect is a reminder of earlier times when the planets' moieties (a sphere of influence around a planet) described the various relationships between the planets.

For instance, the Moon's moiety is fifteen degrees *(Fig. 33)*, a broad area surrounding the Moon whereby it can give and gain access to another planet as it moves swiftly through the zodiac.

When the Moon's moiety comes into contact with a slower moving planet, especially by conjunction, the two planets influence one another, something which we would now call an aspect.

This was regardless of whether their two signs were identical when the collision of energies took place.

The Moon could be in one sign and the planet alongside it could be in the following sign, so while they closely shared position, there is nothing to connect them in the way of gender, quality or modality.

For instance, a Moon at 27 degrees of Leo would conjunct Venus at 2 degrees of Virgo, but the two signs share no similarities.

Sometimes signs which follow one another will share the same passive quality, i.e. Aries and Taurus are both dry, or Aquarius and Pisces are both wet, but this does not seem to be enough to over-ride their basic differences.

Some astrologers argue that there can be no such thing as an 'out-of-sign' conjunction or an 'inconjunct' as this indicates that the two signs have nothing in common.

As the diagrams of the aspects suggest, it is far easier to disregard an out-of-sign trine as the elements do not match.

For instance, a Moon at 27 degrees of Leo will share a separation of 125 degrees with Venus at 2 degrees of Capricorn, which is within the orb for a trine aspect, but Leo and Capricorn are not in the same element which is usual for a trine.

Instead they have different genders, elements and active qualities (hot and cold) so the similarities between two signs in trine are completely missing in this example.

The same rule of possibly disregarding or looking at a reduced impact applies to an inconjunct square, because there is already so much happening in this aspect.

If the same Moon at 27 degrees of Leo had an angle of separation of ninety five degrees to Venus at 2 degrees of Sagittarius, the mathematical division by four would be intact, but as both planets are in the same fire element, the natural stress that should occurs between planets in a square aspect is mitigated by the signs, and the astrologer has to ask themselves whether this 'inconjunct square' is truly representing the same difficulty of an authentic square aspect.

Even ignoring an out of sign or 'inconjunct' opposition as an aspect is a possibility given that it virtually misses the mark on every level, i.e. if the Moon were to be once more in 27 degrees of Leo and Venus was 185 degrees away at 2 degrees of Pisces, the mathematics means they are within orb, but there is something wrong with this picture.

Leo naturally should oppose Aquarius, not Pisces, and the ruling planet of Leo (Sun) does not oppose the ruling planet of Pisces (Jupiter).

Nor do Leo and Pisces share gender, active quality or modality.

The correct term for planets in similar degrees but in signs five signs apart is not a Ptolemaic aspect and only occurs when the circle is divided by twelve, thereby creating aspects at thirty degree intervals.

One of these aspects is a 'quincunx' which has an angle of separation of one hundred and fifty degrees.

If the Moon was at 27 degrees of Leo and Venus was in similar degrees of Pisces then by modern standards the aspect between the two planets would be a quincunx.

An inconjunct describes a completely different aspecting situation, and as such, the two terms should not be interchanged or confused for one another.

The Sextile: Two Signs Apart – A Different Modality

Same Active Contrary (Hot/Cold): Different Passive Contrary (Wet/Dry)

The sextile is a Ptolemaic aspect with the shortest angle (60 degrees) between two planets.

It is an aspect which has links between signs of the same gender and as such will match masculine to masculine or feminine to feminine sign.

The masculine signs contain the hot quality and are also identified as the diurnal signs in keeping with the rules of planetary sect.

The feminine signs contain the opposite active quality of coldness and are called the nocturnal signs of the zodiac.

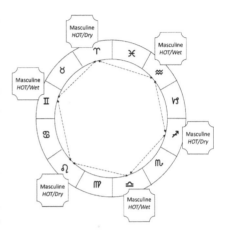

Fig. 58 The Masculine Sextile (hot to hot)

When a sextile occurs the two planets are beholding one another, in other words, they can see and acknowledge one another's presence in the circle because they have something in common.

Through the commonality of the active quality of either heat or coldness, the planets can communicate and, as the sextile is described as a 'soft' or easy aspect, it is a mutually beneficial dialogue which takes place between the planets.

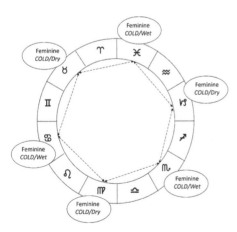

Fig. 59 The Feminine Sextile (cold to cold)

The Square: Three Signs Apart – Same Modality

Different in Active Contrary (Hot/Cold):
Same or Different in Passive Contrary (Wet/Dry)

The square has a separation of three signs and is a right angle (90 degrees), sometimes called one quarter turn of a revolution.

In mathematical terms, the right angle is a critical angle as it marks a change in the circle from an acute angle (less than 90 degrees) to an obtuse angle (greater than 90 degrees).

In other words, it is a turning point and this concept crosses over to the astrological interpretation of the square aspect.

Ptolemy makes the point

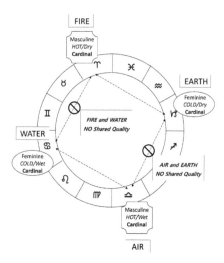

Fig. 60 The Quadruplicities: The Difference Between The Squares Of Cardinal Signs

that the quartile aspect (square) is discordant because it is a configuration between signs not of the same kind, but of different natures and sexes.[96]

Whilst all squares share the same angle and will experience their link through the modalities of cardinal, fixed or mutable quadruplicity, not all squares work in the same way.

Ninety degree angles can be split between signs with some level of compatibility (by sharing

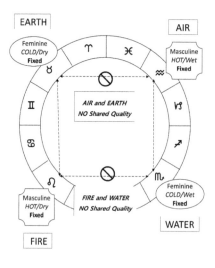

Fig. 61 The Squares of Fixed Signs

their passive quality), and those which have no commonality in gender or quality.

The right angle reflects a waxing or waning square, either beginning the journey and arriving at a critical turning point of 180 degrees, or moving towards the end of the circle's journey at the longest 270 degree turning point. But this fact does not interfere with the difference between one square and another.

Aristotle's Model of the Elements holds the clue as to why one square may create more drama and is more likely to exasperate a tricky situation, than another square that seems to handle situations competently.

Fire has no common bond with water and earth has no common bond with air, so squares involving either of these combinations are likely to be difficult and not as easily dealt with in the chart.

However, fire has a common bond with earth provided by their dry quality, just as water and air have a common bond through their wet quality, so these two potential combinations may be able to work together better than those which share no commonality.

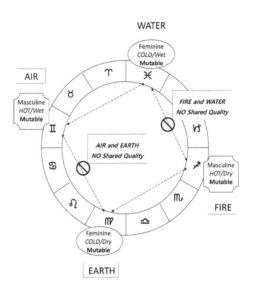

Fig. 62 The Squares of Mutable Signs

The Trine: Four Signs Apart – A Different Modality

Same Active Contrary (Hot/Cold): Same Passive Contrary (Wet/Dry)

The trine aspect has the highest level of compatibility between gender and diurnal or nocturnal signs as the signs share identical active and passive qualities and create aspects between like elements.

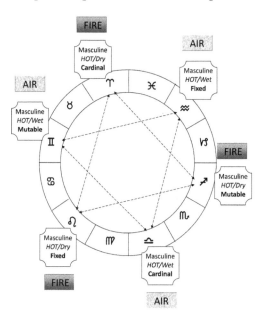

Fig. 63 The Masculine Trine

This should ensure that nothing goes wrong when a trine aspect is activated.

However, Hermes warned his readers against complacency where a trine between planets was concerned, saying that a trine produces a greater level of good or bad than a sextile.[97]

There is little resistance in the trine due to the compatibility of the four qualities, and whatever happens, whether good or bad, happens at incredible speed.

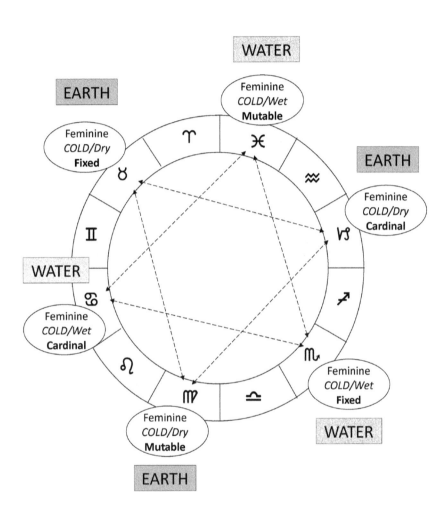

Fig. 64 The Feminine Trine

Oppositions: Six Signs Apart – Same Modality

Same Active Quality (Hot/Cold): Different Passive Quality (Wet/Dry)

"Opposition unites.
From what draws apart results the most perfect harmony.
All things take place by strife."

Heraclitus (535-475 BCE)

Six oppositions exist within a chart and this aspect sets itself apart from the previous aspects for several reasons.

When planets find themselves facing across the chart from one another, they are automatically placed in a position which suggests friction, aggression, inflexibility and resentment towards one another.

Even planets which are normally compatible in nature can experience displeasure and agitation when they are diametrically opposed across the span of the zodiac.

Planets at either end of the opposition will tend to fall into their most extreme and negative behaviours as they are unwittingly caught in a battle between age-old enemies.

Thema Mundi's placement of signs and the order of ruling planets is a subject which has been discussed in Friends and Enemies *(Chapter Four)*.

However, it is worth noting that when planets are in opposition they are in an aspect where the archetypal owners of their signs are two planets with an axe to grind.

For instance, any planet in Cancer will have the Moon as the dispositor of its sign, and should this planet oppose another planet in Capricorn, then Saturn becomes the dispositor of the second planet.

Now there are two problems: the opposition between the innate nature, characteristics and essential qualities of the two opposing planets, and the underlying friction between the Thema Mundi chart's prototypes of Cancer and Capricorn, that is, the Moon verses Saturn.

This battle is further compounded by the fact that the house axis will reflect the opposition of the signs' owners and whatever the house axis represents, the issues experienced in the pairing of houses will become the battlefield for the skirmishes of both oppositions – old and new.

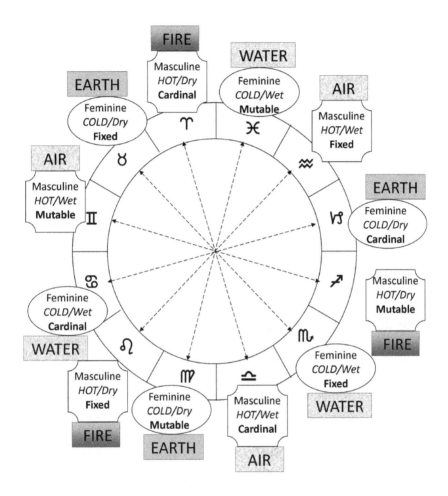

Fig. 65 The Six Axes of Opposition

CHAPTER SIX

Signs of the Zodiac

In the 16th century CE Johannes Schoener described the sign of Cancer as *"the house of the Moon, watery, cold, moist, phlegmatic, feminine, nocturnal, moveable, reptile, mute, sickly, and of many children."* [98]

By defining Cancer by these words the reader knew which divine power directed the sign by its planetary ruler *(the house of the Moon)*, the sign's elemental identity within the environment *(watery)*, its likely response to danger *(cold)*, the sign's processing patterns for information *(moist)*, its temperament model *(phlegmatic)*, gender characteristics *(feminine)*, sect preference *(nocturnal)*, and its place in the seasonal calendar *(moveable* is another term for cardinal*)*.

They also knew its likely physical constitution *(sickly)* and its symbolic animal, in this case the crab, *(reptile, mute, of many children)* because the crab makes no audible sound, and produces a multitude of offspring in its fertile periods.

These abridged classifications curtailed the need for lengthy discussion on the sign yet still provided all the information relevant when considering the relationship between a sign and a planet.

The reader needed to know if a sign was a harmonious blend with a planet's intrinsic nature as well as understanding how a planet might react to a particular sign.

Within Schoener's description of the signs lie both the essential qualities which connect one sign with another, and also specific astrological definitions which give them their own individual characteristics.

Cancer aligns with the two other water signs of Scorpio and Pisces by sharing qualities, temperament, gender, sect division, physical state of health, and its animal status.

However similarities between any three signs of an element end here as quadruplicities, the division of cardinal, fixed and mutable, will separate the element into one sign for each modality.

The planet that stands behind the signs sits at the very top on the list of differences between the signs, and is significantly higher in priority than the impact of quality, element or modality.

Cancer parts ways with Scorpio and Pisces when we consider each water sign's planetary ruler as the Moon rules Cancer, Mars rules Scorpio and Jupiter rules Pisces.

The triplicity of water signs share many common qualities and may play beautifully together in the cosmic sandpit, but when Mumma or Poppa Planet comes to pick up their beloved offspring, the differences between them become glaringly obvious.

But before examining the significance of rulership differences, the first consideration to take into account is the variation in the three types of modality.

Differences in Modality: Cardinal, Fixed or Mutable

The seasons of the year define the difference between each of the three signs in all four elements.

The four Cardinal signs, Cancer, Libra, Capricorn, and Aries were called moveable signs as each in their own way are concerned with initiating action.

These signs which occur at either the point of solstice or at the equinox are the zodiacal springboard for a new season's launch and celebrations abound to mark these four critical points in the sun's calendar.

The Fixed signs, Leo, Scorpio, Aquarius and Taurus, take possession of the central month in each of the given seasons, and promise some consistency in the weather patterns of their particular season.

The fixed signs actively resist change and can restrict the free flow of energy as they hold fast to honour their relevant seasons. Their innate reliability can serve the four signs well as this is a virtue which comes naturally to them, but the cardinal and the mutable signs require training and commitment to learn stability from the fixed signs.

Virgo, Sagittarius, Pisces and Gemini are the Mutable signs, sometimes called the common signs, which mark the last month in each season and show the changeability of their signs through unpredictable shifting weather patterns.

Mutable signs were also known as the bi-corporeal signs as their zodiacal images consisted of two separate forms.

Gemini as the twin boys of Greek myth, the human Castor and divine Pollux; Pisces as the two fish swimming away from each other but joined by the celestial knot; and Sagittarius, a centaur, a wild half horse and half man creature. Virgo is also bi-corporeal as she is the virgin carrying either the gifts of the harvest, or a child on her hip. Both images are a reminder that Virgo is summer's mutable sign and productivity is part of the celestial maiden's gift to mankind.

Various esoteric writers believed the modalities also signified a Chaldean doctrine known as the Lord of the Zodiac, or Grand Man, a spiritual trinity of the Father, the Power and the Mind.[99]

The cardinal signs were the Fathers of the soul, or the Paternal Foundation, a creative force whose virtue lay in initiating and directing the flow of spiritual energy.

Following the cardinal signs were the fixed signs, known as the Powers, or the Formulators, who held the deep reservoirs of infinite energy in check.

Their job was to continually support the Fathers, and their virtue lay in their attributes of persistence and tenacity.

In Hebrew lore, the fixed signs became the Cherubim, in the Brahmin system they are the Maharajahs, or Lords of the corners of creation, and in Christian doctrine they are the Tetramorphs, a four-fold form of dragon or human (Aquarius), lion (Leo), bull (Taurus) and eagle (Scorpio), who are linked to the four evangelists for Christ, respectively Matthew, Mark, Luke and John.[100]

The mutable signs were called the Minds of the Grand Man, and their task was to act as mediator between the cardinal and the fixed signs.

Renowned for their quickness of mind, these four signs were the reconcilers of the universe, created to arbitrate between the impulsiveness of the headstrong Fathers and the rigidity of the recalcitrant Powers.

The common signs display their versatility and adaptability by adopting certain traits which are common to both the cardinal and the fixed signs, rewarded for their role as a buffer between the two extremes of the other modalities.

Differences in Dispositors: A Planet's Ownership of its Sign

Planetary rulership is one of the most important principles of astrology as it gives a planet the power to animate the zodiac signs and it ties the chart together through the connections of house to sign (the cusp) to planet (ruler of sign).

The Thema Mundi chart sets out the planets' rulership signs connecting planets in a unique way which differs from the mathematics of aspecting and giving notice of the 'behind the scenes' dialogue which is constantly active in the planets' relationships.

The term for ownership of a sign is 'dispositor' and is used to describe the planet who owns the sign, when a planet finds itself in a sign other than the one it rules at the highest level of essential dignity.

When a planet borrows a sign belonging to another planet, the dispositor (owner) has a vested interest in the borrower planet.

Likewise, the borrower needs to know the state of its sign's dispositor, as its condition often determines how well or badly events will turn out for the borrower.

For example, if Saturn is in Pisces it is disposited by Jupiter, so not only must we consider how Saturn behaves in a water sign which is a mutable, feminine, nocturnal, cold and wet sign, but we need to know how Jupiter, the owner of Pisces, is placed in the chart.

Is Jupiter in good condition or poor condition according to sign, chart placement, sect, direction (retrograde or direct), and aspect to the other planets?

Once you have looked at Jupiter and made a judgement on its situation, then you are more likely to know what to expect from Saturn.

If the astrologer is not used to this practice it can seem like a backward movement to look at another planet when attempting to focus on Saturn, but in this case, Jupiter will determine whether Saturn in Pisces is well-behaved, or whether it is struggling to fulfil its potential because the sign's ruler Jupiter is in trouble.

If Jupiter is poorly placed, then the negative attributes of Pisces become more evident, and Saturn is more likely to fail because its own behaviours will reflects this, becoming highly strung, irrational, paranoid or totally inert through fear or laziness, when it is required to perform its Saturnian duties.

The good scenario for Saturn in Pisces is if Jupiter (its dispositor) is in dignity, or in one of the good houses, in diurnal sect, or not bothered by aspects which damage its health.

Alternatively, if Jupiter is located in one of Saturn's own signs of dignity, then the two planets can come to a 'gentleman's agreement' to care for each other's sign.

The term for this is 'generosity' and this would be the case if Jupiter were alongside Saturn in Aquarius as generosity means that no aspect exists between the two planets.

If Jupiter was placed in Saturn's other sign of Capricorn, generosity turns into mutual reception because technically there is a sextile aspect between Pisces and Capricorn.

Mutual reception occurs when two planets have borrowed each other's sign, so that there is an unspoken agreement between them to honour the other's sign, almost like an exchange in a house-sitting arrangement where each looks after the other's home for an agreed period of time.

In good faith each party, in this case the planet, agrees to treat the home well in the belief that the other occupant will honour the same set of guidelines in their home.

However, this particular mutual reception is unlikely to work well because Jupiter in Capricorn is in the debility known as fall, so the good faith gets destroyed and Jupiter tends to become the house-sitter from Hell.

Sometimes it is wrongly assumed that signs and planets are interchangeable and that when discussing a sign the boundary between the inactive sign and the energy of the planet becomes blurred in the description.

For instance, Aries was considered to be so archetypically Martian that when Pluto came into being in the 1930's it was unthinkable that Aries should continue the pattern of new planetary rulerships and be taken away from Mars to become Pluto's new sign.

This strong affiliation between sign and planet can result in the astrologer struggling to define the difference between two components of astrology which have dissimilar purposes and unequal powers in the chart.

The best way to clarify this situation is to apply the following analogy to describe the distinction between a sign and a planet.

Imagine a puppet on a stage and the puppeteer who pulls the puppet's strings and causes it to move and dance for the audience.

Without the puppet-master there is no animation and no life, yet in most instances the skill of the puppeteer lies in being able to fade into the background and let the puppet tell the story.

Signs can and do get passed around from planet to planet, and like the puppet that becomes a heap of scrap material and wood without the essential qualities and skill of a range of different puppeteers, so too does a sign have little meaning without the planet.

Schoener's description of Cancer is a list of descriptions in the same way as we might list a puppet's components or material, but nothing breathes life into Cancer until a planet resides in the sign, or its ruling planet, the Moon, begins to activate the house with Cancer on the cusp.

Each puppet-master or planet has a different story to tell, and the sharing of Cancer is the way in which they are destined to tell it within the confines of a chart, which very much acts like the stage on which the puppets will perform their various acts.

It should be noted in this analogy that the puppeteer (planets) are not the type of puppet-master who fades into the background. Their presence on the stage (chart) is domineering and perpetual and whilst they tell their story through the puppets (signs) it would be unwise to ignore their activity in favour of the distractingly playful puppets which they manoeuvre on stage.

Defining a Sign: Qualities, Element, Modality, Dispositor

Each of the twelve signs can be explored through the lens of their qualities, modality and ruling planet in the same order as Aristotle's world-system begins with the highest and lightest element of fire and ends at earth, the fourth and heaviest of the elements.

This method of examining a sign provides an opportunity to explore their similarities and to accentuate their differences through modality and ownership by one of the seven original planets.

The Thema Mundi chart is perfect in the sense of symbolism and in the synastry between the signs and their ruling planets. To disrupt or destroy this order through the inclusion of Uranus, Neptune and Pluto as planetary rulers is a terrible mistake.

These three latecomers definitely need to be included in the chart's design but it is far better to view them as 'stand alone' energies, affecting and interacting with the other planets, rather than attempting to incorporate them into a system of rulership which has worked perfectly for more than two thousand years.

The only sign-sharing that can possibly have merit is the one discussed in the previous chapter on al-Biruni's Table on the Friendships and Enmities of the Planets. This Table makes it clear that signs can be shared between the domicile ruler and the exalted ruler of a sign but there is protocol to be followed and no planet willing gives away one of its signs without 'strings attached' and favours agreed upon by the two negotiating powers.

A planet's visibility in the night sky is "sacrosanct" (literally, *'hallowed by a sacred site'*), and although moderns know by the grace of science of the existence of three new planets, Saturn does not share with Uranus, Jupiter does not co-rule Pisces with Neptune, and Mars would never (never!) relinquish its power over Scorpio by sign-sharing with Pluto.

The Element of Fire
Aries: Leo: Sagittarius

Hot in Action

The Fire element is created through the burning of solid, liquid or gaseous fuels to produce energy and provide heating, but this element cannot be sustained unless it is constantly fed by one or more of these materials.

Its relationship with the other elements is integral to its existence, as to truly release its energy, fire needs a combination of both earth (solid fuels such as wood, charcoal, peat, coal or grains) and air (for oxygen) to thrive as an element. Water is fire's opposite in both qualities, being cold and wet, and is needed to control fire's burn and to temper its extremes and prevent fire from causing untold destruction through its hot and dry qualities.

Fire utilises its hot response to create energy in an intense and fast manner as though it instinctively grasps the fact that this element has a short lifespan, and must be directed into physical expression as quickly as possible.

In sympathy with fire are the two elements which sit on either side in Aristotle's model. The air element shares fire's hot quality and reacts with speed or alacrity to any new challenge and the earth element has dryness to describe its physical matter in a similar fashion to fire's passive quality.

The fire triplicity needs the mundane world to feed its passions and earth, at the other end of the scale as the heaviest of the elements, graciously accommodates fire by providing the physical means by which the lightest element can achieve worldly success.

The air element is also required to assist fire by planting the idea in the first place and then to fan the flames by suggesting a cause that needs encouragement, a battle that must be fought, or an ambition that requires fulfilment so that fire can direct its hot energies towards the immediate challenge.

Our relationship with this element is somewhat ambivalent as we love to harness its energy for our benefit but we are constantly reminded how catastrophic its effects can be if it is not held in check.

Fire with too much freedom can do more harm than good and it is an element which requires just the right amount of temperance (moderation or voluntary self-restraint) if it to get the best from its natural enthusiasm.

Too much control or constant attack or negative criticism and fire loses its energy, becoming suffocated or dispirited by micromanagement or others' insensitivity to its plans.

The hot response turns from outward spontaneity and initiative to self-doubt and second-guessing the important decisions.

If the situation is not rectified by a change in circumstances fire's heat risks becoming internalised and instead of building the courage to act, fire breeds secret flames of rage, bitterness or despair.

Dry in Thought

The quality of Dry is naturally inclined to separate information into compartments in order to give full attention to each thought, idea or concept in a discrete, thinking process.

In this way, all information can be properly examined and analysed without interruption, clutter or bias.

This method of thinking can produce insightful or brilliant solutions to a problem but there can be difficulties in translating these solutions into a workable model.

Often the dry quality struggles with re-assembly and the integration of all parts to create the model in its entirety is fraught with impossibilities and impractical solutions.

Those individuals whose thinking patterns are most comfortable in the dry mode believe this left-brain thinking gives them the advantage of clarity and objectivity. Their skill lies in methodically examining information and drawing conclusions based on the breakdown of data.

They can face criticism from others who judge their dry thinking as rigid, obsessive or limited in its possibilities as the integration of others' opinions or suggestions is not a natural option for them.

Other methods of problem-solving may be outside the scope of their capacity and alternate solutions which have not occurred to them may be viewed with suspicion or scepticism.

Fire Element = The Combination of Hot and Dry

A combination of Hot and Dry qualities creates the Fire element which acts quickly and decisively on thought patterns which view each segment of new information as unique and separated from past circumstances and therefore have little or no effect on present conditions.

In the same way as wildfire rarely burns back on itself, retrospection is not part of the fire model.

Therefore, each challenge requires a fresh and new approach as any planet placed in the fire element will want to 'reinvent the wheel' and can become agitated when others suggest that the individual is wasting their energy on something that already exists and does not require reinvention.

The fire signs are blessed with a child-like optimism along with a strong conviction that the planet in fire will be the one to solve the unsolvable.

Planets in fire signs often display a strong will and whatever the planet signifies, it will hold firmly to its convictions and defend its actions. The planet is intolerant of interruptions or delays, and this trait can lead to extreme or volatile behaviour geared towards gaining attention or inciting heated debate.

Routine work can be unbearably boring for this combination of qualities as repetition is more in tune with cold response, and known procedures allow little room for the dry quality's desire for new and interesting possibilities on which to focus the mind and keep alive fire's intellectual spark.

Modality and Dispositors

Differences between Aries, Leo and Sagittarius

ARIES : Cardinal Fire : Ruled by MARS

"Those candle flames were like the lives of men. So fragile. So deadly. Left alone, they lit and warmed. Let run rampant, they would destroy the very things they were meant to illuminate. Embryonic bonfires, each bearing a seed of destruction so potent it could tumble cities and dash kings to their knees."

Brandon Sanderson, *The Way of Kings*

Several factors combine to ignite Aries' short fuse. Its ruling planet has the measure of Aries' *embryonic bonfires* which are both fragile at the beginning and deadly when a raging Mars is out of control.

Aries is a cardinal sign that carries a primal urge to instigate action. It is unlikely to bear the strain of its energy being contained for very long and becomes agitated if thwarted or wasted by inconsequential matters or bureaucratic mismanagement.

Aries is owned by Mars, a planet which struggles between wanting to be left to its own devices and needing the fuel of others' involvement to keep alive its burning fires.

Both planet and sign need just the right amount of friction to energise them as both are highly sensitive to stimuli in the immediate environment but enjoy the adrenaline rush of meeting deadlines and overcoming obstacles.

Too much friction and Mars' strong survival instinct shifts into gear, resulting in Aries answering the call of a distressed Mars with its hot response and moving into the fight or flight mode, especially when Mars feels under threat or deems itself to be controlled by others' whims.

However, Aries' combination of hot and dry qualities can mean that exhaustion sets in if it tries to react with the same accelerated level of speed or effectiveness at each new drama.

And at the same time, try to process all individual pieces of data with an equal amount of enthusiasm and vigour.

Aries needs time to withdraw and regroup, to gather its energy ready for the next project or the next battle. Any planet situated in Aries must understand that retreat is not always a sign of failure but rather a timely respite which is necessary in order for the planet to evaluate goals and to plan its next move.

Similar to the candle flame Aries needs both guidance and encouragement as it runs the risk of burning out of control and running rampant, or losing its confidence and being snuffed out by others' negativity or disinterest.

The knack lies in good management as a planet in Aries often reacts strongly to any authority which it does not respect or which hinders the planet's freedom to make its own decisions.

With Mars as Aries' dispositor, any planet in this cardinal fire sign will rebel in such a manner that it ends up burning all its bridges and having to start anew – not a problem for Mars, but it may not suit the nature of the planet (Moon or Venus perhaps) which finds itself placed in Aries.

The combination of a masculine sign Aries with the masculine planet Mars tends to emphasise the hunter or warrior quality of this fire sign, and its natural instincts are to attack or capture on the physical, emotional or on the intellectual plane.

A planet in Aries expects a prize at the end of the hunt otherwise it will fret that the energy consumed was not worth the return. Hot response for Aries means a fast physical reaction and can create restlessness in mind and body and a jittery energy that is constantly on the lookout for challenge, movement or physical activity.

A born leader (although not always a wise one) with a dynamic temperament and a ready access to high levels of energy, Aries dreads the advancement of age as it triggers the deeply rooted fear of the hunter who risks being discarded by the tribe when their glory days are counted as moments in the past.

Dry thinking for this sign can mean the individual spends little time reflecting on past achievements as they are naturally geared towards the future, and if the future looks bleak to them, the ruling planet Mars despairs that opportunities have evaporated and all potential has been exhausted.

Containment or physical restriction can mean they become reckless, loud or agitated if they cannot find an immediate or satisfactory release, as this hot, dry sign displays an explosive nature, especially when they are frustrated by inactivity.

Planets in Aries

Planets in Aries display Mars-like qualities becoming agitated if the planet's innate desires cannot be satiated or its full potential cannot be realised.

For instance, Sun in Aries will fight for glory and in defence of its reputation, Moon in Mars' sign will compete for affection and fiercely protect its emotional or physical attachments, and Mercury in the cardinal fire sign will passionately defend its right to have opinions.

In a male's chart an Arian Venus will be attracted to the female warrior type, whilst Venus in Aries in a female's chart will compete with every other woman, make love a lusty game, and then fight for autonomy when 'captured' by a relationship.

Jupiter in Aries will exaggerate every opportunity to exercise its fight or flight response, and Saturn in Mars' sign will be too hot-headed, arrogant or impulsive for its own good.

Saturn in Aries is in fall, making it a dangerous sign for Saturn if it is too brash or tries once too often to bluff its way out of a situation.

It must always be remembered that in all of these planetary possibilities, Mars' condition will need to be carefully examined, in order to judge whether a planet in Aries can reach its potential or it is hampered by being placed in the masculine sign belonging to Mars.

LEO : Fixed Fire : Ruled by THE SUN

Some would say that the fixed sign of Leo achieves the highest honour by being adopted by the Sun for its own sign.

Vettius Valens (1st century C.E.) wrote

> *"the all-seeing sun, nature's fire and intellectual light, the organ of mental perception, indicates kingship, rule, intellect, intelligence, beauty...the ordinance of the gods"*[101]

suggesting this fire sign carries lofty ideals and high principles with the Sun as its ruling planet.

The hot response for Leo differs from the other two fire signs by acknowledging the responsibility which comes with leadership and prides itself on leading by example.

Leo is similar to Aries in that it possesses the desire to be dynamic and active and it relishes working towards a goal but their lords are different and whilst Aries follows Mars' direction, so Leo will follow the Sun's light and warmth.

Sometimes the zodiac signs can mimic the attributes of their ruling planet. For instance, Aries is associated with the colour red and Mars is a red planet.

Likewise, Jupiter, the largest planet in the solar system, is often reflected in the grandiose gestures of its own sign Sagittarius or in the roaming depths of the watery imaginative Pisces.

The two signs of Venus reflect the glorious *Lucifer*, or Morning Star, and Taurus and Libra share the light of Venus through a desire to be loved and worshipped according to their respective elements.

Leo differs from all of these signs by its link to a symbolic Sun and this means that Leo can go through phases or seasons similar to the physical sun. Like the puppet that takes on the characteristics of its puppeteer, so too can Leo echo the Sun's seasons as it passes through its yearly pattern.

Japanese multimedia artist, singer and peace activist, Yoko Ono (1933-) wrote the following poem and it speaks volumes for the Sun's seasons and their relationship to the seasons of Leo:

> *"Spring passes and one remembers one's innocence.*
> *Summer passes and one remembers one's exuberance.*
> *Autumn passes and one remembers one's reverence.*
> *Winter passes and one remembers one's perseverance."*

Leo passes through similar phases to the Sun's changing seasons and any planet which finds itself in Leo is likely to feel the impact of these phases through their activity by lending their own nature, characteristics or significations to the experience.

Sometimes these seasons work hand in hand with a person's age, but this is not always the case.

In the same way as the Sun's seasons come and go, it is not impossible to experience the delight of a Spring Leo in a person of advancing years, especially if they have a personality which reflects a 'tapping into the fountain of youth' attitude, and who continues to meet each new day with vigour and spirit.

Or to meet a young Winter Leo whose outlook on life is bleak, or one who has become stuck in the phase in their youth and has struggled for years to leave the shadows of winter behind so they can move once more into the Sun's light.

To meet the four varieties of Leo perhaps the first introduction should begin with the Spring Leo. This energy possesses an innocence born from inexperience yet at the same time is ambitious, brash and optimistic as the Spring Leo keenly searches for new adventure by which it can test its mettle.

A Summer Leo is exuberant, glorious and triumphant in its success.

But like the hottest of sunny days, Summer Leo can overheat thereby creating mannerisms which are brazen, domineering or arrogant, and may not realize that it can be over-shadowing others' efforts or needlessly causing offence.

It is a Leo which can only be tolerated for short periods of time before needing to be dampened down by an external force.

The Autumn Leo uses hot response more for reflection than action as it has plenty of opportunity to capitalise on its success.

This is a season which is advancing towards winter and therefore has a deep reverence for life and an appreciation tinged by the awareness of Time passing.

Autumn Leo basks in rich memories and enjoys this stunning season of grace and beauty so any planet placed in Leo which experiences this phase of deep contentment is one very fortunate planet that has the potential to bring happiness to the native's life.

Autumn Leo is likely to be magnanimous in giving time and advice, often sharing its experiences with younger players who want to reach the top.

If destiny has played out well for the Autumn Leo it warms others with its generosity of spirit but it is inclined to show flashes of heat when it is challenged or when it fears losing a privileged position it has fought hard to win.

The Winter Leo still bears the mark of its hot quality but depending on how hard the years preceding the winter season are perceived to have been, it can go one of two ways.

All seasons of Leo believe that perseverance delivers rewards, but if honours have not been forthcoming and sacrifices made by Winter Leo have been for naught, then another side of this complex sign can become evident to the observer.

A Winter Leo can feel humiliated by thwarted ambitions or a lack of eminence in the workplace or within society's ranks and Leo's heat and dry thinking mode can focus on feeling as though Fate has treated this individual badly.

Frustrated hot response has the potential to evolve into barely contained rage over an extended period of time, and whilst this type of internalised fuming still keeps the Leo sign warm, it is by no means a comfortable heat for either the individual, or for those who surround them.

Alternatively, the Winter Leo can spend its energy on a type of false humility which outwardly lauds those whose lives appear more successful than their own, but who silently seethes on the comparison between others' good fortune and their own missed opportunities.

Especially when they believe that their own talents and qualities far outshine the skills of their object of interest.

This side of Leo looks passive and could be mistaken for being a colder version of its sign, but hot energy is internalised and becomes like molten lava, and there are times when its poisonous containment results in physical ailments or mental disorders.

Dependant on a number of factors, the dry quality of Leo can be both a gift and a source of frustration, since the persistence and focused tenacity of dry thinking can mean Leo is unwilling to give up when everyone else has abandoned an idea.

This type of thinking can create a breakthrough in a particular field of interest, and depending on which of the planets is placed in Leo, is often the mark of an independent and self-sufficient individual.

It may take time but once a planet in Leo has focused on a target it will use its own unique properties to visualise the goal and work relentlessly towards achieving its objective.

In its extreme, this type of mental toughness can turn into total inflexibility and can lead to obsessive deliberation whereby Leo fractures its information.

The planet in Leo is then either unable to connect back to reality or to move forward through its natural linear progression to arrive at the next sequence in their cogitations.

Leo's trick lies in knowing when to persevere, and when to walk away. Sometimes moving from one phase or season to another will trigger Leo's hot response into making the decision to abandon an idea and move on to another project.

Valens says the Sun, rather than Mercury, is the organ of mental perception, so it should be noted that the seasons of Leo are more about the mind's subjective view of life's circumstances rather than the individual's age or their actual situation.

Planets in Leo

The fixed nature of this sign can mean that Leo gets stuck in one or more of these behaviours and it is important to remember that this seasonal phasing is not confined to the Sun in Leo, but can also apply to any of the other planets finding themselves in this sign belonging to the Sun.

Within the bounds of its own nature, each planet experiences Leo as a constant round of season-like behaviours, and any planet in Leo has the potential to display the hot, dry qualities of this sign which may or may not be compatible with what that planet is trying to achieve in the chart.

It is also critical to understand that when looking at a planet placed in Leo it is necessary to be aware of what the Sun is also doing in the chart.

If the Sun is struggling, then so too is Leo, and this reflects back on the performance of the planet in the sign of Leo, as the Sun's condition often provides a clue as to which particular season the planet in Leo is likely to experience more often than the remaining three seasonal possibilities.

SAGITTARIUS : Mutable Fire : Ruled by JUPITER

The Archer or the Centaur sets Sagittarius apart from the previous two fire signs, Aries the Ram and Leo the Lion, by introducing the figure of a human into the list of the fire signs' astrological symbols.

Both images of Sagittarius give the impression of a sign keen for action and happy to deal with danger but there is a marked difference between the intentions behind each of its images.

The archer takes careful aim and holds their breath until the release of the deadly arrow, whilst the primitive man-horse creature races into battle and strikes at its enemy without fear or favour.

The combination of qualities, modality and ruling planet suggests a sign which has multiple options and can direct its active hot quality towards leaping forwards into action with heavy hooves pounding across the land like the centaur.

Or for Sagittarius to activate its dry thinking mode for the archer to concentrate in the din of battle on separating its mark with precision and careful forethought so the arrow hits its intended victim.

Sagittarius' versatility and Jupiter's rulership of the mutable fire sign means that moving from the brash courage of the centaur to the dry calculations of an archer causes Sagittarius little concern so long as marksman or horse are both free to move quickly and react instinctively to produce their own version of heat and energy.

The mythic images for Sagittarius use heat in a different way but they share Jupiter's nature in constantly looking forwards, the centaur speeding to get the next adventure, and the archer making a split second decision to let loose the arrow, not to where its mark is, but *where it will be* in the immediate future.

Ptolemy considered Jupiter, the ruler of Sagittarius, to be a benefic with a temperate nature because the planet was neatly placed between the extreme cold of Saturn and the burning heat of Mars in the Chaldean Order.[102]

Under normal chart conditions if a planet was bordered on either side by two malefics it suffered the debility of 'besiegement', but rather than threatening this celestial giant by their proximity, instead Saturn's cold and Mars' heat created the golden mean of a perfect temperature for this fortunate planet.

As a fire sign, Sagittarius takes Jupiter's temperate nature and warms it up, stimulating activity by leading and organising in a somewhat haphazard way which allows others the freedom to join in during the planning stages or at the final execution of an idea.

Sagittarius is not as attached to the title of Leader as the other two fire signs, but it does like to be recognised as the teacher or philosopher when it lights fires beneath others' tinder dry ambitions or their desire for knowledge.

Gender-wise, both Sagittarius the sign and Jupiter the planet are masculine and together sign and planet give an impression of self-assuredness, a strong will, and a passionate nature when it comes to taking action.

The quality of dryness encourages decisive behaviour as it processes each part in isolation and returns it to the whole, driven by Jupiter to correct wrongs and seek practical solutions.

Overconfidence can mean this sign backed by the mighty Jupiter thinks it knows the right answer in any situation and believes it can manage anything if given half the chance.

As a dry thinker Sagittarius rarely casts its mind back to past experiences as it is more concerned with the present or is constantly on the lookout for the excitement inherent in future possibilities.

Unfortunately this pattern can be Sagittarius' weakness as one of life's philosophers because a true philosopher must have the courage and humility to look back and reflect on past mistakes in order to truly understand Jupiter's version of the big picture.

Sagittarius is a combination of hot and dry, and as such, any planet in this sign can take these qualities to an extreme level, to the point where the planet's influence causes the native to manifest as the zealot, or the one who believes there is only one true path.

For this ardent believer its qualities join forces to convince them of the rightness (or righteousness) of their cause, whether its roots are based in a religious, philosophical, or spiritual background.

Sagittarian passion can ignite fire's natural enthusiasm and can quickly morph into religious *fervor* (Latin, heat). Dryness blocks outside influence, isolates doubt, and channels the thoughts so that Sagittarian logic demands one solution to all problems.

The danger for any planet placed in Sagittarius (and disposited by Jupiter) is that in its most extreme mode, the planet operates in such a way that it creates a polarising effect in the affairs of the house in which it is located.

In the field of psychology, this extreme type of dry thinking is known as 'splitting,' or black-and-white thinking[103] and is the failure in a person's thinking to bring together both positive and negative qualities in order to reach a cohesive or realistic conclusion.

The individual tends to think in extremes resulting in their own and others' actions and motivations considered as all good or all bad with no middle ground,[104] a situation which is best summed up by a quote which originates from the Bible.

"Whoever is not with me is against me, and whoever does not gather with me scatters"

Jesus of Nazareth, *Matthew Ch 12v.30*, from the *Synoptic Gospels of Matthew, Mark and Luke*

While this is an oversimplification of a complex problem, Sagittarius, more than the two other fire signs, compounds the potential for this possibility by harnessing its two qualities, hot and dry, and placing them on the altar of its ruling planet.

Jupiter is extreme by both astronomical and astrological terms, considering that it is the giant of our solar system, with an equatorial diameter eleven times that of Earth, and with twelve satellites to our one moon.

With Jupiter possessing the grand title of 'greater benefic' and having a reputation for being *'an index of the moral nature of the native'*,[105] it is easy to see how an individual, under the influence of such a planet, could get carried away by a misunderstanding of their own importance.

Jupiter provides Sagittarius with ideals that carry a dual purpose.

Firstly, it convinces the individual that there is spiritual security in the higher ideal *(if you're not with me)* and secondly, it feeds the fire of opposition *(then you must be against me)* and provides a platform from which to preach to others on the merits of their beliefs.

Planets in Sagittarius

By its very nature Jupiter seeks to embrace a philosophy, but rather than taking a more temperate view, it often feels duty bound to extend its theories to include others who they believe may not have reached their same level of enlightenment.

When the other planets are placed in Sagittarius, they are all open to Jupiter's influence as the owner of this sign, and each of them will choose to exhibit a different perspective of this one-sided thinking in accord with their own natural significations.

Mercury especially, runs rampant in Sagittarius, and for a planet in detriment Mercury does not seem to notice that it lacks self-discipline, tact and purposeful focus when Jupiter is its dispositor.

Nineteenth century painter Vincent Van Gogh had Moon and Jupiter together in Sagittarius.

When he said:

> *"There may be a great fire in our soul, yet no one ever comes to warm himself at it, and the passers-by see only a wisp of smoke."*[106]

you can feel not only his anguish at being ignored as a painter, but also the self-righteousness which distorts impartial thinking and encourages the type of Jupiterian splitting which ultimately led to the destruction of this artist's physical strength and his peace of mind.

The Element of Air
Libra: Aquarius: Gemini

Hot in Action

Hot may seem an odd choice for the element of Air especially when we are inclined to think of cool breezes and draughty hallways in winter, but this element's active quality is highly sensitive to inequalities in temperature and air pressure, and its constant movement demonstrates its desire to create moderation wherever extremes exist in the atmosphere.

Air brings more than changes in the weather, as its power has been harnessed as an energy source since the day mankind created sails to propel ships, and wind-powered machines to grind grain and draw water.

In terms of physical speed, a hot response for air is not so much about the quickness of the body in reacting to danger or challenge, but is more central to the speed of the mind and how quickly a threat can be identified, a choice made, and a mode of action initiated, when reading the situation at hand.

The air element is often not visible to the eye unless it is stirring up the other three elements; fanning a fire, moving dust particles or leaves on a tree, or creating waves on water.

And yet, it is constantly in a state of motion, large enough to alter weather patterns and move mighty oceans and yet tiny enough to enter our lungs and create the oxygen we need to survive.

In the same manner as air interacts with the elements, the air signs' reaction to external stimulus is instinctive and lightening fast, and their speed in being able to process information is breathtaking in its scope and understanding.

Wet in Thought

The quality of wetness suits the air signs so well, as this element of nature is divinely engineered to bring opposites together.

All three air signs share a fluid quality with internal thought patterns designed to think in abstract form, create new theories, and convert concepts into definite possibilities.

Similar to the right-brain hemisphere, wet thinking produces a fantasy-oriented mind, combining creative thinking patterns with emotions and intuition.

When ideas flow from one concept to another anything is possible, if the mind can but conceive of it.

In writing mode the wet signs pay more attention to coherence and meaning rather than the mechanics of spelling and punctuation as they are intent that the written word should reflect their visual images and original ideas.

Air Element = The Combination of Hot and Wet

A combination of Hot and Wet qualities creates the Air element signs that act on impulse at the same time as forming impressions and putting together ideas, concepts and possibilities in order to quickly pass them on to others.

The ancients called the air signs a sanguine temperament, and communication and the speedy exchange of ideas are an indispensable part of this element, as the air signs gladly discuss their findings with anyone who will listen.

The sanguine temperament's reputation for being friendly, talkative or comfortable in social settings, is born from the combination of two qualities which create an element that constantly looks for external stimulation and generally enjoys the company of others.

Through the hot response, the energetic process of thinking and verbal exchange is accentuated, and the air type is often flexible in speech and action, especially considering that part of the intellectual process is self-expression and open debate is an arena where the air element is confident and powerful.

However, air's flexibility can give way to agitation or exaggeration if they are feel they are not being listened to, and especially if a dry thinker is the one to challenge their thinking patterns.

Air does not appreciate being told that their rationalising abilities are inferior simply because they are deemed to lack the right facts to back their opinions. Or that their ideas lack objectivity because air allows emotions or perceptions to enter into their decision-making process.

Luckily air has the mental agility and adroitness to bamboozle dry thinkers (fire and earth) and to get the better of any verbal opponent who challenges their statements.

Modality and Dispositors

Differences between Libra, Aquarius and Gemini

LIBRA : Cardinal Air : Ruled by VENUS

The cardinal modality is linked to the four signs which mark major turning points in the earth's journey around the sun.

The cardinal signs initiate each new season, and the Sun in the first degree of Libra is an equinoctial point which heralds the season of autumn in the northern hemisphere.

Venus, as Libra's ruling planet, is the driving force behind this hot, wet sign which is driven by the desire to interact and form intimate and beneficial bonds with others, in order to strengthen alliances, or to create joy and pleasure through relationship.

The heat contrariety for Libra lies in its yearning to be understood and to be accepted and loved by another.

One to one communication is important to Venus' sign, and better still, if social and leisure activities can provide emotional and demonstrative outlets for this sign that craves human interaction.

The planet in Libra is a good actor and can appear in public as though nothing upsets their equilibrium, but in private the hot quality combined with moisture produces fuming and emotional outbursts in keeping with Venus' propensity to avoid making a scene, but to passionately vent their displeasure when behind closed doors.

The hot quality also brings forth the signature of an expressive and entertaining storyteller but one who can be prone to exaggeration if enjoying the limelight too much.

"There is no such thing as perpetual tranquillity of mind while we live here; because life itself is but motion, and can never be without desire, not without fear, no more than without sense."[107]

The energy needed to create outer images of harmony and balance activates Libra's hot response, and both qualities of heat and moisture are particularly taxed if the exterior peaceful image masks inner conflict or unrest.

True, Venus can never be without desire, but fear of losing loved ones is never far from Venus' thoughts and with such an active imagination, Libra sometimes finds it difficult to find a comfortable balance between peace of mind and mindfulness.

Peace of mind is a numbing sensation brought about by a feeling of being safe and protected.

Order, harmony, serenity and tranquillity are all terms used to describe peace of mind and perhaps this is the mind utopia for which Libra secretly yearns.

On the other hand, mindfulness is described as a mental state achieved by focusing one's awareness on the present moment.

Mindfulness maintains a nonjudgmental state of heightened awareness of one's thoughts, emotions and experiences on a moment to moment basis.

Inasmuch as the Scales of Libra idealistically seeks perpetual tranquillity of mind, it needs to be aware of the two states of mind and to make a conscious decision on whether it chooses peace of mind or mindfulness.

Its thinking process is from the wet contrariety, and truthfully, the latter state is probably more compatible with a mind that stores a never-ending flow of intermingling thought, perception, emotion and memory.

Libra is one of two signs ruled by Venus, and whilst we have become accustomed to this fact, there is a level of incompatibility which exists between the planet and its sign.

In the descriptive lists on Libra it is described as a masculine diurnal sign, and this is in conflict with Venus, which is a feminine planet of the night representing women, dance and ornamentation.

However, the very nature of air's passive quality is moisture, capable of melding these conflicting statements between sign and planet, and producing a fertile imagination by integrating the best qualities of the two genders of feminine planet with masculine sign.

Libra's romanticism is part of its general allure and the cross pollination between the two components of astrology, and the two genders, has the potential to produce a powerful aphrodisiac.

In its best moments, the wet quality for Libra is the love of bringing together beauty, grace and rhythm, either through music, the spoken or written word, or through movement.

In its worst moments, Libra stockpiles information (like wet wood in winter) for a time when it is useful, or when it must be gathered to make a decision, or to light Libra's fire within, but sometimes too much information stored causes indecision, forgetfulness or poor organisation skills.

Planets in Libra

Planets in Libra seek to find a balance according to their own nature, and whilst this may not always be an easy task, each planet must wrestle in their own way to find the ideal balance between what is virtuous, and what is not, according to what principles they represent as a planet.

Each planet in Libra must look towards the dispositor of its sign (Venus) for guidance, and some planets can do this gracefully, whilst others struggle when obligated to serve Venus in such a manner.

For instance, the Moon is comfortable with its fellow nocturnal planet so there is little strain when Moon in Libra looks for a way to balance its nurturing, between keeping itself happy whilst tending to the people it loves.

Jupiter in Libra needs to take care in its pleasure excesses, in case it becomes too greedy or destructively hedonistic, but otherwise it is quite happy to follow the instructions of its fellow benefic planet.

However, the Sun, Mercury and Mars all take issue with Venus as al-Biruni's Table illustrates in Chapter Four.

The Sun is *'injurious to'* Venus because Libra is its sign of fall, and the Sun struggles to get a true sense of itself when it is constantly judging its own value through another's eyes.

There is no problem when Sun in Libra is loved, as this is the lens through which a Libran views its own value, but if a love should sour, then these images are ones that plague the Libran Sun and fills them with self-doubt and loathing, especially if they in turn are loathed by the ex-loved one.

Mercury in Libra would love to believe itself to be fair and equitable in the decisions it makes but the truth is that Mercury *'is mutually hurtful with'* Venus, and this means that a Libran Mercury is always influenced by the desire to please everyone, with its information causing it to dither, prevaricate, flatter or avoid confrontation, when really, it should be telling the truth and 'letting the chips fall where they may'.

Mars is also *'mutually hurtful with'* Venus, as Mars in Libra grapples with its sign of detriment and tries to find equilibrium between timidity and rashness, fear of rejection and unbridled anger when it cannot control itself.

Venus is helpless to dampen its malefic tendencies, especially when Mars' worst behaviours appear when it is in debility.

When Saturn is disposited by Venus it revels in the experience given that Libra is Saturn's exalted sign.

A number of astrologers believe that the dignity of Exaltation outdates that of Rulership, so it is interesting to note that perhaps Libra belonged to Saturn well before Venus took ownership over this sign.

Marcus Manilius' didactic poem *Astronomica* is considered to be the first astrological work in Latin[108] written in the early years of the first century[109] and in it, Manilius describes a native born under the sign of Libra in this manner,

"He will be acquainted with the tables of law, abstruse (obscure) *legal points, and words denoted by compendious signs* (legal abbreviations)*; he will know what is permissible and the penalties incurred by doing what is forbidden; and in his own house he is a magistrate holding lifelong office. Under no other sign would Servius*[110] *more fittingly have been born, who in interpreting the law framed legislation of his own. Indeed, whatever stands in dispute and needs a ruling the pointer of the Balance will determine."*[111]

We might surmise from this text that when Saturn is found in Libra it indicates an individual who creates laws or a creed unique unto themselves, and strictly adheres to those laws, regardless of what the rest of the world thinks of them.

This form of personal integrity may be flexible up to a point, given Libra's hot and wet qualities, but it also creates a non-conformist who isolates themselves from others and creates a pull between both ruling planets, Saturn, who is happy to stand alone, and Venus, who aches for human companionship and acceptance.

AQUARIUS : Fixed Air : Ruled by SATURN

Most traditional writers believed that Saturn preferred the sign of Aquarius over Capricorn, as this fixed air sign meant Saturn was warmed by the sign's contrarieties, and became more temperate in its nature due to the comforting qualities of heat and moisture.

Saturn's brittleness eased a bit, and it could afford to be more lenient, and more easily swayed by debate under the influence of its sanguine sign.

However, in comparison with the other two air signs Aquarius is definitely less flexible, more insulated or withdrawn and a little colder in behaviour because of its rulership by Saturn.

In contrast, Libra and Gemini are two affable signs who are ruled by more socially adept planets, Venus and Mercury respectively, and are air signs who seek the company of others and fully commit to their sanguine temperament.

Perhaps the best argument in linking yet another air sign with Saturn (Libra is Saturn's exalted sign), but this time by rulership, is to remember that Saturn is, all things considered, a planet of consequences.

Saturn is known for drawing a line in the sand and priding itself that it knows how to keep to this line through diligence and discipline.

In order to do this, Saturn needs to constantly redefine and review what exactly this line means for it, and a fixed air sign is the perfect vehicle for this type of intense contemplation.

It is imperative for Aquarius to use its hot and wet qualities to keep its boundaries clearly defined because if Saturn crosses the boundary by compromising its principles, then it ceases to be a line and instead becomes a squeaky gate that destroys Saturn's integrity, and makes every move thereafter an agonising decision over right and wrong.

Another reason why Aquarius is an appropriate sign for Saturn's rulership is to remember that there are two ways by which Saturn maintains its boundaries.

One way is through the use of physical borders (Capricorn) and the other, and perhaps the more insidious, is to maintain separation through the control of information or the repetitious reinforcement of lies in order to instil a particular mindset.

The term 'brain-washing' is apt for an air sign which has the passive quality of wetness and the ruling planet of Saturn, and it is important to understand that sometimes fighting what we are conditioned to think can become one of the greatest battles of our lives.

In contrast to Aquarius, Saturn's other sign of Capricorn is an earth sign which works to keep its physical environment well under its control.

Build a barrier big enough, and Saturn will keep the division intact and ward off any advances to break it down.

But even the strongest Capricorn defences can be breached if the cardinal sign cannot resist a moving force with enough momentum to eliminate a physical obstacle.

Any planet situated in Aquarius is ruled by a subtler version of Saturn which works on the mind, defeating the possibility of challenge even before it arises.

If the planet in Aquarius repeatedly tells the chart owner that they will fail, the mind is likely to capitulate under constant onslaught of doubt and negativity becoming compliant, subservient and easily controlled by Saturn's fears.

"I don't want my daughter to break any glass ceilings. I'd rather she never contemplated their existence. Because glass ceilings, closed doors, boys clubs are notions, they're ideas, and they're not tangible. You can't see, touch or feel them."[112]

Capricorn may be the wall of iron, but Aquarius is the glass ceiling. Subtle, tantalisingly close, but often impenetrable because the mind does not believe a breakthrough is possible.

Like all intangibles, it does not matter if you cannot see, touch, or feel them, they are a real presence in the mind, and are ultimately, the more formidable of obstacles.

Brainwashing, mind-control, coercive persuasion, whatever the term, it is designed to change someone's beliefs or attitudes using intense teaching and indoctrination for the purpose of controlling the present and future thoughts and actions of that individual.

Saturn's ownership of Aquarius does this by repeatedly telling someone that something is true (creating its own reality), whilst at the same time blocking out or preventing any 'counter-truth' which might destabilise the original information.

Nor does Saturn need a dark room or a menacing masked torturer to achieve this mind control.

Day to day experiences can have the same lasting effect on the psyche, and other planets need to be active and present to provide a more balanced and optimistic view of life to prevent the boundaries for the planet in Aquarius from becoming insurmountable.

Aquarius shares another link with its ruler Saturn, as both sign and planet are masculine in gender and diurnal by sect, therefore, there is a sense of *bonhomie*, literally 'good man' in French, between the sign and its dispositor.

This natural connection leads Aquarius to actively pursue information to bring honour, good reputation and success to the individual, as these are important states of being for Saturn, and increases its value to the Sun, the ruler of the diurnal sect.

Under this sign, the wet quality establishes thought patterns which collect information in a somewhat random manner, and use it to shore up Saturn's authority, making for a quick-witted mind and a natural leader.

As a wet thinker Aquarius is gifted with being able to start with the answer and work backwards, so that a challenge can be met with a list of facts to support the information.

This Saturnian sign possesses a concrete thinking process in that it is capable of maintaining its thoughts in a fluid motion, easily accessible and usually backed up with good articulation and impressive presentation of factual information.

In a less enlightened manner, Saturn uses Aquarius to link information together in a far more subjective way than this sign is willing to admit, piling up misleading or depressing data that reinforces images of oppression or victimisation, especially where clashes with authority figures are concerned.

Planets in Aquarius

Planets in Aquarius meet Saturn through this sign, and will use their own resources to work around this formidable planet.

Here the joint qualities of hot and wet combine to attack the problem, and present the planet with acceptable working solutions.

The Sun in Aquarius battles Saturn's opposition across the Thema Mundi chart, as Leo and Aquarius face off on opposite sides of the chart and the Sun is debilitated in Aquarius.

Saturn cools the Sun's ardour and causes self-doubt, so this is a good example of the individual needing to break Saturn's hold on the mind and to find more positive patterns to encourage self-confidence.

Aquarian Moon convinces itself that it will be the first one to break attachments and walk away, only to find that when it happens in reality, their emotional wounds are deep, and the independence they thought they would cherish is accompanied by a loneliness that cuts to the core.

When Saturn is the dispositor, Mercury in Aquarius prides itself on honesty and clear thinking, but gets caught in the fixed trap of being unable to change its facts midstream, and Mars in Aquarius is distracted by the voices in its head, and worries that it will never have sufficient courage to crack the glass ceiling that perpetually looms overhead.

Venus and Saturn are friendly towards one another because Saturn asks for Venus' sign for its exaltation, so Venus in Aquarius, whilst often choosing independence over commitment, does not appear too heart-broken by its decision to change relationships to suit its own needs.

Whilst Jupiter in Aquarius is still disposited by Saturn, it is not as harmful as Saturn's other sign, whereby Jupiter in Capricorn is in fall.

This Saturnian sign is both warm and moist which suits Jupiter's own temperament, plus the two planets are both diurnal, so Jupiter in Aquarius enjoys both the sign and the mental stimulation which an air sign provides to a lover of education, philosophy and knowledge.

GEMINI : Mutable Air : Ruled by MERCURY

The mutable sign of Gemini occurs at the third month of the northern spring; a season epitomised by the hot/wet qualities, and is ruled by the planet Mercury.

Perhaps for these reasons, Gemini is the easiest of the air signs to identify with its two contrariety qualities.

Gemini's heat lies in its generally enthusiastic and cheerful nature, suiting Mercury who adds restless energy to keep the mind active, and heralds the compulsive talker constantly on the go.

Mercury tends to be androgynous in nature. It changes gender according to its placement before or after the Sun, or becomes the same sex as the other planets when in aspect to them, so this part of Gemini's changeability will be dependent on what its ruling planet is doing in any given chart.

A distressed Mercury adds more instability to Gemini's expression, so their speedy energy is engaged in making rapid changes in temperament depending on what triggers Mercury's anxieties.

One minute demonstrative and the life of the party, the next withdrawn and introspective, Gemini has all the traits of a sign reacting in a hot manner to the circumstances under which its ruler is placed.

Mercury is the quintessential significator for communication, speech, memory retention and mental acumen, so it seems this planet is literally 'in its element' in a hot, wet sign.

It may seem reasonable for Mercury to naturally migrate towards an air sign in preference to an earth sign for exaltation, but perhaps this has something to do with Thema Mundi when Mercury's astronomical position in a sign alongside a Leo Sun, places it in Virgo rather than Gemini, which lies on the other side of the Moon's sign.

Wet thinking relishes the possibility of delving into the past and connecting any similarities from what has been, to what is happening now.

This is Gemini's passion as it loves puzzles, intrigues and conundrums and there is no better mystery than the link between past and present.

The concept of *de-ja vu* fascinates all wet thinkers, but perhaps Gemini is the most taken by this idea of experiencing the same act at two different moments in time.

This kind of thinking outside the box is extremely attractive for Mercury as it seeks mental stimulation and enjoys thinking creatively.

"The secret thoughts of a man run over all things, holy, profane, clean, obscene, grave, and light, without shame or blame."[113]

'The secret thoughts of man' fascinates any planet in Gemini as there is no thought which is deemed to be too boring or too trivial for a sign that thrives on detail and loves the subtlety of nuance in thought, language and expression.

Part of Gemini's compulsion to understand the broad range of possibilities lies in its search for both self-expression and self-acceptance and it constantly looks for what is alike and what is unalike to its own attitudes, opinions, expressions and emotions.

All this must be done by a planet which finds itself in Gemini and some planets relish the task whilst others are exhausted by Gemini's natural exuberance.

For a sign which is often demeaned by being harshly judged as 'superficial' by some astrology definitions, this hot/wet sign is anything but superficial.

Is it fascinated by the machinations of mankind?

Does it find human nature an on-going soap opera? Certainly!

But there is also kindness and hope behind Gemini's desire to know every last fact of what is going on in others' lives, and what Gemini does with the information it collects and stores away is largely up to the condition and state of its ruling planet, Mercury, as it is Mercury who will decide what to do with the assembled facts.

One of the vital rules in traditional astrology states:

Whatever action a planet begins, the ruler of its sign (the dispositor) will complete.

For instance, a great looking planet with a sign whose owner is poorly placed will begin the race well, but it is destined to run out of puff before the end. The more debilitated the ruler of the sign, the more dramatically spoiled is the finish and Gemini is no exception to this rule when Mercury finds itself in a terrible state in the chart.

Planets in Gemini

Any planet in Gemini's hot air sign is keen to actively participate in life and to explore every avenue in order to maximise on its potential.

The wetness of Gemini's sign means that this planet will search in the same manner as a right-brained hemisphere, using face recognition, by reading emotions, in visual imagery, or in holistic thinking patterns which collates feelings and thoughts into one model.

Once the planet has done its job, Mercury takes over, simply because Gemini is on loan to the planet and a mercantile planet such as Mercury, knows that loans must ultimately be repaid by the borrower.

Planets in Gemini react quickly to any stimuli which best suits that planet's nature and the brain reacts quickly to record information which is useful for the planet in Gemini to take advantage of any scraps of information which may help it to materialize its potential.

For instance, Moon in Gemini feeds off sudden changes in its immediate environment and both protects the body and stimulates the emotions so that the native can quickly adjust physically and emotionally to new situations.

Depending on the gender of the individual, Venus and Mars in Gemini will look for partners who have similarities to themselves, but with enough differences to still make the opposite sex interesting to them.

Jupiter struggles in its masculine sign of detriment as Gemini tends to send Jupiter off in a spin with its careless or scattered collection of data and that can make Jupiter sound foolish or ill-prepared to defend itself if it moves onto ground where generalisations, gossip-mongering, or grandiose statements will be its undoing.

Gemini warms up Saturn and makes it a little more gregarious but like Jupiter, if Saturn does not do the work to back up its facts, it risks losing others' respect or jeopardizing its level of authority.

The Element of Water
Cancer: Scorpio: Pisces

Cold in Action

Cold response is concerned with the conservation of energy and therefore a number of characteristics can be seen to come from this response.

Those who predominantly act from a cold response appear resistant to change, or frustrate others with their seeming unwillingness to move forward to the next stage of life.

They enter something akin to a dormancy stage and may seem to be overly fearful or unenthusiastic when confronted by a new situation.

The hot response signs of air and fire can be harshly critical of such apparent inactivity and unfairly judge their cold counterparts using negative adjectives such as indecisive, unmotivated or even lazy to describe a cold quality's behaviour.

The cold signs are feminine and they instinctively survive using caution and observation in keeping with their gender and nature.

Cold response signs resent being pushed into anything hasty as they prefer to slow things down in order to acclimatise to change in their own time.

Their energy and vitality levels are lower than hot response signs, and this means they use their energy wisely and economically, so as not to waste effort. The resultant behaviour of a cold sign is that it often appears to display a more conservative and contained nature than its masculine air or fire counter- elements.

For the cold signs energy is something to be saved rather than wasted on pointless displays of power, speed or strength, especially given that it is more difficult to collect and store energy for the water and earth signs.

It takes the cold signs time and effort to go into action, but once there, the action is prolonged and fortified by sheer willpower, and has a clear and conscious target as energy is precious and requires time to regain or replenish its reserves.

For these reasons, conservation of energy through inertia rather than inactivity (as to *resist activity* can be as tiresome as doing something), reflection, and passive behaviour is part of the cold signs' *modus operandi*.

Words like coagulate, curdle, congeal, and clot describe the physical act of something changing from a fluid into a substance of thicker or glutinous consistency.

Applying the active contrariety of coldness to matter causes it to congeal or freeze, to hold a more solid state until warmth (the opposite contrariety) can be added to restore it, if possible, to its original state or take it to another preferred state.

Heat or friction is added to warm cold up but it must be a constant source of heat, as it is natural for things to 'lose heat' and return back to a cooler state of being if heat is not maintained.

Coldness is about preservation, slowing down or even aborting change if that is what is desired. This buys the necessary time to observe, contemplate, improve, or even relish a moment which cannot be repeated.

Steps must be taken to control something which is changing too fast as genuine fear of being replaced or discarded is a real and present threat for the cold quality signs.

Wet in Thought

Wet thinking is built on the concept that everything is inter-connected to the past, present, and the future.

Wet thinking is concerned with joining seemingly unrelated pieces of information together, so that information flows from one source to another creating links and forming bonds between ideas, memory, perception, and opinions.

Sometimes thought has no specific form, and creates fleeting or half-formed impressions rather than detailed so-called logical analysis.

This type of thinker may instinctively know the right answer, but does not know the process by which they got there, and can get agitated or defensive if pressured to analyse their methods of arriving at a conclusion.

Water Element = The Combination of Cold and Wet

A combination of Cold and Wet qualities creates the water element comprising of three signs that hold back their initial response so that they can work through their emotional state before proceeding to the action stage.

This element understands on some primal level that all information has an effect on the deeper level of feeling states, so movement forward is not just about preserving their energy for future action, it is also about finding the *appropriate* action to move through life with the least amount of resistance.

Flowing water will follow the water course set by its earthly constraints, the banks of the river and the contours of the land determine how fast and in which direction water will flow, and this makes water the one element which will take the path of least resistance, in order to preserve its limited energy.

In earlier times, a person whose chart had a high water content was judged to have a phlegmatic temperament, and unlike our modern concept of water as an element which readily exposes its emotions, the authentic phlegmatic temperament was expected to possess quite the opposite nature.

Phlegmatic described a person with a sluggish, self-possessed or stolidly calm disposition, almost to the point of apathetic or impassive when it came to the emotions.

Obviously this seemingly calm exterior was designed for a number of reasons and most of them concern the individual's survival.

Firstly, water was a feminine element and women during most periods of history were expected to blend into the background as wives, mothers and lovers.

Any emotion shown by women was to be mistrusted as many of the earlier texts on the Moon or Venus, both feminine planets, clearly indicate in the two planets' significations.

Secondly, Plato, the Greek philosopher from 500 B.C.E., proposed the notion of a tripartite soul which comprised of a rational part, a spirited part, and a far inferior appetitive part to the soul.

The appetitive part was governed by its desires and emotions, and as such was prone to leading its counterparts into terrible places where the soul ought not go, according to Plato.

The repression of emotions meant that the rational side of the soul was winning the battle against corruption or destruction, and it was ultimately far better for the soul, if the appetites (emotions) were controlled by the elevated parts of the soul.

Thirdly, whilst a calm disposition may be the exact opposite to the water element's true nature, it does conserve energy, maintain privacy and buy time, all of which works in the favour of the cold quality.

And finally, the wet quality which complements water's passivity, if not wasted on emotional outbursts, is able to focus on the mind's inner landscape where the imagination is fertile and escape from the mundane world is not only possible but is actively pursued by the water element.

Information is a sensitive trigger for emotion, so the water personality requires a good deal of internalised cold energy to process incoming data, given that the mind is processing through a number of diverse avenues using colour, rhythm, visual imagery and intuition to collate and bind the information into useful data for future reference.

If being phlegmatic meant that ideas, concepts and infinite possibilities occurred within a mind freed from judgement and restriction, then it seems sensible that a heavy water element would be quite happy to confound and mystify a critical outside world which harshly judged their temperament.

Modality and Dispositors

Differences between Cancer, Scorpio and Pisces

CANCER: Cardinal Water : Ruled by THE MOON

The Moon stands at the head of the celestial procession, and as the fastest moving planet and the one we witness changing shape with her proximity to the Earth, she embodies the inconsistencies of the material world.

By her very character the Moon symbolises the changeable nature of all living things, and in the same way as she reflects the sun's light in the evening hours, the Moon also embodies the sun's passage through the years and decades, as she marks the physical effects of birth, maturation, decline, and death.

There could be no more appropriate sign than Cancer to claim the Thema Mundi's ascendant as its own, and for its ruling planet to signify the body's life, health and vitality.

"We can fill our lives with generous deeds, with loving words, with art and song, and all the ecstasies of love. We can flood our years with sunshine – with the divine climate of kindness, and we can drain to the last drop the golden cup of joy."[114]

Cancer is a sign of emotional highs and lows, and a sign which is capable of deep compassion, generous deeds, and loving kindness.

The passive contrariety of wet draws all things together, talks of similarities rather than differences, and urges information to flow from one source to another, so that every thought and experience has connection.

Perhaps another reason for giving Cancer over to Thema Mundi for its Ascendant is that as much as it concerns coming into being through conception, birth and growth, Cancer as the rising sign of the World Horoscope also carries the very positive virtue of Hope.

Hope that our humanity will link us together, rather than pull us apart, hope that we learn to honour and respect our differences instead of hating and mistrusting one another for them, and that *'a divine climate of kindness'* means that ultimately, we can create global harmony for the environment and for ourselves, and that hopefully we do not destroy the Earth in the process.

Planets in Cancer look to the Moon to describe how the physical world will unfold for that particular planet.

Planets placed in a cold wet sign such as Cancer is, may have to learn patience, humility or compassion, and according to their own essence, they may or may not struggle with this concept.

Each planet which experiences Cancer through sign placement will be disposited by the Moon, and will therefore be required, like the cardinal sign, to go forth and search for the thing or person it loves in order to learn lessons in nurturing, patience, defence, service and sacrifice.

As well as being a cardinal sign, Cancer is also a sign of cold quality, and there will be some planets which will feel restrained by Cancer' cautionary and protective movement, which is not unlike the sideways, crab-like motions of its namesake.

Planets in Cancer

Planets which naturally carry heat such as the Sun and Mars are likely to find Cancer extremely frustrating and may fight against Cancer's natural propensity to keep its feelings hidden or to remain silent to protect itself.

Mars' nature is far too impulsive for the Crab, and there is little doubt that Mars feels the sting of being in fall in this sign, as it is not so much the qualities that Mars fights against (Scorpio too is cold and wet) but rather it resents the restriction placed on it by the dispositor of Cancer.

The concept of *a divine climate of kindness* is so foreign to Mars that when it finds itself in the sign owned by the Moon, it grapples with unfamiliar emotions and feels its energy taken hostage by a cold/wet sign that seems to achieve very little in Mars' eyes.

Mars does not object to emotions *per-se*, because certain emotions drive courage, passion and the commitment to a battle, but more considerate feelings such as kindness, gentleness and the awareness of others' feelings, plunges Mars totally out of its depth and it is all at sea when it feels weakened or vulnerable under the influence of Cancer's emotions.

Saturn too suffers in Cancer considering that it is in a sign of its detriment, and one of the major problems for Saturn in Cancer, is the dichotomy of distance and separation verses love and attachment.

I wrote earlier of the danger of Saturn's line becoming a squeaky gate and placing Saturn in Cancer is one way in which the line can be crossed, as Saturn's integrity can be sacrificed for the sake of its sign's owner.

The Moon can coerce or force Saturn to its own bidding when Saturn is in Cancer, and this is a very uncomfortable and detrimental place for Saturn to find itself, caught up in the whims of an extremely changeable and unpredictable planet as the Moon.

Jupiter fares better, as Cancer is its sign of exaltation, but even then, the Moon's condition will determine the height and duration of Jupiter's exaltation as the Moon can be a fickle dispositor (it rules Fate after all), and its changing phases can mean that Jupiter, or any other planet for that matter, is forced to submit to the changing fortunes brought about by the Moon.

SCORPIO: Fixed Water : Ruled by MARS

The fixed sign of Scorpio presents a different side of water from its free-flowing sibling, as Cancer's cardinality suggests movement, currents ebbing and flowing in unison with the Moon's phases.

In contrast Scorpio lies in dark pools of water quietly hidden away in marshes and swamps where shadows play on the surface and the land has become saturated and can no longer absorb any more liquid.

The ruling planet of Scorpio is Mars, and while the element of water seems incongruous with such a war-like planet, it pays to remember that life can turn from an easy ride into a treacherous fight for survival in the blink of an eye.

Scorpio uses its cold wet qualities to keep guard over those it cherishes so that should any sign of danger arise, Mars' sign can act with purpose and deliberation in order to contain the threat and restore safety.

"Biologically speaking, if something bites you, it is more likely to be female."[15]

The feminine sign of Scorpio is a perfect foil for Aries, the masculine sign ruled by Mars.

A planet in Scorpio will look to protect rather than attack, will value strategy above brute strength, and will prefer effective extermination to wanton destruction.

In contrast, the same planet in Aries will be willing to accept collateral damage, feeling justified by the philosophical argument that sometimes there are 'casualties of war' which are regrettable but necessary to restore order.

Feelings get hurt and enemies are made, especially when the planet in Aries is in hot pursuit of something it desperately desires, but Mars' masculine sign is willing to take these risks if it can see a prize at the end of its combat.

This is not an option for Scorpio's interpretation of its ruling planet, as Mars is after all placed in the water sign, and for water it is a higher priority to preserve life and to protect those it loves than to destroy those who oppose it.

Planets in Scorpio (even the Moon) deplore destruction for the sheer sake of it, and the mode of operation for Mars' feminine cold sign is such that any planet in its sign will contemplate each decision and weigh up the consequences, wait patiently for the right moment, and then strike its enemy (and only its enemy) in what it deems to be the appropriate manner, and at the appropriate time.

Scorpio dislikes the role of protagonist, as generally speaking, it is a sign that likes to keep its head down and stay out of trouble.

In true phlegmatic style, Scorpio prefers to maintain a calm and collected demeanour, prides itself on being competent and good under pressure, and prefers to hide its emotions so that it draws the least amount of attention.

Planets in Scorpio

If a planet in Scorpio feels that it has been backed into a corner then this sign will bring forward its natural instinct to strike, and the planet concerned will determined how and when it will protect itself, and is usually pretty effective, given that its sign is owned by the warrior planet, Mars.

However, Scorpio is a water sign and as such, it is fully aware of the harm it is capable of inflicting, and therefore is strangely empathetic towards its enemy.

This is especially true for both Venus and the Moon in Scorpio, and gives some insight into why both planets are distressed in this sign.

The strangely intimate relationship between two antagonists is hard for most planets in Scorpio to understand, as the chart owner can fiercely defend the motives of its enemy, whilst still wishing to destroy them.

Perhaps it is only another water sign which truly comprehends the duality of emotions, whereby love and hate create a co-dependent relationship, as planets in Cancer or Pisces can experience similar negative relationships.

Planets in Scorpio are often caught in a dilemma between the sign's qualities (and its dispositor Mars), and the nature of their own significations.

Ironically, the feminine planets, Venus and the Moon, are both disadvantaged when they are in the same gender sign of Scorpio, Venus is in detriment and the Moon is in fall, so understandably these two planets are often nervous of, or act defensively towards, the female relatives, colleagues and friends who pass through their lives.

Regardless of whether the native themselves is male or female, they are likely to view members of the female sex as a threat when Venus is in Scorpio, and depending on the state of Mars, there may be good reason for such mistrust where women are concerned.

The aging process helps to alleviate these suspicions if strong bonds with women are able to be made, but the initial response to any new woman on the horizon, is to take care until they have assessed the possible impact this individual may make to their lives.

When the Moon is situated in Scorpio, the mother is often perceived as being controlling, abusive, overly emotional or manipulative, and there is a genuine struggle for the individual to feel physically and emotionally safe under such a debilitated Moon.

Scorpio belongs to Mars, and a Moon in Scorpio can reflect the warrior qualities of this sign's dispositor, but as Scorpio is also a cold wet sign, sometimes there exists a war of attrition between mother and child whereby one side seeks to gradually wear down the other through a series of small-scale skirmishes often engaged over an entire lifetime.

No-one wins in these kinds of emotional conflicts, but as a fixed water sign Scorpio has established the battle lines early in life, and is unlikely to abandon them for fear of appearing weak or vulnerable to their enemy, even if it is one's own mother.

The masculine planets do not fare much better under the scrutiny of Mars.

A Sun in Scorpio is often the sign of a matriarch-ruled family, as father has either stepped out or handed over control to his strong or controlling female counterpart.

This can create issues past childhood, especially if the child has been used as a pawn in the battle for power between mother and father.

Saturn and Jupiter are masculine planets, but in this feminine sign, they tend to indicate either powerful women or underhanded men with two different modes of action.

Saturn in Scorpio does not handle authority well as both malefics, Saturn and Mars, have their control issues and do not like to be challenged or dominated by others.

Jupiter in Scorpio likes to collect secrets, but is not so good at keeping them safe, so intrigues and sabotage can be the undoing of mighty Jupiter in this sign.

Whatever the planet in Scorpio is doing, it is wise to keep a close eye on Mars' position in the chart as it is the dispositor for Scorpio, and whilst the planet itself indicates how the trouble starts, it is the ruler of the sign who determines how the battle is likely to end.

PISCES: Mutable Water : Ruled by JUPITER

The mutable sign of Pisces is perhaps the most versatile of all twelve signs.

Its element is water, its modality is mutable and its lord is Jupiter, the planet with most expansive and exploratory nature of all seven planets.

Water is the stuff of life. Nothing can exist without it, and of all the water signs, Pisces exemplifies rain washing down on the earth, causing tiny rivulets to form if only for a few moments, gutters to fill and overflow, and water droplets like tears to wash away care, sadness and fatigue.

Pisces identifies with the transcendent nature of falling rain, as Jupiter reminds us that in spite of the vastness of the universe, still no two drops of rain are identical. For this reason, just like the raindrops, people need to be celebrated and deserve in equal measure to receive the benefits of love, praise and acceptance from the world.

Pisces may be the dreamer who retreats into the phlegmatic temperament in order to find their own Jupiterian kingdom within, but there exists a pragmatism to Pisces which tolerates a world gone mad with greed and hate.

The nature of rain is that whilst it is cold, it also has a cascading flow that captures every available surface, moving everywhere at once, searching for cracks to run through and filling every dry nook and cranny with moisture.

Pisces knows that the world is not perfect, but like the rain, its sees opportunity everywhere and seeks to fill parched spaces, if only for a moment, with its own life essence.

A planet with the cold qualities of Pisces may sometimes hold back from adventure, and may hesitate, while another in the sign of its co-ruled Sagittarius (perhaps in the aspect of square) might tear ahead without fear.

Both planets must still look to Jupiter to direct them, and for the planet in Pisces, part of this search involves having the courage to look within its own essence to find its potential, and to bring forth its unique characteristics.

Whilst human nature is drawn to the fiery enthusiasm of Jupiter's masculine sign, and Sagittarius' enthusiasm for life is certainly contagious, it should be remembered that for the planet in Pisces, the journey within often requires far more intestinal fortitude to search with kindness, and to accept the truth when it becomes evident, even if that truth results in exposure to raw emotions.

J.R.R.Tolkien created many brave wanderers and truth searchers in his fictional trilogy *The Lord of the Rings,* many of which are fine examples which display the admirable qualities of both signs belonging to Jupiter.

The main character is the hobbit Frodo Baggins, who is visited by Gandalf the Grey, a wizard who tells Frodo that he must destroy the Ring and return peace and harmony to all the kingdoms of Middle Earth.

Frodo is aided in his quest by Samwise "Sam" Gamgee, his gardener and faithful friend, Legolas the elf, Gimli the dwarf and Boromir of Gondor, but perhaps the closest friendship which Frodo experiences (apart from Gandalf) is his relationship with the complicated and endearingly human character, Strider, a Ranger of the North.

The enigmatic and mysterious Strider is on a quest of his own making, as it is revealed that his true identity is that of the deposed king, Aragorn II.

Tolkien's trilogy is as much about Aragorn's journey to reclaim his throne as it is about the infamous Ring, so much so, that his third book is titled *The Return of the King,* and Aragorn is worth a special mention here, as he displays many of the characteristics which are reminiscent of Jupiter's sign of Pisces.

Tolkien's poem in his first book *The Fellowship of the Rings* is referring to Aragorn who hides not only his identity, but also his inner strength and his true value, behind his quiet demeanour.

The first line of Tolkien's poem is a clever reversal of Shakespeare's famous line from *The Merchant of Venice* (1596) *"All that glitters is not gold."*

Tolkien's poem reads:

> *"All that is gold does not glitter,*
> *Not all those who wander are lost;*
> *The old that is strong does not wither,*
> *Deep roots are not reached by the frost."*

> J.R.R. Tolkien, *Lord of the Rings*

Aragorn perpetually embodies the phlegmatic temperament, as he is often described as emotionally withdrawn or undemonstrative, sometimes grim or sad, but with unexpected moments of levity.

In the trilogy, Aragorn has acquired otherworldly gifts from his childhood with the elves, a subtle reminder of the invisible link between a mundane world and the ethereal world which Pisces often seems to stand astride with a foot in both camps.

Like Aragorn, who has a repository of Elven wisdom and owns the gift of foresight, a planet in Pisces possesses a level of intuition and an uncanny access to knowledge from an unknown source, which is information that goes far beyond the usual standards of wet thinking mode.

Aragorn is both wise and strong, yet suffers from crushing self-doubt in several episodes in Tolkien's books, especially when the group's mentor and protector Gandalf appears to lose his life in the battle with the supernatural being Balrog.

Aragorn's grief at the loss of his friend is real and is not diminished until the wizard returns as an elevation of his former self with the title of Gandalf the White.

It is not hard to imagine that any planet situated in Pisces might share a certain rapport with both Tolkien's characters, as Pisces is a water sign which, when aligned with a planet, finds the necessary impetus from its ruler Jupiter to drive the planet to explore its motivations, and to doubt the wisdom of its decisions.

Gandalf's transformation from Grey Wizard to White Wizard is synonymous with Jupiter (Pisces' dispositor) and its ability to demand any planet finding itself in Pisces to 'up the ante' by making more of an effort to do Jupiter's bidding.

The borrower planet can feel as though Jupiter is asking for far too many favours from a planet in its sign, and Jupiter's increasing demands on a planet in Pisces can reverberate throughout the chart.

Like Gandalf and his fluctuating powers against his evil nemesis, the condition of Jupiter will be critical as to whether Jupiter can deliver the promises it makes, when the planet does its bidding as unexpected or diminished results can be distressing for both the planet and the chart's owner.

The feminine nocturnal sign of Pisces is matched with Jupiter, a masculine diurnal planet and sometimes the imbalance of sect and gender creates issues for both sign and planet.

Jupiter learns the lessons of gentleness, humility and sacrifice through its water sign, as it is generally a skilled puppeteer when it comes to the signs.

However, when Pisces is the puppet there is a requirement for patience and understanding so that in the end, the puppet master learns as much as his valued toy.

Planets in Pisces

It is a mixed bag so far as the planets' comfort with Pisces is concerned.

Pisces wins some points simply because it belongs to Jupiter, a planet which creates very little drama for the rest of the crew.

Theoretically only two planets encounter trouble with Pisces' dispositor, as both Mars and Mercury are classified by al-Biruni as *"mutually hurtful with"* Jupiter.

Pisces does not bring out the better qualities of Mercury for several reasons.

Firstly, the water element is not particularly compatible with a planet which prides itself on its ability to view information objectively and its claim to possess clarity in thought, speech and memory.

Water is too free flowing for Mercury to feel completely at home, and although air is also a wet quality, Mercury feels more in tune with the speed and energy of its hot active quality.

Water is cold as well as wet, and its slowness and cautionary behaviour is inclined to bog Mercury down with either too much detail, or too much emotional attachment to information.

Pisces is also the sign of both Mercury's detriment and its fall since the opposing sign Virgo is honoured in the dual role of Mercury's domicile sign and also its sign of exaltation.

For this reason, Mercury and Jupiter are at odds with one another as between them they rule the four mutable signs and consequently take the position of opposites in two right-angled axes.

Mars has no debility in Pisces but the exaltation signs of both Mars (Capricorn) and Jupiter (Cancer) oppose one another in Thema Mundi and for this reason, Mars would prefer not to be in a sign owned by Jupiter.

The animosity which these two planets share may come as a surprise to modern astrologers as these two planets in aspect are often considered to signify a good experience for the individual, with Jupiter ramping up the energy of Mars.

However, a traditional astrologer may not be so keen to see these two planets co-mingling their energies, and especially if the aspect which connects them is a square or an opposition.

They may both be masculine and superior planets (in the realm above the Sun) but this is where their similarities end.

Jupiter is a diurnal benefic, and Mars is a nocturnal malefic, and when they meet through a hard aspect Mars has the capacity to harm Jupiter, even more so if Mars is debilitated in the chart.

The Sun, Moon and Saturn bear Jupiter no ill will so any of these planets are happy to have Jupiter as their sign's dispositor.

Sun and Saturn are diurnal planets so they share the same sect as Jupiter, and a Sun in Pisces or Saturn in Pisces works quite well, especially if the person is born during the daytime.

The second line of Tolkien's poem is especially pertinent for any planet when Pisces becomes the sign by which it must express its own energy.

'Not all those who wander are lost' is a powerful reminder from Jupiter to the other planets that, like them, it is a wanderer in the night sky, but whilst the other planets have chosen different paths in which to express their own unique qualities, Jupiter has retained its love of wandering into foreign places and searching for frightening new possibilities to expand the mind and challenge the body.

Jupiter is giving them fair warning that they too will yearn for new pastures, will wander through watery meadows and high peaks in their own imagined landscapes, and will be called to sacrifice something they love (just like Aragorn) when they are placed in a sign belonging to Jupiter.

The Element of Earth
Capricorn: Taurus: Virgo

Cold in Action

A Cold response means that any action taken will occur after careful planning and the contemplation of all possible avenues as any action must be both economical and purposeful in its execution.

When the cold quality perceives a threat it takes time to reflect on a suitable response which is then carried out with deliberation and efficiency.

This active contrariety expects to reach an effective result and does not believe in wasting energy by repeating a process which may not have been successful the first time around.

Albert Einstein (1879-1955) once said:

"Insanity is doing the same thing over and over again and expecting different results"

and earth understands this, as their sanity depends on doing the same thing over and over and getting exactly the same results.

Earth craves predictability, and if earth were to re-write Einstein's definition for what they believed was insanity, it would read like this :

"Insanity is doing different things over and over and expecting the same results".

The cold quality is quite happy to keep repeating a pattern or a routine, but only if the outcome is successful, or if the amount of energy used is proportional to the reward achieved at the end of the process.

For this reason, the cold signs prefer consistency and routine in their lives so that movement through their daily tasks is seamless and requires the least amount of physical or mental exertion on their part.

They find comfort in a steady life with few dramatic turns and upsets and are usually easy-going people who enjoy a peaceful and agreeable environment both in the workplace and at home.

Regardless of others' requests for urgency or quick decisions, the cold quality individual is unlikely to bow to the demands of those who do not understand that Time is precious and should be savoured, not wasted by people who want deadlines and think that going fast, is going better.

The need for space to withdraw from life's frantic pace is crucial to this cold quality as periods set aside for quietness, reflection or inactivity are necessary for the cold response signs to gather their energy in privacy so that they can re-enter the world with a sense of inner calm.

Dry in Thought

Dry thinking creates the belief that thoughts and memories can be divided into compartments and can be recovered at a later time when the information is needed.

One of the best examples of committing information to memory via the passive dry quality was used by the Greeks and Romans to memorise and give speeches that could last for hours at a time.

The method of *loci* is essentially a visual filing system which allows the individual to separate and file information in the mind in such a way as it can be easily retrieved when needed.

The modern term for this technique is 'memory palaces' or 'the journey method' and is used to recall a virtually unlimited number of items in a fixed order.

The concept behind memory palaces is perfectly suited to dry thinking as the mind has the ability to separate information so that when it is required to, it can visualise an area which is extremely familiar to the individual, and to attach a memory to each familiar place.

It may be a person's residence or an often taken journey which is used as the background but there are items in the house or points along the way which have become deeply embedded within the unconscious and these are used to trigger the memory.

These points or locations (*loci*) are concrete items which serve as imaginary hooks for the mind to visually hang a memory or connect to whatever it is that is required to be remembered.

In the memory palace method, the person memorises a complete list of items in a room and imagines a connection between the concrete item and the memory.

In the journey method, the person remembers a list of physical items on the way such as the bus stop, a tree, the crossing, the street light, etc.

When the information needs to be recalled the individual visually moves around the house picking up the singular mental reminders as it goes, or mentally takes the journey and picks up thoughts at all the familiar vantage points.

Earth Element = The Combination of Cold and Dry

A combination of Cold and Dry qualities creates the earth element.

These three signs have a reverence for life and usually have a perception of a world order to which they can commit according to their modality and the planet which rules the sign.

Part of an orderly world (and a world order) is the tendency to believe that rules should be followed in a particular way and a planet in earth is prone to accumulate lists (often in their heads), and on paper or computer to record charts, data and all kinds of information which will support their own personal point of view on how systems should run and how things which are broken can be fixed.

Borne from a nature which is efficient in action and has deep energy reserves, planets in the earth signs have a need to secure their environment in such a way that they will not be caught unawares by any new development that has not already cropped up as a possibility within the individual's mind.

The idea of options (usually three in number for some odd reason) is part of the dry thinking which accompanies their cold response quality so it is important for earth to have visually explored their options so they cannot be taken by surprise.

The careful and meticulous piecing together of data is important for a planet in earth to build slowly toward a future that is both solid and secure, and the planet in question will aim for it with purpose and a tenacious ability to persevere until it succeeds.

Often other elements feel as though the same conversation with earth keeps happening, and if you are earth's sounding board, you may feel as though they are mentally stuck in a mind rut, but it is critical for whichever planet finds itself in the earth element, to work through a methodical thought process (even a repetitious one), especially if change is fast approaching on their horizon.

Unexpected change initiated by others creates distress in the earth element, and depending on which planet is in its sign will dictate how the individual deals with the stress of sudden upheaval or broken routines.

Aristotle considered the earth element to be the heaviest of the four elements, the least likely to change its state and the most predictable in its reaction to stress or catastrophe.

Words like solid, unaffected, grounded or organic remind us of this element, even the word 'earthy' brings to mind the richness of soil and the safeness we feel when we 'plant our feet' firmly on the ground.

Earth tells us it is not going anywhere, and although scientists warn of approaching disaster, humankind clings to the idea that we can rely on our planet to continue to pass through its slowly rotating seasons as it feeds us, shelters us, and (hopefully) continues to provide a future, for generations to come.

We need air, fire and water in order to survive, but the paralysing fear that fills us when we think of the possibility of Earth's destruction gives some indication as to our dependency on its continued existence as we struggle to survive within its physical realm.

Modality and Dispositors

Differences between Capricorn, Taurus, and Virgo

CAPRICORN : Cardinal Earth : Ruled by SATURN

The sign of Capricorn is still an initiator like its other cardinal cousins, but its mobility is not as noticeable as fire and air, as they both work from a hot response.

Rather, Capricorn is more measured in its movement, deliberate and economical especially as it prides itself on being orderly and well prepared for any eventuality.

Any planet placed in Capricorn is likely to conserve energy and to act with purpose and deliberate intent.

Saturn's rulership of this sign makes hard work of even the simple tasks, as perfection is expected in all enterprises, and this can mean that Capricorn is hesitant in starting new projects especially if there are time constraints, or if there is any doubt that endeavours will not result in success.

A planet situated in Capricorn gets something that comes for free with the sign, but unfortunately it is not a gift the planet is keen to accept from Saturn.

The fear of failure is inbuilt in Capricorn, and is so real that it is almost physically debilitating for the individual with it in their chart.

For any planet in this situation it is worth remembering that there is a fine line between realism and pessimism, and sometimes Capricorn can be inclined to confuse the two concepts.

"Ever tried. Ever failed. No matter. Try Again. Fail again. Fail better."[116]

Realism is favouring practicality and accepting life's physical restrictions.

Realism is seeing things clearly and honestly, the way they really are, and accepting them with grace and wisdom.

Pessimism is choosing to see things in a negative light, and to automatically believe that there are restrictions to something, before actually making an honest assessment of its feasibility.

In short, pessimism encourages cold and dry qualities because in truth, it is choosing the path of least resistance.

It is imperative for any planet that finds itself in Capricorn to constantly fight against this mind set, given the combination of its qualities, and the fact that its dispositor is Saturn (in itself a cold dry planet).

"You're on Earth. There's no cure for that."[117]

Dry thinking for Capricorn can bring a certain rigidity of thought, as whilst it is unlikely to produce rash decisions or hasty opinions, this Saturn sign often records the negatives and can produce a moody or depressed turn of mind.

A planet in Capricorn sets high standards for itself and is inclined to use its linear thinking model to go over every detail in order to get perfect results.

Not all planets are comfortable with this *modus operandi,* as their own quintessential qualities may be at odds with a sign that expects perfectionism in every act.

This dilemma can prove both physically and intellectually wearing on the chart's owner especially if other parts of their chart are heavily balanced towards the fire or air elements.

The earth element is wonderful for grounding, and some people love being a list maker or daily planner, but too many planets in Capricorn can be exhausting, when even small acts require so much energy to reach impossibly high expectations.

Planets in Capricorn

Thema Mundi makes the point that Saturn is a natural enemy to the Sun and Moon, and for this reason, neither luminary is particularly comfortable in the sign of Capricorn.

The Moon even less so, considering that it is in detriment in this sign.

The Moon's sensitivity and fear of rejection is especially heightened in Capricorn, and it can be difficult for the Moon to express or experience many of its lunar significations, under such a heavy yoke as Saturn.

Significations such as the body's health and its ability to recover from illness, the mothering statement, emotional satisfaction or even a general sense of well-being can be compromised by Saturn's presence.

Mercury in Capricorn is a careful thinker and planner but generally speaking is not overly worried by this sign.

Likewise, both Venus or Mars in Capricorn are comfortable with Saturn as both share a bond with the greater malefic, Venus lends Saturn her sign of Libra for his exaltation, and Mars borrows Capricorn from Saturn for its exaltation, and provided that Saturn is in good condition, the two planets are not overly bothered by their situation in this earth sign.

Jupiter, on the other hand, finds itself in fall in Capricorn and Saturn dries up Jupiter's good humour by being a difficult dispositor to a planet that dislikes restriction and boundaries.

In many cases, if a dispositor is in rulership, it provides excellent protection for its borrower planet. However, in the case of Saturn in Capricorn, the potential for conjunction is high, and Jupiter and the luminaries find Saturn's close proximity unnerving. Saturn can directly impact on them through the conjunction, as well as serving as their dispositor, and this situation can exacerbate the strain on these three benefic energies rather than alleviate their distress.

TAURUS : Fixed Earth : Ruled by VENUS

Taurus the Bull possesses a gentle persistence in keeping with its fixed state in the category of earth element signs.

Taurus' cold response is spent savouring the five senses, being captivated by its physical surroundings, and absorbing the abundance of natural energy which largely goes unnoticed by the other signs.

When Taurus absorbs energy borrowed from the earth, it dedicates itself to mimicking the world around it by producing similar sounds or movement or by creating practical adaptations of what it observes in the natural world.

"Drink your tea slowly and reverently, as if it is the axis on which the world earth revolves – slowly, evenly, without rushing toward the future. Live the actual moment. Only this moment is life."[118]

Venus is the glorious Morning Star (*Phosphurus*) and Evening Star (*Hesperus*) which rules this earth sign, and the bond Venus and Taurus share between a feminine planet and a feminine sign creates a natural ease and a shared passion for aesthetic beauty, which is not always easy for Venus to share with its masculine sign of Libra.

This attachment can mean any planet placed in Taurus is likely to want this same easy connection with those living in its immediate environment, and this can mean the individual seeks to gain approval from others, and may be inclined to quietly sacrifice its own will for those people for whom it holds a deep affection.

A planet in Taurus expects loyalty, given that it is faithful in its affections and will be inclined to be steadfast and rock solid in its friendships even if, as an earth sign, it has been slow to build these emotional bonds in the first place.

Taurus carries the quality of dryness which allows any planet in this sign to capitalise on methodical thought patterns when carefully gathering ideas and information, and then as an earth sign, to turn these ideas into creating something of beauty or practical worth.

Somewhat of a perfectionist in all manner of ways, Taurus becomes fixated on getting it right, even if it means displaying less Venetian traits and isolating itself, or denying itself pleasures in order to not be affected by outside distractions, so that it can concentrate on the immediate project at hand.

Like all dry thinkers, Taurus indulges in the belief that it deals exclusively in reality, that it sees things the way they are, but being ruled by such a romantically-orientated planet, it can be more idealistic than the other dry signs, and once stuck on its own version of reality Taurus is hard to be persuaded that its facts are mistaken or are somewhat tailored to meet their own perceptions.

Planets in Taurus

The Moon is exalted in Taurus and this luminary is a perfect match for Taurus, given that it signifies everything of a physical nature, and this earth sign has such a natural affinity with the mundane world.

Small comforts like a cup of tea provide a Taurean Moon with the feeling that *'Only this moment is life'*, and provided that Venus is in good state in the chart the individual finds much comfort in the simple moments, always present, but often unappreciated in everyday life.

The Sun, Jupiter and Saturn, whilst being diurnal planets, have no argument with nocturnal Venus and are quite content to find themselves in her amenable sign.

However, Mars shares a strained relationship with Venus, as they are mutually hurtful to each other because both planets own signs which place the other in detriment.

Mars finds Taurus far too slow and stolid for its need to be alert and quick on its feet.

Mercury has a similar issue with Taurus, as it does not always appreciate having to slow its pace so that Taurus can check each fact carefully, and then go over the same ground again, to check the validity of its information one more time.

One advantage for Mercury in Taurus is the ease in which it can master the method of *loci,* the retentive learning pattern to retain memories or information which was mentioned earlier.

The journey method of visualising physical objects and attaching information or memory joggers to them, so that the mind can easily recover data is perfect for this Mercury, if it is prepared to take the time and effort to become familiar with the principles behind the *loci* memory patterns.

VIRGO : Mutable Earth : Ruled by MERCURY

The mutable earth sign of Virgo uses its cold quality for the purpose of arranging life in a neat methodical manner, simply because it struggles with sudden change or an unexpected break in routine.

Similar to the other two earth signs, Virgo draws its energy from the temporal world, seeking balance and harmony in nature in order to settle the mind and strengthen its sense of purpose and deep commitment to caring for the physical realm.

"A mountain is composed of tiny grains of earth. The ocean is made up of tiny drops of water. Even so, life is but an endless series of little details, actions, speeches, and thoughts. And the consequences whether good or bad of even the least of them are far-reaching."[119]

A planet in Virgo is inclined to over-think everything, and Mercury often exhausts the mind by picking at the *'tiny grains of earth'*, and trying to analyse every last one in one version of its dry thinking model.

The planet situated in a mutable earth sign consumes energy purely in an effort to meet its own high standards, and the same planet in the feminine sign of Virgo needs to be patient as slower access to large reserves of energy is limited and earth's energy requires constant replenishment.

Any planet in Mercury's slower sign displays irritation when it feels forced to take time away from what it perceives to be a mountain of tasks and jobs, abandoned for such a small reason as exhaustion or mental and physical burn-out.

This can create a vicious cycle whereby the planet in Virgo frets when it should be resting and berates itself for apparent physical weakness, until guilt cuts the recovery time short.

The individual is inclined to over-compensate for any inactivity by forcing themselves to work even harder to 'catch-up', or vows to meet the next round of unrealistic expectations they have set for themselves with renewed dedication to the task. Exhaustion sets in again, and the wheel continues to turn.

Mercury rules both mutable signs of Gemini and Virgo, signs which share their ruler but are diametrically opposed in Aristotle's model according to their gender and qualities.

Coming from the same cosmic lord, the analogy they present is akin to distant cousins who have very little in common except for their celestial kinship.

Gemini is the cosmopolitan cousin, sleek, assured and confident with the qualities of a hot and wet air sign with a sanguine temperament.

Shy Virgo on the other hand has a melancholic temperament, and represents Gemini's country cousin, a feminine sign linked to the land and less showy than its sophisticated relative.

Virgo's mode of action is cold and its thinking pattern favours the dry method, so although Mercury shares rulership, the two signs are qualitatively foreign to one another.

Gemini's thinking patterns flow and connect ideas, perceptions and visual images which Gemini pursues with gusto.

Virgo's precision breaks down information into separate concepts, analyses it carefully and without haste, and then recreates the model in a more practical fashion so that it can be put into practice on a material basis, and if wrong, patiently starts the whole process again from the beginning.

Totally different in qualities, and yet together they serve Mercury beautifully as they cover this planet's varied requirements to apply reason and solve problems, to collect and collate information and to broadcast knowledge as efficiently and hopefully as truthfully as possible, for a planet which has the Trickster as its emblem.

Virgo may have the soundness and stability which defines its earth element, but its lord Mercury is fickle and changeable being able to flip gender, redefine its qualities, swap sect preference and generally alter its nature according to the influence of any planets nearby or in aspect to it.

Luckily both Mercury's signs are mutable as Mercury literally 'goes with the flow' and any planet which finds itself in Mercury's sign will have to be open to its dispositor's whims, and learn to adapt even when one of these signs belong to the earth element.

There is a fine line between prudence and pragmatism, and any planet in Virgo needs to temper its melancholic temperament with a clear understanding of the subtle difference between the two terms.

If a person is being prudent they are using caution and sensible judgement to discipline their own actions.

Prudence was classically considered to be the mother of all virtues, because its strength lay in its ability to judge between virtuous and vicious acts, and to actively choose virtuous conduct at the right place and time.

The word is derived from the Latin *prudential* (foresight) and is often associated with insight and knowledge and later came to be identified as 'practical wisdom'.

If a person is being pragmatic (Greek *pragma,* 'deed') they are also using sound judgement and being practical, but in a completely different way, and for different reasons from someone who is acting prudently.

This individual is being pragmatic by doing what works best for any given situation, and would consider themselves to be realistic, as they make their decisions based on a thought process which runs the gamut from prediction, to problem-solving, and taking action.

A pragmatic person is running through the possible outcomes in their head, solving the inherent problems as they see them, and then taking appropriate practical action.

Basically the difference is this: Imagine you are walking down the street and you see someone being robbed by someone else who is big and frightening.

You are being prudent if you have the wisdom (foresight) to pick up a heavy object as a weapon and run to their rescue.

You are being pragmatic (the sensible deed) if you turn a corner and call the police instead of intervening in the melee.

Which act is the more practical?

And is one scenario more ethically correct than the other?

The answers to these questions are for Virgo (and planets in Virgo) to ponder at their leisure.

Planets in Virgo

Mercury's sign can mean trouble for the two benefics, Venus and Jupiter, as Virgo is Venus' sign of fall and Jupiter is in detriment in Virgo.

When Mercury disposits Venus, it is inclined to sharpen the tongue and cause caustic comments or to replace pleasure with cynicism, and can be overly critical of women in general.

Venus in fall can create problems in relationships where they may not have existed, if Venus were positioned in any other sign.

A Virgoan Venus needs to remember to relax and enjoy what is, rather than what may be in the future, as examining in painful detail every *'tiny grain of sand and every tiny drop of water'* runs the risk of suffocating their relationships in negativity, as nothing so fragile as love stands up well to this amount of in-depth scrutiny.

Jupiter struggles when placed in either of Mercury's two signs.

Gemini rushes Jupiter into false statements and poorly made decisions which are more optimistic than they are wise.

Virgo, on the other hand, is cold and slow and far too weighty for Jupiter to enjoy this sign, and Jupiter tends to turn towards being pompous or dogmatic in its attitudes and preaches rather than discusses differences in opinion.

The remaining planets, Sun, Moon, Mars and Saturn take their chances with Virgo as they have no direct conflict with Mercury, and are more inclined to modify their behaviour according to how their extremely versatile (and somewhat unstable) dispositor is situated in the chart.

CHAPTER SEVEN

The Twelve Houses

"If you want a golden rule that will fit everybody, this is it: Have nothing in your houses that you do not know to be useful, or believe to be beautiful."

William Morris (English textile designer, writer, socialist and Marxist, 1834-1896)

So said William Morris during his lecture on *"The Beauty of Life"*, and whilst I have deliberately taken the quote out of context, there is a ring of truth to it when applied to the twelve houses in the astrological model.

The twelve houses provide an earthbound pin-up board for humankind to post all the subjects which interest, obsess and frustrate them during a lifetime.

Subjects such as body image, extended family, love, work, pets, and health problems fit into the golden rule where houses are concerned and although there are times when houses contain things which are neither useful nor beautiful, they still remain an insightful tool by which our tiny universe can bridge the gap to the divine Universe.

Even questions concerning 'the point of my existence' crop up during a consultation and it is always tricky to find answers to adequately satisfy a client particularly when the goal posts keep shifting on this particular subject as the answer differs from client to client.

As for the planets, they keep shuffling like a pack of cards through the zodiac, mingling and rearranging and sliding past one another until the time comes for the soul's materialization on Earth.

Within the mundane framework of the houses the 'accident' of birth deposits a planet in a particular house according to the sign, and the degree of the sign which a planet is passing through at the time of the native's birth.

Once the planet settles into its designated house it has a look around the neighbourhood to see where its rulership signs are located in the chart.

Well and good if the planet catches sight of one or preferably two of its rulership signs (the planet's placement sign needs to aspect its rulership sign), but that does not always happen, and this is a type of blindness for the planet, technically known as 'aversion'.

If a planet in a house is *'useful or beautiful'*, then it probably has a good level of essential and accidental dignity, and is likely to fulfil most of its brief to the best of its ability.

As time moves forward through a period of twenty four hours, the chart will continue to change as the Sun's position in the sky (and depending on its own sign according to the time of year) will determine which of the signs are rising at the time of birth.

The Light From The Ascendant: Good and Bad Houses

The Ptolemaic aspects are listed by Claudius Ptolemy (1st C) in his *Tetrabiblos,* and are the major aspects which divide the circle according to geometric angles and the mathematical degrees which exist between each aspect.

Ptolemy writes that oppositions occur when signs face one another across the diameter and that an opposition contains two right angles and is six signs apart.

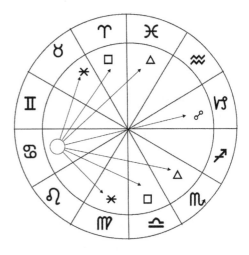

Fig. 66 Thema Mundi with Ptolemaic Aspects Radiating from the Ascendant

He says the trine contains one and a third right angles (120 degrees) and is four signs apart, whilst the quadrate (a square) is three signs apart and contains a right angle of exactly ninety degrees.

Lastly, the sextile is the smallest angle at sixty degrees which is two-thirds of a right angle and has a separation of two signs.

The duplication of Thema Mundi with the sign of Cancer placed at the ascendant or first house cusp is used here *(Fig. 66)* to demonstrate the Ptolemaic aspects and their relationship to the theory of the meanings of the twelve houses.

The aspects described by Ptolemy radiate from Cancer to show aspects which form to the right and left of Cancer. Cancer will share the same gender as Taurus and Virgo and so will form a sextile aspect to both of these feminine signs.

By cardinal modality Cancer will square both Aries and Libra; by the link between the water element Cancer will trine both Pisces and Scorpio; and by the opposition across the first and seventh houses, Cancer will oppose the sign of Capricorn.

The direction of an aspect was important to the traditional astrologer as a dexter (right-sided) aspect meant the sign which had already risen, and a sinister (left-sided) aspect meant the sign which would rise at a later time.

In this example, Taurus would be the dexter sextile and Virgo is the sinister sextile to Cancer.

In square aspect, Aries is the dexter quartile to Cancer (ten signs away) and Libra is the sinister quartile (four signs away) from Cancer at the ascendant.

Pisces is the dexter trine and Scorpio is the sinister trine to Cancer.

The opposition at Capricorn is judged as neither dexter nor sinister as it is exactly 180 degrees from Cancer and therefore, is technically both behind and in front of Cancer.

The word 'sinister' has many meanings, and the relationship between a word meaning both "left hand" (Latin *sinestra*) and "ill-omen" originates from ancient times when the flight of certain birds was used for fortune-telling purposes.

Ravens, crows or eagles were the messengers of the gods and the Greek seer would face north and wait to see if birds would fly past on their right, that is, at the east in the direction of the sunrise.

If this happened the seer would declare it to be a good omen from the gods.

However, if the birds flew to the seer's left side, at the western horizon of sunset, it was considered to be an indication of the gods' displeasure and an omen of approaching disaster.

The Romans used the same bird-watching techniques (Latin, *avspecium*) but the Roman priest would reverse the directions, instead choosing to face south rather than north.

Sunrise is now on the left-hand side at the east, and birds flying from the left meant a good omen for the Romans, whilst birds flying on their right-hand side was a bad omen because on the right-hand side lay the western horizon.

Astrology (and etymology) has taken its terminology and most of its practices from the Greeks and so sinister or 'left hand' relates to the western point, and dexter or 'right hand' relates to the eastern point.

To put these directions into perspective in terms of an astrology chart, imagine that you are the Greek seer whose altar lies at the centre of the chart.

If you turn your body to face north you are now looking directly at the Imum Coeli (I.C.) at the base of the chart.

If you then extend your right arm and point to the east (the ascendant), this is a favourable position because this is where the Sun rises each morning.

Now extend your left arm and point to the chart's descendant.

This direction is less favourable because this is the point where the sun 'dies' at the end of each day and is why for the Greeks, the left became 'sinister' and an ill-omen from the gods.

The same principle applies when you remain in the centre of the chart and this time turn your body to face towards the ascendant in the east.

Now when you extend your right hand you are pointing at planets which have appeared to already risen over the ascendant.

Extending your left hand will direct you to planets which are yet to rise over the ascendant.

The terms for direction may seem archaic, but it is important because it affects the interpretation of the houses *from the perspective of the ascendant*.

The elevated houses above the ascendant are dexter and therefore considered the best of the houses, whilst the sinister aspects from the ascendant cast down to the houses placed below the horizon.

Cancer may form sextiles to both Taurus and Virgo, but if the signs were translated to houses in a chart, Taurus (a dexter sextile) would be the cusp of the elevated eleventh house whilst Virgo (a sinister sextile) would find itself on the cusp of the third house below the horizon.

The same rule on direction applies to the quartile or square aspect between Cancer and Aries which is ten signs away at the zenith or the apex of the chart.

Aries is a dexter square to Cancer and is the sign featured at the highest point, signifying the most important house in the chart according to Firmicus Maternus.

Libra is the sinister square to Cancer, and whilst the fourth house is an angular house, the house at the nadir or base of the chart, often indicates hidden treasures and is no match for the elevated tenth house.

In terms of judging whether an aspect to a planet is dexter or sinister, the planet is approached in the same manner as the ascendant.

In other words, from the centre of the chart the astrologer looks at the planet and views the aspects to the right of the planet (dexter aspects) as giving advantage to the more elevated planet, and the aspects to the left (sinister aspects) as bestowing greater power to the original planet being examined.

The diagram below *(Fig. 67)* contains three planets in the chart. Planet A has been used as the focal planet but the rules of direction and placement, i.e. dexter and sinister position, can just as easily be applied to Planet B and Planet C. From Planet A's vantage point, Planet B is to its right and therefore lies in a dexter position to Planet A and has an advantage over the central planet in the diagram. Planet C on the other hand, lies to the left of Planet A and is therefore judged to have less influence on Planet A than Planet B.

So far as rising is concerned, Planet B rises before the two other planets, and Planet A rises before Planet C, which is the last of the three planets to rise on the day in question.

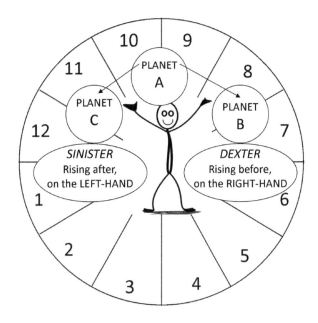

Fig. 67 Dexter and Sinister Positions within the Chart

Dexter and Sinister Squares: The Concept of 'Over-powering'

Dorotheus of Sidon (1st Century C.E.) subscribed to the belief that dexter was a stronger position to take in an aspect and uses the term 'over-powering' to describe a planet in square aspect which is ten signs away (a waning square) and therefore on the right-hand of a planet being examined by the astrologer.

For example, in a square aspect between Saturn and Venus, one planet will have risen (or will rise in the future) over the ascendant before the other.

If Venus is the focal planet and Saturn is to Venus' right-hand side then Saturn has the higher position and therefore over-powers Venus .

Dorotheus states: *"If Saturn is in* (dexter) *quartile of Venus, it indicates his (the native's) fall from women, that he will be rejected and devoid of good, and every evil will come to him."*[120]

In the example *(Fig. 68)*, Venus is exalted in Pisces and whilst the native may be having a fabulous time with wine, women and song, there is a penalty to pay, and Saturn will be the one to enforce the punishment.

It may be the native's health which suffers (Saturn in the first and Venus ruling the sixth house of poor health).

The father may disinherit the native or cut their allowance or salary (Venus in the fourth and Saturn ruling the second house of wealth).

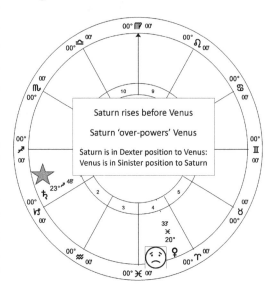

Or the native's friends may grow tired of him/her when they have trashed the house, drunk all the alcohol and exhausted his/her funds thereby leaving them financially ruined or extremely unpopular with their neighbours.

(Venus in the fourth house is ruling the eleventh and sixth houses whilst Saturn in the first house is ruling the second and third houses).

Fig. 68 Saturn in Dexter Square to Venus – Saturn 'over-powers' Venus

However, if the reverse is true, and the focal planet again is Venus, then Saturn in the second example is placed in a sinister position to Venus and Venus then gains the greater power over Saturn in the quartile aspect *(Fig. 69)*.

Dorotheus states:

> *"But if Venus is over-powering Saturn, then the native will be weary and difficult, but he will be blessed with a good wife who will be better than he in lineage, one who is admirable in herself together with her agreeing with his parents."*

The native, presumably male, has some health issues but he has made a good marriage which has hopefully improved his social standing – *"better than he in lineage"*.

(Saturn in the twelfth, ruling the first house, the body, and the second house of wealth, whilst Venus is ruling the tenth house, social status, and the fifth house of children or entertainments).

His wife (Venus in fall in Virgo) may however nag him or be overly critical of his personal habits, or his tendency to waste money on frivolities (Venus rules 5th house), or his inability to earn sufficient money to support her (Debilitated Venus square Saturn ruling the first and second houses, and both planets are cadent).

She may also have trouble conceiving or be unable to provide children in the marriage (a cadent Venus in fall ruling the fifth house square Saturn in the house of sorrows, 12th house).

Or his wife may remind him too much of his controlling mother who thinks her new daughter-in-law is just perfect for her son – *"one who is admirable in herself together with her agreeing with his parents"* (Venus in fall ruling tenth house, Saturn in the twelfth house of hidden enemies).

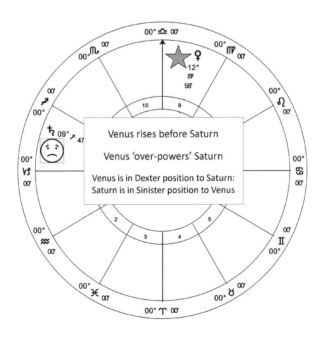

Fig. 69 Saturn in Sinister Square to Venus – Venus 'over-powers' Saturn

Firmicus Maternus and The Twelve Houses

> *"The first house is the place in which the ascendant is located. In this house is to be found the life and vital spirit of men; from this house the basic character of the entire nativity is determined. It is also the first cardinal point (angle) and the cornerstone and basis of the whole nativity."*[121]

Firmicus Maternus, *Matheseos*

The Thema Mundi chart *(Fig. 70)* shows Ptolemaic aspects between Cancer and seven other signs. These aspects are related directly to the houses and the total number of houses which receive light from the ascendant are eight in total (the ascendant is included in the number).

Good aspects (sextile and trine) demonstrated houses which benefitted the native, and hard aspects (square and opposition) represented houses that were challenging but ultimately rewarding, especially since they were the angular (or cardinal) houses in the chart.

The diagram shows the signs either side of Cancer, Gemini and Leo, are not in aspect to Cancer. Nor are the signs which oppose Gemini and Leo (Sagittarius and Aquarius) making an aspect to Cancer. These are the four signs which are in 'aversion' to the sign of Cancer.

Aversion means blindness as Cancer cannot see Gemini, Leo, Sagittarius or Aquarius. There are exceptions to these rules, such as antiscia, contra-antiscia

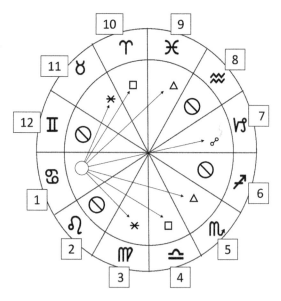

Fig. 70 Aspects and the Houses: Eight Houses Receiving Light

and like-engirdling, which allow signs to see one another through other similarities besides the traditional aspects.

Nor is Cancer the only sign to experience aversion. Each of the twelve zodiac signs will experience this same blindness to the sign immediately to the right or the left and the two signs which oppose their immediate neighbours.

The original Ptolemaic aspects stand true as aspects which determine the strength and nature of the twelve houses and the four signs which do not aspect the rising sign correspond to the four houses in a chart which do not receive light from the ascendant.

These four houses were classified by Firmicus as either passive and/or debilitated houses. The second and the eighth houses were passive, as although there was no light from the ascendant, they were succedent houses and therefore had one redeeming feature, that is, by being houses which followed the angular first house and seventh house respectively.

Worst of all houses were the passive and debilitated houses, the sixth and twelfth house, which received no light (aspect) from the ascendant and were also cadent houses – after 'cadaver' as they fell (like dead bodies) into the angular houses and had no power of their own.

The houses' names and their order of strength originates from Firmicus Maternus' *Matheseos,* Book Two, Chapters 15 to 19 where he discusses the houses and their meanings *(Fig. 71).*

The names of the houses, in Greek, Latin and English, are based on the principle that the ascendant is both the source of light which animates through aspect, and also the fount from which all life springs in the chart.

Firmicus Maternus begins his explanation on the houses by stating there are four cardinal points in the nativity.

The Ascendant, Descendant, the *Medium Caelum* (Zenith), and the *Imum Caelum* (Nadir), which the Greeks usually call by the following names: *Anatole* (East, Sunrise), *Dysis* (West, Sunset), *Mesuranima* (Meridian, Zenith), *Ypogeon* (below the Earth).[122]

When Firmicus uses the term 'cardinal' it should not be confused with the cardinal signs of Aries, Cancer, Libra and Capricorn, but rather Firmicus is using the word to describe the four angular houses as the fundamental, pivotal or premium houses of the chart.

Firmicus then says there are four other houses in the nativity which follow the cardinal points, and are favourable in power, as each secondary house will gain light from the ascendant by either a sextile or a trine aspect.

Firmicus' secondary house category contains two succedent houses (fifth and eleventh house) and two cadent houses (third and ninth house).

These four houses in Greek and English are *Thea* (Goddess), *Theos* (God), *Agathe Tyche* (Good Luck) and *Agathos Daemon* (Good Spirit).

The remaining four houses Firmicus describes as being *"all (four) feeble and debilitated because of the fact that they are not aspected to the ascendant."*[123]

The second and the eighth houses are known as the Gates of Hell.

The Greek word for the second house is *Anafora* (rising up from the Underworld) and the eighth house is called *Epicatafora* (casting down into the Underworld).

The sixth house is Bad Luck *(Cace Tyche)* and the twelfth house is Bad Spirit *(Cacodaemon)*.

Firmicus lists the relative strengths of the houses and has been included in the diagram of the Houses *(Fig. 71)*. The list begins with the strongest (1st) and finishing with the weakest house (12th) in the following order: first, seventh, tenth, fourth, eleventh, fifth, ninth, third, second, eighth, sixth, and finally, the twelfth house.

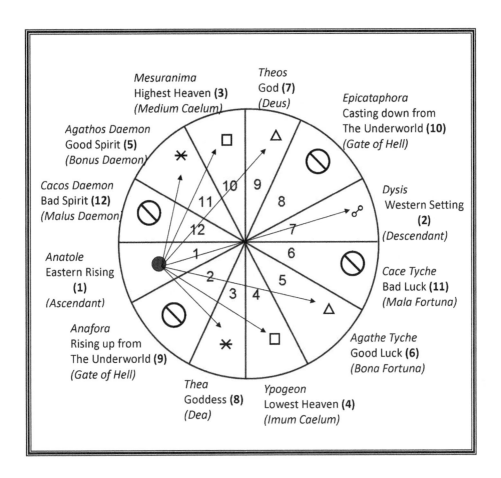

Fig. 71 Identities and Strengths of the Houses according to Firmicus Maternus listing the houses with their Greek names and English translations, Latin names (bracketed) and the order of their relative strength (the number in parentheses).

Note that Firmicus lists the angular houses (1st, 7th, 10th, 4th) followed by the harmonious houses, then the feeble houses and lastly, the debilitated houses.

In each case where an axis is featured, the dexter aspects or elevated houses are listed in priority before the sinister aspect or lower houses in the chart, i.e. 10th before 4th; 11th before 5th ; 9th before 3rd house.

However, when the feeble and debilitated houses are listed, the sinister aspect precedes the dexter aspect in the list, and the second house precedes the eighth, and the sixth precedes the twelfth house in order of the strength of the houses.

The translation of Firmicus's *Matheseos* by Jean Rhys Bram also includes a diagram with one word meanings for the twelve houses, and this diagram has been reproduced below (*Fig. 72*).

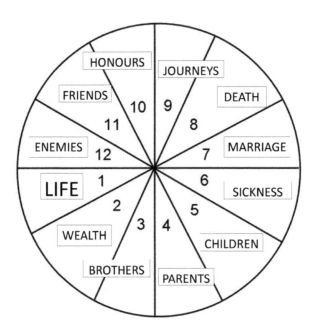

Fig. 72 One-word meanings for the Houses from Firmicus Maternus (Matheseos, Book 2)

Discordant Aspects To The Ascendant: The Cardinal Points

House Name: *Descendant*
Position: *Seventh House*
Area of Influence: *Marriage*
Preference: *No. 2 in the order of 12 houses*

Firmicus identifies the seventh house as second in strength behind the ascendant, and allocates this house to marriage.

He also warns that this house is detrimental to the ascendant, given that the aspect of opposition connects the seventh house to the ascendant.

By its very nature, the word 'opposition' suggests resistance, difficulty and open combat.

In politics, it is the opposition party's right to try to block the government in power, and to question any legislation which they feel needs alteration or restraint, or that disagrees with their own policies.

Within the confines of an astrology chart, the people who are represented by the seventh house act in much the same way towards the native (owner of the chart) as they do in the Houses of Parliament.

Both ascendant and descendant have a special relationship with the Sun, and between them, they rule the horizon over which the Sun appears to rise at the ascendant, and approximately twelve hours later, appears to set across the descendant each day.

This is the most important diameter of all six axes because it is the one which sets the entire chart, and, although the descendant is purely a reflection of the opposite sign to the ascendant, it still counts as the house which is second behind the ascendant in strength.

Greek philosopher Heraclitus (504 BCE) said:

"Opposition unites. From what draws apart results the most beautiful harmony. All things take place by strife."

It seems appropriate then that the house which opposes the ascendant should signify both those we love, and those who vex us.

In a positive light, the seventh house rules marriages, business and love partnerships, and in general, all nature of allies who choose to support the native.

It is the house of contracts, both those which are legally binding, such as marriage or business partnerships, as well as contacts for payment of services.

For this reason, the seventh house is the house of litigation and civil law disputes.

Seventh house describes professional to client relationships, and as such covers specialist advice for which the professional receives remuneration.

Professionals from fields such as medicine, dentistry, legal services, real estate agencies or engineering consultants are services which the individual may themselves not be trained in, and therefore pays a specialist in the field for their advice, and if required, to act on their behalf by using their expertise to solve a problem.

> *"Opposition is true friendship"*
>
> William Blake (1757-1827)

I suspect contracts of a less formal kind are also included in the seventh house, and these are informal agreements or bonds of commitment, which are often unspoken but are extremely important to the native's continued support throughout their day-to-day life.

For instance, catching up with a running buddy for some exercise would be a fifth house friend.

Joining my associates for a drink after work to relax would be eleventh house friends.

But phoning a friend in the early hours of the morning and expecting them to pick up the phone, or to be bold enough to tell you an unpalatable truth, this is the kind of 'friendship contract' that I believe is covered by the seventh house.

We may not want to hear their advice about our partner, work situation, children, or even our own behaviour, but like the political party which opposes the government, they serve as a sounding board by telling us truths we are unwilling to tell ourselves.

And we reciprocate by responding in kind and fulfilling the same role for them.

The axis of any two houses which oppose one another in the chart will share certain qualities, but will differ in others, and the axis of the ascendant and descendant is no exception to this rule.

For instance, if the ascendant is in a feminine sign, then so will its opposite house be in a feminine sign.

That means that one house will be in water while the opposite is in the element of earth.

These two elements share the same active quality which is cold, and they share the same quadruplicity, whether it is from the cardinal, fixed or mutable modality.

However, the first and seventh house will come into a state of opposition when it comes to their passive quality.

One house, perhaps the ascendant, will want to approach life through the wet quality, and this will have a water sign on the cusp as water is a combination of cold and wet, whilst the opposite house (seventh house) will use its passive quality of dryness to resist or defy the ascendant through the earth element (cold and dry).

If the same axis has masculine signs in opposition then one side will be fire (hot and dry) and the house at the other end of the horizon line will have an air sign (hot and wet) on its cusp.

Each time the gender and modality will agree, but the 'not so' passive quality will disagree.

But even more important than the clash between wet and dry, is the fact that the opposition between any house axis will highlight the conflict which exists between the two ruling planets of the signs.

The Table of Friendships and Enmity (Chapter Four, *Fig. 37*) is the key to why one sign will object so strongly to its opponent, not because of the qualities' incompatibility, but because these planets are powerful puppeteers who will fight across the chart for domination over one another.

The signs are merely their puppets, so if one looks and acts slightly differently from the other, it is not a big deal, but if the Moon's sign (Cancer) opposes Saturn's sign (Capricorn) then in every chart we encounter, we have a struggle of cosmic proportions.

House Name: *Medium Caelum, Highest Heaven*
Position: *Tenth House*
Area of Influence: *Honours*
Preference: *No. 3 in the order of 12 houses*

Ptolemy states that the opposition and quartile (square) are discordant, because they are configurations made between signs which are not of the same kind, but of different natures and sexes.[124]

In terms of the opposition, Ptolemy's quote refers to the opposing nature of the ruling planets which are hostile towards one another in the Thema Mundi chart.

The square is discordant for other reasons as there may not be any difficulty between the two lords of signs which are placed at a ninety degree angle.

The modality squares are a case in point.

Two of the square aspects are ruled by the same planet as the sign of Gemini squares Virgo and both signs are ruled by Mercury, or Sagittarius squaring Pisces brings forth Jupiter which is the lord of both mutable signs.

The square aspect is discussed in Chapter Five on the Qualities, and it has been noted in the chapter that the major difficulty for a square concerns the four qualities (hot, cold, wet and dry), which are often at odds with one another and this creates the tension and discord within the square aspect.

For instance, if the ascendant and descendant axis features the feminine elements of earth and water then the fourth and tenth signs will be a combination of the masculine elements of fire and air.

The same quandary will occur if the first and seventh house horizon has masculine elements of fire and air, then the fourth and tenth houses will share the same modality, but the feminine elements of water and earth will disagree with their masculine counterparts through the aspect of a square.

One point must be made clear.

This model follows the rules of the whole sign chart system.

That is, charts which begin at zero degrees of a different sign on each cusp so that all twelve signs (and their lords) are represented in the chart.

This will be regardless of the sign in which the Midheaven (the highest point in the chart) is situated.

In a quadrant style chart the Midheaven (MC) begins the tenth house but this is not the case in a whole sign chart.

Chapter Eight follows this chapter on the houses and discusses the differences between the two styles of charts in detail.

The whole sign system has been adopted here for the purpose of discussing the houses' archetypal meanings, as the whole sign method is the style in which Thema Mundi was described by Firmicus Maternus in *Matheseos*.

In the whole sign system, all female signs will have their tenth sign culminate with male signs, and vice versa.

In real terms, this means that the initial hesitancy and desire for self protection common to all female (water or earth) signs on the ascendant, is challenged by the square aspect which leads to the tenth house.

Ascendants with feminine signs will learn to compete or to press forwards to make the most of any advantages in order to claim physical space or acknowledgement in the outside world, which for them, is mainly dominated by men.

Good planning and routine will help the earth ascendant to succeed in a career that requires intellect and communication (air MC), but the water ascendant can be extremely sensitive when the fire element stands at the summit of their chart.

The ruler of the water sign ascendants, be it the Moon, Mars or Jupiter, will find strategies to protect the ascendant as there are certain emotions which bind two elements which have none of the qualities in common.

The water ascendant may recognise the fiery emotions contained within the chart's MC and rather than withdraw from them, may instead embrace emotions such as passion, excitement, zeal, ardour and enthusiasm.

For the male signs on the ascendant (fire or air), the drive to push forward into the world is challenged by the need to look inwards or to act with compassion in affairs which concern the tenth house.

Feminine signs on the apex often represent service-orientated professions and if satisfaction is to be gained from tenth house rewards the male ascendant will need to learn that physical strength (fire) or decent skills in communication (air) from the first house will stand them in good stead once they enter the workforce.

This discord between the houses on the horizon and the houses at the right angle, which Firmicus collectively calls the cardinal points, is often experienced at an early age when the combination of the two houses creates the parenting axis and represents the native's past and future lives.

Firmicus says it is in the tenth house that we find life and vital spirit, all our actions, country, home, all our dealings with others, professional careers, and whatever our choice of career brings us.

Firmicus adds that from this house *"we easily see the infirmities of the mind"*[125], but he does not proceed to explain this statement.

The diagram of the houses' one-word meanings (*Fig. 72*) lists both parents in the fourth house, and this joint description of father and mother in this house differs from some of the later writers, e.g. Bonatti, Ibn-ezra, Schoener and Lilly to name a few, who list the fourth house as father and the tenth house as mother.

The tenth house signifying the mother is not so much because the tenth's other significations are aligned with mother in any particular way.

Mother takes position in the tenth house purely because it is opposite to the fourth, and father is well established as being signified by this house.

In Greek times and for many centuries after, the ability to own and bequeath property or real estate was a father's right only, and fathers could acknowledge their bloodline by leaving property to their legitimate (or at least, recognised) offspring.

Hence, the link between father and the fourth house.

The mother gets the tenth house by turning the chart (deriving the houses) because she is the partner of father, and so her house is placed seven houses away from the fourth, in the tenth house.

The later diagram entitled *Example One: My Father (Fig. 77)* derives the houses from the fourth house and shows father's partner in the radical (natal) tenth house.

The square aspect symbolises the manifestation of victory through trial and adversity, and as there are two squares which radiate from the ascendant, there will be two phases which manifest through either the waxing square (at the fourth house) or at the waning square (at the tenth house).

The waning square is the long journey, being placed ten signs away from the ascendant. It is symbolic of the native's journey both through the chart, and through Fate's pathway to find *'life and vital spirit'*.

Firmicus lists the houses in the order of their strength and, as all traditional authors do, he begins the list with the first house.

However, when he writes about the tenth house he says:

"This place is the first in importance and has the greatest influence of all of the angles."[126]

He is definitely making a point here, and rather than contradicting himself, I believe he is drawing the reader's attention to the fact that the tenth house is the pinnacle of life's journey, which is not reached just once, so that the native can then rest on their laurels, but must keep striving towards as goals change and new challenges arise throughout life.

The tenth house may have *"the greatest influence of all of the angles"*, but every journey must start somewhere, and the place to start is where the light shines the brightest at the ascendant.

The tension that a square creates between unalike qualities and dissimilar genders is symbolic of the constant battle to achieve, hold on to the prize and keep the momentum to fight competition, all of which is signified by the elevated tenth house.

House Name: *Imum Caelum, Lowest Heaven*
Position: *Fourth House*
Area of Influence: *Parents*
Preference: *No. 4 in the order of 12 houses*

The relationship between the ascendant and the fourth sign is a waxing square, and the latent qualities of the fourth sign can be either under-developed or overlooked by the native.

The fourth house, or *Imum Caelum,* shows us family property, substance, possessions and household goods, and because it is at the lowest point of the chart, also pertains to hidden and recovered wealth.[127]

The perception of 'hidden wealth' in the fourth house was literal at the time of Firmicus' writings. However, it becomes a metaphor for what happens when a square from the bowels of the chart puts pressure on the ascendant.

For instance,

> an ascendant in a water sign is likely to react emotionally when the square aspect from an air sign keeps changing and threatening stability in the fourth house,

> an earth ascendant becomes doubly inflexible when pushed by the fire at the base of the chart to hurry up and take action,

> a fire ascendant gets agitated and 'fired up' when the water at its base give off vibes that makes fire feel vulnerable or uncomfortable,

> and an air ascendant feels bogged down and suffocated by earth's rigidity and slow pace at home base.

Under the pressure of any of these scenarios, the native has little choice but to push onwards, even though they will expend a great deal of energy on trying to resist the signs from the opposite gender on the vertical axis of the fourth and tenth houses.

Regardless of whether the ascendant is in earth or water signs both female elements are highly resistant to change, and whilst the fire and air combination on the right angled squares believes they are encouraging and stimulating the possibilities for change, from their vantage points, the female signs on the horizon will view this behaviour as agitation and bullying from the sidelines.

Likewise, the male ascendant signs of the fire or air element have the natural urge to make themselves known to the world and strive for power or acknowledgement, but hit the tension of the square when it comes to the fourth and tenth axis.

All that male energy on the horizon must learn service and humility through joint or shared effort is the prize at the end of the journey, and for ascendants not geared towards inner reflection or honest self-evaluation, the fourth house will test their sincerity and intention, whilst the feminine tenth house climax, can leave them feeling a little queasy or uncharacteristically unsure of themselves.

No amount of male assertion or exertion from the ascendant will cure the dilemma of mixed gender, and the individual with fire or air ascendant signs may take heed from the words of Austrian philosopher Ludwig Wittgenstein (1889-1951):

"A man will be imprisoned in a room with a door that's unlocked and opens inwards; as long as it does not occur to him to pull rather than push."

Harmonious Aspects To The Ascendant: Favourable Houses

"A comfortable house is a great source of happiness. It ranks immediately after health and a good conscience."

Sydney Smith (English writer, 1771-1845)

House Name: *Bonus Daemon, The Good Spirit*
Position: *Eleventh House*
Area of Influence: *Friends*
Preference: *No. 5 in the order of 12 houses*

The secondary set of four points does not share a similar plane of modality as the ascendant.

Rather, these four favourable houses are joined to the ascendant through good and harmonious aspects.

They are houses which receive light and blessings from the ascendant which provides each house with the option of fine opportunities, bona fide daemons, good fortune and powerful skills if the native knows how to use these houses wisely and well.

Firmicus lists the eleventh house as the fifth in strength, and the dexter sextile which exists between the sign on the ascendant and the eleventh sign is linked by the same gender.

Male to male signs, or female to female signs, provide an automatic ally for the ascendant ensuring that a house which Johannes Schoener (1477-1547) says is dedicated to friends, counsellors, political supporters, hope and favour, is also a house where Jupiter finds its joy.[128]

Other authors claim that the eleventh house indicates wealth or great advancement and that the planets will bestow gifts on this house depending on their nature.

Valens says that the benefics brought forth the greatest goods, whilst malefics in this house *"will not have the power to do anything evil"*.[129]

Firmicus claims that even Saturn produces moderately good fortune in the eleventh house and the potential is there for the native to follow in the footsteps of a successful father, provided it occurs after the native's thirtieth year.

Jupiter in its joy brings the greatest good fortune and great fame for a person born during the day-time.

Mars in the eleventh increases income and assures popularity with the people and high office, whilst the Sun on the rise to its highest position on the Midheaven, provides benefit from powerful family connections especially if aspected by the benefics.

Honours are heaped upon the native, whilst the continued goodwill of friends protects the native from harm when the Sun is in the eleventh house.

Venus is accidentally dignified when she is in fifth house, the house opposite to the eleventh house.

Firmicus' judgement on Venus in the eleventh house shows a distressed Venus in a house in which, surprisingly, she does not rejoice.

If Venus is an evening star (she rises after the Sun) and she is aspected by malefic, Venus in the eleventh house will make the native sterile, and cause them to have difficulties in achieving a successful state of matrimony.

Firmicus also warns of sexual liaisons which promise a fall from the king's or society's favour and create scandal and malicious rumours if Venus is located in the eleventh house.

However bad the situation may become, Firmicus assures the reader that Venus in the eleventh will mean that the native is aesthetically pleasing and sociable, and under the right influence from the Moon, can still achieve great fame and power.[130]

Finally, Mercury can bring intelligence and great proficiency in a variety of professions if it is found in the eleventh house.

House Name: *Bona Fortuna, Good Fortune*
Position: *Fifth House*
Area of Influence: *Children*
Preference: *No. 6 in the order of 12 houses*

The fifth house is powerfully connected to the ascendant through a trine aspect.

In a Whole Sign chart the element on the ascendant will complement the same element in a different modality on the fifth house cusp.

This powerful and harmonious aspect is meant to provide the native with the gift of children and the fifth is the location of Venus as its house of joy.

The house of good fortune brings constant benefit to the native through the trine aspect and Firmicus makes the following statements on what one might expect when the superior planets (Saturn, Jupiter or Mars) are situated in the fifth house.

Firmicus says, Saturn by day makes very powerful men whom life has blessed with benefit, whilst Jupiter indicates great increases in prosperity, and Mars in a night-time chart decrees great glory and wealth, and all manner of good fortune.

Those who have the Sun in the fifth house are agreeable and successful, and win all their desires, largely through the help of their friends.

The Sun in the fifth house is a nocturnal chart (Sun below the horizon), but this does not seem to affect the possibility for good outcomes from the diurnal luminary.

Malefic planets conjunct the Sun in the fifth house are not able to exercise their malevolence directly onto the native because of the benevolence of this house, but Firmicus says they can harm the native's children.[131]

The inferior planet Venus, in its house of joy, indicates those who are honourable, benevolent, and who easily attain their goals.

They will be a close companion to famous men, and gain great benefits and patronage from women, be prize-winners and victors in all contests, whilst Bonatti claims *"Venus rejoices in the fifth because it is the house of joy, delight, and dance, and she (Venus) signifies this."*[132]

Mercury in front of the Sun in the fifth house will be in charge of great riches, produce many children, and be seen by others as having a good and divine character, but will be misers with their money.

But Mercury placed behind the Sun (nocturnal Mercury) has little luck with saving money and Maternus warns *"Whatever gold, silver, or other property was entrusted will be dissipated in profuse outpourings."*[133]

The only good fortune a nocturnal Mercury seems to achieve here, is that it indicates some kind of administrative post, or a teaching position, and somehow, as managers of wrestlers.

This may seem bizarre, but the fifth house can be extended to include managers or agents of those who engage in the entertainment business or careers produced from leisure activities (personal trainers, gym managers, tennis coaches, etc).

Firmicus provides no deliberation for the Moon placed in the fifth house as some of text on the Moon's position in the houses has been lost.

House Name: *Deus, God*
Position: *Ninth House*
Area of Influence: *Journeys*
Preference: *No. 7 in the order of 12 houses*

The trine is an important aspect which captures the light of the ascendant and links it directly to the ninth house of the Sun God.[134]

This aspect brings power and favour to the native by creating a direct line between the ascendant and the ninth house by both houses being in signs from the same element.

The idea of humankind being created in the image of God is not so difficult to understand given the 'sameness' of the element that binds the two houses together.

Schoener says that the ninth house is the house in which we *"seek piety, truth, the divisions of mankind, long journeys, wisdom, divination, philosophy, and the interpretation of dreams."* [135]

Firmicus states this house is where the social class of men is found and that the ninth house concerns itself with religion and foreign travel.

Firmicus says that Saturn in the ninth (in a day chart) will make famous magicians, renowned philosophers, temple priests and according the signs in which Saturn finds itself, seers, diviners and astrologers.

However, if the native is born at night, Saturn in the ninth indicates the wrath of the gods and hatred of emperors. [136]

His list of occupations is strange to our ears, but the text can be translated into more modern terms under the list of ninth house's significations of education, learning, philosophy and religion.

Magicians become dabblers or experts in the sciences, temple attendants are spiritual devotees and seers covers a huge range of individuals interested in matters which do not concern this world.

And astrologers? Well we are still here, as scattered and diverse in technique and location as they were in Firmicus' day, but still hanging in there.

Jupiter in the ninth house makes interpreters of the gods (priests) but he adds that sometimes Jupiter's placement here indicates losses and fevers of the mind.

This last phrase suggests religious fervour or zeal, and it is certainly possible that Jupiter loses perspective in this house, where the boundary between the macrocosm (god) and the microcosm (human) is very thin, and Jupiter is tempted to explore further by crossing from one side to the other.

Mars in the ninth is seen as quite favourable in regards to life and fame, and if Jupiter is also placed on the ascendant at the time of birth the native will win whatever they seek.

There may be difficult journeys but Mars in the ninth indicates great administrative power, learned and famous orators and will provide great military prowess.

A ninth house Sun is in its house of joy, and Firmicus' text reflects this accidental dignity for the Sun.

A religious life is anticipated with the native worshipping divine images and gaining fame and honour by honouring the gods in voice and actions.

The father of the native will be fortunate but both the native and the father will have many changes in life, often involving long journeys.

Venus does not fare so well in the ninth house as she indicates physical dishevelment, unholy prophesies and predictions, and constant attack by demons.

Sometimes Firmicus' text shows a lack of astronomical awareness in practical terms, as he continues to discuss Venus in the ninth house in a night-time chart, which would mean that the Sun was below the horizon and Venus was in the ninth house.

Even if the Sun had only just set, the distance between a sixth house Sun, and a ninth house Venus, is much greater than is physically possible, as Venus has a maximum span of only forty seven degrees from the Sun and these two houses are generally separated by a larger number of degrees.

Certainly by whole sign a ninth house Venus by night would be impossible as Venus would need to be at least sixty degrees from the Sun for this to be the case.

Finally, a ninth house Mercury needed the influence of another planet to sweeten its mood as an unaided (or possibly unaspected) Mercury in the ninth created quarrelsome, contentious arguers. Those annoying individuals who claimed to know all things above everyone else, were malevolent in nature, but were unable to complete tasks due to their own lack of care.

House Name: *Dea, Goddess*
Position: *Third House*
Area of Influence: *Siblings*
Preference: *No. 8 in the order of 12 houses*

The sextile between the ascendant and the third house brings power and favour to the native, by describing the people who will support them as they go about their daily life.

People such as siblings, close relatives, friends, neighbours or peers are the groups who envelop the individual with their care and attention.

Third house also signifies the ease of travel through familiar places which are neither dangerous nor wearisome, which mean a quick return to home base, hopefully with the benefit of increased profit or useful goods brought home for the native's comfort.

The number of miles covered in a trip away from home is not the point of third house travel.

Rather it concerns the level of familiarity with the journey and the landmarks which are predictably placed along the way.

Third house travel instils a sense of security in the native, a feeling of boredom and a sense of ownership over one's regular seat of passage.

Those individuals who travel hundreds of miles regularly can verify that third house journeys are mundane, but are not always measured in distance from Point A to Point B.

Third house travel is the kind of movement where you arrive at your destination (work, home, school, the shops), but are not exactly sure that you remember the process along the way.

One might pray to the goddess for conditions of the day to be favourable, or send up a prayer for fine weather, a good crowd in the marketplace (airport/bus depot) or an act of kindness from a neighbour.

These are third house prayers for help in the realm of the familiar and are vastly different to the serious travel prayer, where one goes straight to the ninth house of the gods.

With ninth house prayers, the tourist/adventurer/pilgrim bargains or pleads for protection against the unknowable perils of travel through an alien or hostile terrain containing strange customs, perilous voyages, and foreign languages.

Goddess is the name of the third house, and the Moon is in her joy here, where constant change and activity is part of daily life, and her blessings may be seen as having a twofold benefit.

In the Chaldean Order, the Moon is the luminary of the night, and the last planet touched by the soul on its descent to Earth.

For this reason, she represents the bridge between the spiritual realm and the natural world, and the Moon rejoicing in the third house indicates a far more practical use of her expertise as the signifier of all things physical in this world.

The ascendant describes all matters pertaining to the consistency, health and maintenance of the physical body. The harmonious sextile which passes from the first sign to the third sign (same gender, same active contrariety), means the ascendant can direct the third house to assist it in fortifying the native's constitution.

The third house needs to master skills as quickly as possible, so that movement and tasks become easy and economical, requiring little effort and no conscious thought when manipulating the human body and the materials used in daily life.

The axis of the third and ninth house is one of constant learning and assimilation of information, and the ease or difficulty of the flow between the two houses will be determined by the rulers of the opposing houses.

As an example, learning to drive a car is a ninth house experience.

It is terrifying in the beginning. Learning all the gadgets in the car, knowing how and when to apply the rules of the road, being aware of other drivers on the road and navigating the streets to find the expected destination, all of these factors are exhausting both physically and mentally for the learner driver.

The ninth house of new experiences and new journeys (even if only few miles for a learning driver) is the house where the constant assembly of foreign information and its collation for eventual easy access takes place in the chart.

After much time, practice and constant repetition, the newly learned skill of driving a car passes from the ninth house to the third house.

The brain starts to relax and the body's automatic responses take over so that the driver no longer thinks in specific detail about the process of driving a vehicle.

It is only when something known changes into the unknown – learning the gears in a new car, driving in a new area, road works, or a sudden situation with a potential for danger – that the ninth house is required to kick back in, and the mind and body quickens to deal with the foreign situation or avoid the danger.

One of the saddest experiences occurs when illness, disease or accident strikes an individual, and they struggle to master simple tasks which they learned when they were a child.

Third house skills like holding cutlery, tying shoelaces or simply knowing how to walk, become ninth house battles requiring enormous amounts of tenacity, patience and courage to retrain brain and muscles to work in unison again and perform acts which previously were so easy for the body.

The third house is where we learn and automatically memorise the considerable skill that is required to manoeuvre our mass through the physical plane, so it seems only fair that the Moon should rejoice in a house which brings forth natural talents that help to define our immediate environment, and seamlessly become an extension of our individual physical prowess.

Thirteenth century writer Guido Bonatti says the common denominator between the Moon and the third house, is that they both signify things which change from one purpose to another quickly, and are those things which repeat themselves.

The happy coincidence of finding a Moon in the third house in the natal chart means that the owner is better equipped or physically competent to adapt to, and swiftly navigate, the territory between birth and death.

For this reason, it is always important to note if there is anything which may further assist in cementing the archetypal relationship between the first house and the third house such as:

1) The involvement of the Moon with the third house by placement or rulership,
2) Establishing if there is any link between planets in these two houses,
3) Being aware if there is an aspect between the ruling lords of the ascendant and the third house.

Inconjunct (Non-Aspects) To The Ascendant:
Passive Points – Feeble and/or Debilitated Houses

All charts will have four signs which bear no aspectual relationship to the ascendant.

The signs either side of the ascendant, and their corresponding opposites will be in a different gender, and a different modality, to the sign on the ascendant.

For this reason, the four houses will receive no direct light from the ascendant and Firmicus labels these houses as 'passive' in nature.

They are houses which are hidden from the first house, and in order for them to work effectively in the chart and bring them out of their passivity, there needs to be a way for them to link to the ascendant.

A Ptolemaic aspect (conjunction, sextile, square, trine or opposition) between the two lords of the houses (the ruling planets) will wed the passive house to the ascendant, and the nature of the aspect will describe the type of marriage.

A conjunction is a strong bond, and the planets themselves will determine if the connection is wedded bliss or a nightmare.

The easy aspects of sextile or trine means there is a natural flow of energy between the two lords as they link through their signs' gender, qualities or element and this will bode well for affairs which are signified by a specific passive house.

A square or opposition lacks the harmony of the other aspects and denotes tension and possible strife between the two houses, but at least the aspect has illuminated the passive house and brought it to the attention of the ascendant.

These conditions are very specific and are dependent on the planets' situation in each chart.

For this reason the value of the passive houses to the ascendant is limited, and it will depend on the planets who rule the four houses, namely the second, eighth, sixth and twelfth houses, to make themselves known to the ascendant for these houses to have a positive impact on the person's life.

The cardinal points (angles) often present vexing and time consuming difficulties for the native due to the quartile (square) and opposition aspects, but they are visible obstacles and therefore can be met and conquered through strategy, experience and foresighted planning.

The favourable houses ease the pressures of life, and bring joy and respite when it is the most needed, and are a reminder, even in the darkest hours, that while there is light there is life.

And then there are the problematic houses, where shadows lurk, and fear or uncertainty are never far away.

Firmicus' term for these houses can be misleading because passive houses are not so-called because they are inactive or unresponsive, but because they are not aspected to the ascendant and therefore the native cannot anticipate in advance, the issues which they will create throughout the lifetime.

These four houses are inclined to blind-side the native by creating misfortune 'out of the blue' and all the worry, fear or perceived preparation for the dramas to come are of little use to the native when situations arise from these sources.

At their worst these are the houses which signify financial ruin, death, illness, accident or imprisonment and are houses where fear abounds and perceived calamity is skulking just around the corner ready to pounce at the most unexpected time.

At their best, the passive houses are irritating, perplexing, frustrating or exhausting and that is pretty cold comfort when planets are situated in any of these four houses.

The Second and Eighth Houses: Feeble, But Not Debilitated

House Name: *Anafora, Rising Up from the Underworld*
Position: *Second House*
Area of Influence: *Wealth*
Preference: *No. 9 in the order of 12 houses*

It may seem strange to add the second house of money to the list of passive houses when the effort required to accumulate money is anything but passive, but the daily grind required to ensure the seamless tide of money coming in exceeds money going out, is wearing on both body and soul.

If various Greek philosophers were correct, and the soul manifests in physical form on Earth in order to evolve, then you can imagine how vexed the soul must be when the body keeps distracting its purpose with demands for food, warmth, comfort and shelter.

Firmicus says that the second house shows the native's personal hopes for wealth and determines material possessions.

He calls it the Gates of Hell because the Sun is starting to arise from the underground and will soon cross the ascendant to herald a brand new day.

Planets located in the second house will directly influence the finances but an empty house does not mean that the native is destitute or without any visible means of support.

It is the duty of the lord of the sign on the second house to manage the native's financial stability and the condition of the ruling planet (by essential and accidental dignity) will determine how well or how poorly the native handles the pecuniary affairs of their life.

The ruling planet will show if they live above their means, how they can earn income, if they save their money, and even the origin of their wastage or unnecessary expenditures.

In terms of economic stability, if Mars is situated in the second house in a daytime chart, the indication is for great evils and great misfortune, whilst Saturn brings great reversals of fortune and the native will be inclined to waste any family inheritances.

The benefics fare better, as Jupiter can inherit from strangers, and if Mercury aspects the second house Jupiter then great riches and many possessions are predicted for the native's wealth.

However, if Saturn or Mars aspect a second-house Jupiter from any direction, this will transfer the chart's owner from respectable entrepreneur towards dishonourable or illegal occupations.

Firmicus says that the Sun in the second makes the native agreeable and respectable, but that they will be anxious and fearful during their lives as they are hindered in many ways purely because the Sun is not particularly comfortable in any of the four passive houses.

A Mercury in the second which rises after the Sun in a daytime chart will indicate a native of humble class, of criminal disposition, with no knowledge of letters, and destitute of all means of livelihood.

This will only happen occasionally, as Mercury's maximum separation from the Sun is 28 degrees, so to be in the second house would require the Sun to be in the late degrees of a sign *but risen above the horizon*, with Mercury in the sign following the Sun.

But if the same Mercury is in a nocturnal chart (the Sun is yet to rise) it will make money-lenders or managers of other people's money.

Finally, the fortunes of Venus in the second house will be greatly affected by whether the native is either a diurnal or a nocturnal chart.

If the native is born during the night (nocturnal chart), Venus will produce designers of important crafts, and the native will be charming, agreeable in love affairs, but often victims of scandal.

If the Sun has just risen over the eastern horizon then the chart is diurnal, and within Venus' 47 degree range of possible placement from the Sun, Venus can be situated in the second house and can produce great reverses of fortune and indicate that the native will marry late, but often unsuccessfully.

It should be remembered that in almost all cases, the clientele for a traditional astrologer would have been comprised of affluent or powerful males, and as Venus reflects very restricted and often negative views on the place of women in society, an out of sect Venus in the second house would indicate someone (usually a female) who marries for material gain rather than for love.

The astrologer's delineation was really a warning to their client to steer clear of marriage or any serious liaison with a beautiful young woman, who was bound to want to spend all their precious money, and thereby 'reverse their fortunes'.

House Name: *Epicataphora, Casting Down into the Underworld*
Position: *Eighth House*
Area of Influence: *Death*
Preference: No. *10 in the order of 12 houses*

The house which opposes the second house is classified by Firmicus as the second passive house, and if the second is the eastern Gate of Hell, which the Sun must pass through in order to be born again each morning at the ascendant, then the eighth house contains the Gate of Hell, where the Sun gets ready to enter the underworld.

In today's world of varying spiritual beliefs, the idea of reincarnation, the rebirth of the soul into another human body, may not sit comfortably with everyone's views on what happens after death.

However, along with astrology, the Greeks inherited or adopted the Egyptian and Chaldean view that souls return many times, and each soul will live an unquantified number of lives on Earth.

The great mathematician Pythagoras (c. 570-495 BCE) preached on transmigration, which means the soul, after the death of one carrier body, can return to Earth in the body of either another human being or in an animal form, explaining the reasons why Pythagorus practised vegan-ism in his lifetime.

The ancients really had little choice but to believe in either the reincarnation or the transmigration of the soul, given that they witnessed the rebirth and death of their Sun-god every single day of their lives.

In their experience, Earth did not rotate around the Sun in order to arrive at roughly the same position every day.

It was the Sun that rose on one side of the Earth and set on the other, and then rose and set the next day in a place which was fractionally different to the day before.

Their belief in the continuity of life was based on the myth that the Sun was born at dawn, grew to be a man by noon and died in old age at sunset.

The Sun then entered the underworld for a period of twelve hours and was resurrected the next morning, so that it could repeat the process for the next day.

Under the terms of this philosophy, there was no fear or trepidation about either set of Gates to Hell or the Underworld because they were a part of the natural process of living and dying and reliving again, even if in a completely different form.

Aristotle's belief in reincarnation may have influenced his determination to define the differences between form and matter, as 'matter' could be interpreted as soul (from which something is made), and 'form' is the vehicle or the body which the soul inhabits.

The constant striving to correctly classify matter was then directly related to prolonged definitions on moral dilemmas and the choices between virtues and vices, and the three-parts of the soul.

If to the philosopher's mind, matter was the soul, then the one variable became the changing form from one body to another as the soul continues to manifest time and time again in a different form (body).

Firmicus says that, from the eighth house is discovered the kind of death forecast for the native.

He also says that it is necessary to know that no planet rejoices in this house except the Moon, and then only in nocturnal charts.

If the waxing Moon is situated in the eighth house in a nocturnal chart, and if she is not harmed by aspects to the malefic, the native can experience good fortune and a bounty of riches.

The planets Jupiter, Venus or Mercury in harmonious aspect to the eighth house Moon, especially if she has essential dignity, can increase the native's fortunes, described by Maternus as

> "riches beyond measure, great glory of material power and outstanding recognition in worldly position."[137]

The eighth house is not a 'use once and dispose' kind of house, as there are other meanings to it besides being the house of the native's death.

By turning the houses, also called deriving houses, any house in the chart can be treated as though it is a first house scenario, and whoever is indicated by the house *(Fig. 76)* can drive the chart from their viewpoint.

The most important point to remember when turning the chart, is that the house that you begin from must be treated as the new 'first house' when counting any subsequent houses.

For instance, to find out more information about the partner from your own chart, begin at the seventh house and make this house the focus of the chart.

The radical (original birth chart) seventh house becomes house 'number one' and the radical eighth house becomes house 'number two', the house of the partner's wealth.

The first house to be discussed in detail was the seventh house, and as mentioned earlier, there are a number of people in our lives with whom we have both formal and informal contracts.

For each one of these people, whether they are friends, partners, business associates, professionals or clients, the radical eighth house becomes their house of finance.

In many cases, a traditional astrologer would perform a detailed synopsis of the eighth house for their wealthier clients, as this would indicate the financial solvency of those seventh house individuals who wanted access to the client's own money.

The Sixth and Twelfth Houses: Feeble And Debilitated

House Name: *Cace Tyche, Bad Fortune*
Position: *Sixth House*
Area of Influence: *Sickness*
Preference: *No. 11 in the order of 12 houses*

The final two houses are unfortunate for two reasons, as Firmicus says they are the two weakest houses of the chart.

Firstly, the ascendant represents the entry of light from the soul into the body, and with no aspect from the ascendant to either the sixth or twelfth houses, there is no reciprocal transfer of light from the house immediately before the descendant or to its opposing axis, the house which sits to the immediate right of the ascendant (viewed from the centre of the chart).[138]

Secondly, both houses are marked by either bad luck (the sixth house), or by the deeds of evil spirits (the twelfth house).

Both debilitated houses are also cadent houses. The term itself gives some clue as to why they are considered weak houses, as cadent is derived from the Latin word *cadaver* meaning 'corpse', and *cadere* meaning 'to fall or perish'.

The third and ninth houses are also cadent as they are situated to the right of the other cardinal points or angular houses, but these are saved from the same fate as the sixth and twelfth, because they exchange harmonious aspects with the ascendant.

They are also the houses where the two luminaries rejoice, and are therefore not as disempowered as two houses considered to be feeble (no aspect) or debilitated (cadent).

This sixth and twelfth axis is where the two malefic planets, Mars and Saturn, are said to rejoice, and whilst Mars may gain accidental dignity from a sixth house placement, and Saturn may be in its joy in the twelfth house, this does not automatically translate to good news for the chart's owner.

There are also mixed messages concerning the presence of planets in these two houses.

Firmicus calls all four passive houses 'dejected' and says in his 'Advice on Interpretation of the Chart' in Book Seven:

"You should pray in every possible way that the chart you are working on should not have planets either malefic or benefic in the sixth or twelfth houses; or in the second or eighth. For these houses are always filled with hostile influences from all planets."[139]

He warns that if a benefic planet occupies these houses, it forfeits its salutary power and its beneficence or protective influence is lost.

Furthermore, if a malefic is found in any one of the four houses, its injurious influence is increased.

If the Moon is joined with a malefic in one of the passive houses, it indicates misfortunes without remedy.

The planet Mars is considered to receive accidental dignity if it is situated in the sixth house, the house of its joy, so it begs the question:

Is Mars' behaviour better or worse when it is found in the sixth house?

Does Mars rejoice in the sixth house, because it can create the right conditions to accelerate the native's blind corners where illness, accident or bad luck lurks?

Or does accidental dignity for Mars mean that it is better behaved, and therefore some of its maleficence is mitigated by its preference for the house?

And as the house itself is cadent, will this also weaken the planet's effectiveness to do harm?

Most traditional authors simply list the joys of the planets in their preferred houses but Guido Bonatti (1282 C.E.) is one of the few who rationalises the linking of planets to certain houses.

Bonatti says: *"Mars rejoices in the sixth because it is the house of deception, infirmities, and servants; and he signifies servants, deceivers, liars, and false speaking men; and therefore he rejoices in this (house) because no other house signifies these things."*[140]

In an earlier passage Bonatti says Mars rejoices in burnings, the spilling of blood, and in every evil deed which is performed by iron or fire, and these are the reasons why Mars is particularly drawn to this (sixth) house.[141]

Perhaps judging Mars' intent is important in reading its effect on the woes of the sixth house.

That is, by examining a number of factors in the chart the astrologer can determine whether Mars intends to do mischief in his house of joy and is keen to become the champion of Bad Fortune.

Or whether he is pacified by the position and protects the native from mishap.

For instance, a nocturnal chart will settle Mars down and bring forward a more benign personality from him, and even a diurnal chart will see Mars tucked safely away from the Sun in a different hemisphere if it is situated in the sixth house.

Essential dignity can improve Mars' behaviour, as does any additional accidental dignity aside from the planet being situated in the house of its joy.

The lord of the sixth house will also need to be inspected, because if the quadrant style house system is in use, then Mars may be situated in a different sign from the sixth house cusp.

An idea which has been floated in the previous chapter on the signs, is that a planet in a house is the initiator of a situation, but it is the planet's dispositor (the owner of its sign) which ultimately determines how the action will be completed.

In the case of Mars in its joy, this malefic may direct the drama which results in poor health or an accident, but the planet which owns its sign, will have the final say on whether the trouble is short-term or has continuing consequences for the native's constitution.

A final note on the sixth house: it is the destroyer of health, and not the indicator of health itself.

So far as the houses are concerned, it is the ascendant and its lord who determines the strength and vitality of the native's constitution, and for this reason, the planet which rules the sign on the ascendant requires close scrutiny when judging the body's vibrancy and its resistance to Mars' onslaught from the sixth house.

The Moon is the planetary lord of the body, and so further examination of the Moon's state according to its essential and accidental dignity, and its sign's owner, will be critical in determining the speed of recovery, and the overall impact of Mars' mischief from the sixth house.

The body's debilitation is one aspect of the cadent sixth house, but there is another, more positive feature to this house. In the whole sign house system the sign on the sixth house will share the same element as the sign on the tenth house, so although the sixth house has no aspect to the ascendant's sign, there is energy from this house to the apex house at the top of the chart.

The elemental trine which occurs between the sixth sign and the tenth sign means that sometimes an unfavourable influence is removed from the sixth house, especially when a planet in the sixth is in a trine aspect to another planet in the tenth house, or is directly to the degree which marks the Midheaven in the chart.[142]

The sixth house can be a place where one slaves away at a project, or in the workplace, feeling unappreciated, under-valued and largely invisible.

However, any connection by aspect to the tenth house, or to the Midheaven, means that the efforts will not all be in vain, and that recognition is on the way.

Sometimes hard work does pay off and the native receives advancement, maybe not equal to, but at least proportional, to the self-imposed drudgery they have endured in the sixth house.

House Name: *Cacos Daemon, The Bad Spirit*
Position: *Twelfth House*
Area of Influence: *Enemies*
Preference: *No. 12 in the order of 12 houses*

Does the same principle apply to Saturn when it is accidentally dignified in the twelfth house, in its own house of joy?

Does Saturn play a protective role in the twelfth house, or does it indicate the presence of a powerful hidden enemy?

Again, to quote Bonatti: *"Saturn rejoices in the twelfth house because it is the house of sorrow, sadness, labor, lamentation, and weeping; and Saturn rejoices in these things and the like."*[143]

Does Saturn give strength through protection, or does it feed the fears and paranoia of the twelfth house?

The entire chart will need to be examined in order to satisfactorily answer questions on Saturn's intent.

We cannot say that Saturn is better behaved because his preferred house relieves him of his destructive tendencies, when Firmicus has stated this is simply not the case.

Likewise, we cannot always tell the difference between a dignified Saturn which protects us against our hidden enemies, or which describes the power behind a hidden enemy, who has the capacity to bring about our downfall simply because the sign of Saturn suggests they have enormous power or resources at their disposal.

The only thing we do know is that Saturn is better behaved in a diurnal chart when the Sun joins Saturn above the horizon.

Everything else requires in-depth delineation of all the planets, not just Saturn, and that in truth, with Saturn in the twelfth house, the potential for both scenarios, rather than choosing one over the other, is more likely to be closer to the truth.

Firmicus does little to supply helpful answers to these questions, but he does warn of the pitfalls of the twelfth house, saying we find defects and illness in this house.

At the end of his summation on the debilitating effects of this house, he adds: *"It is, moreover, the house of Saturn"* so this does not augur well for a good outcome from Saturn when it is found in the house of its joy.

Firmicus also says that planets in the twelfth can describe certain relations, for example,

"The Sun gives definite information about the father in the nativities of both men and women, the Moon about the mother, Venus about the wife, Mars about the husband." [144]

Modern astrologer and translator, Robert Hand, says on the subject of the twelfth house that medieval astrologers *"would prefer the ruler of the twelfth to be debilitated"*[145] as this would cause one's secret enemies to be weak and ineffectual when on the attack.

One of the benefits of turning the chart, or deriving the houses as the practice is otherwise known, is to view its use not so much from where the astrologer might begin the journey, but rather where they might end up in the chart, at the very end of the process.

For instance, if the twelfth house becomes a destination point when turning the chart then several other important significations for the same house become evident to the astrologer.

Thirteenth century astrologer Guido Bonatti uses this technique in all of his descriptions on the houses[146] and his interpretations for the twelfth house are shown in the Table below *(Fig. 73)*.

There are extensions of the twelfth house in Bonatti's Table, which seem odd from our modern perspective, and the text has been modernised to make sense of the turning of the houses.

However, there are at least two significant points here that give some insight into why the twelfth house can be connected with fear.

The twelfth house signifies the illness of my partner (six houses from the 7th) and also the death of my children (eight houses from the 5th) meaning that the fear from the twelfth is not restricted to one's own safety, but is extended to concerns over a loved one's safety, and this is a huge key to understanding the broadness of this house.

Planets in these houses are not a guarantee that these things will happen, but the fear of a debilitated partner or the passing of a child are the stuff that nightmares are made of, and night terrors truly are the appropriate dwelling place for the darkest of the twelve houses in a chart.

JOURNEY BEGINS at	HOUSES COUNTED	OTHER SIGNIFICATIONS FOR TWELFTH HOUSE
1st house	TWELVE houses from the 1st The RADICAL CHART (Natal chart)	Hidden enemies, deceivers, persons who hate, sorrows, prisons, malevolencies
2nd house	ELEVEN houses from the RADICAL 2nd	Friends of my workmen
3rd house	TEN houses from the RADICAL 3rd	Professions of my siblings
4th house	NINE houses from the RADICAL 4th	Religion of my father *(Fig. 77)*
5th house	EIGHT houses from the RADICAL 5th	Death of my children
6th house	SEVEN houses from the RADICAL 6th	Partners of my employees
7th house	SIX houses from the RADICAL 7th	Illness of my partner Illness of my 2nd born child *(Fig. 78)*
8th house	FIVE houses from the RADICAL 8th	Children of my financial advisors
9th house	FOUR houses from the RADICAL 9th	Father or property of my priest
10th house	THREE houses from the RADICAL 10th	My siblings of my boss or mother
11th house	TWO houses from the RADICAL 11th	The wealth of friends
12th house	**TWELFTH HOUSE AS FIRST HOUSE**	**The Nature of MY HIDDEN ENEMY**

Fig. 73 The Other Significations for Twelfth House when it becomes the Destination for Deriving The Houses

Two Models of the Houses

The following pair of diagrams show the twelve houses extended in meaning but still incorporating the original one word meanings provided by Firmicus in Book Two of *Matheseos (Fig . 72)*.

The first wheel, entitled *All About Me (Fig. 74)*, depicts the ascendant as the hub of the astrological wheel and follows the principle that the other eleven houses work as spokes which rotate around the central pivot.

The first house plays a central role in the chart and the model is designed to show this crucial house as the animating principle behind the chart.

The remainder of the houses represent the concerns of the individual who resides in the first house.

The houses relate back to the ascendant in support of the native and for this reason, the topics indicated by the eleven houses are concerned with meeting the native's physical and emotional needs.

Relations, friends, employers, and all the people who surround the native are listed in the following diagram on the houses entitled *The People in My Life (Fig. 75)*.

Whilst the first model *All About Me* is a somewhat egocentric way to view the chart, it reinforces the idea that the ascendant is a unique house with light and a life force, and that all other houses are required to serve the ascendant's (and the native's) needs.

The second house model *The People in My Life* is familiar to horary astrologers as this chart is designed to identify other living beings as well as the native, who is represented once more by the first house.

Horary astrology is the art of answering a specific question using the chart of the moment when the question is first asked of the astrologer.

A combination of the two models given here provides the answer to a question as firstly the person is identified using the second model *(Fig. 75)* of individual figures within the radical (original) chart.

Once the person's identity has been established by the horary astrologer, the radical chart is turned in their favour so that the house which represents the person becomes a type of mock ascendant.

Then the first model of supporting topics *(Fig. 74)* can be put into practice so that the other eleven houses revolve around the artificial ascendant.

The Table *(Fig. 76)* compares the two models and provides a summary for the various meanings for the twelve houses.

Fig. 74 Model One: All About Me

Fig. 75 Model Two of House Meanings : The People in My Life

HOUSES	All About Me	People in My Life
First	ME – As the Animator of My Chart	ME – My Primary Motivation; my body; my behaviour and patterns; my reactions to changes in my environment; my health and vitality
Second	My moveable wealth; my possessions; money made from my livelihood	Those who serve me for monetary gain; skilled labour for services I cannot do for myself (plumber, electrician, builder, etc)
Third	My short journeys; my physical prowess; my neighbourhood; my correspondence	My siblings and cousins; my peers and brethren; my neighbours; my fellow cult members
Fourth	My immoveable wealth; my family property; my gains from hidden sources	My father; my father's family; my mother-in-law
Fifth	My good fortune; my pleasures and entertainments; my love affairs	My children in general; my first-born in particular; my lover; my friend; those who entertain me; my beloved pets
Sixth	My bad fortune; my illnesses and physical infirmities; my accidents; my unrewarded toil and miseries	My fellow workers; servants who are a part of my family (cook, house-keeper, nanny, etc); my small herd animals
Seventh	My contracts and alliances; contentions and disagreements; things to bind and strengthen me; things to weaken and oppose me	My partner and my allies; my open enemies; those people in contract with me (clients, doctor, dentist, lawyer, etc)
Eighth	My death and losses; my misfortune and trials; things that affect my finances for good (loans) and bad (debts)	My bank manager; my accountant; my tax agent; the keeper of my legal will or my partner's money and their agent
Ninth	My religion; my foreign travel; my philosophies; my ability to grow, adapt and learn	My spiritual leader; my priest or guru; my foreign influence; my teachers; those I meet when travelling in unfamiliar territory (physical and spiritual)
Tenth	My destiny and my honours; my glories gained from my career or public status	My authority figure; my mother and her family; my father-in-law; my judge
Eleventh	My Good Spirit; my hopes and dreams; my happiness and attainment of desires	My social peers; my mentors; my friends with influence; those who can benefit me or increase my social status
Twelfth	My Bad Spirit; my sorrows and anxieties; my self-undoing; things that imprison me	My hidden enemies; those who imprison me; those whom society shuns or fears; my large herd animals

Fig. 76 The Two Models of the Twelve Houses.
Model One: All About Me and Model Two: The People in My Life

Turning The Chart (Deriving The Houses)
Example One: My Father

The following two diagrams give examples of how the same chart can be used to represent the life of the native's father *(Fig. 77)* and the life of the native's second born child *(Fig. 78)*.

In this example the house of father *(Fig. 77)* begins at the radical fourth house, represented by the numbers in the centre of the circle.

The numbers on the outside of the circle represent the houses of the father which begin at the radical fourth house and are numbered in a counter-clockwise direction in the same manner as the radical chart's house numbers.

Each of the houses within father's chart will describe a combination of people or activities or his support systems, according to the meanings of the turned chart.

For instance, the radical twelfth house describes my hidden enemies and my sorrows and anxieties, but the Table on Bonatti's Turned Houses *(Fig. 73)* shows that the radical twelfth house can also be used to delineate the nature of my father's religion, his long journeys, or any engagement he may have with elevated learning or professional training.

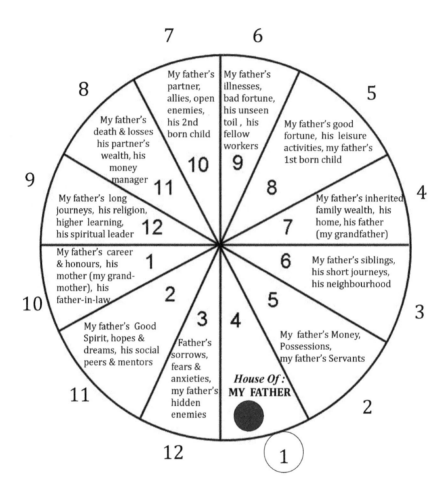

*Fig. 77 The radical chart turned to show the chart
from the perspective of the native's father*

Example Two: My Second Born Child

In the second example of a turned chart the centre of focus has become the native's second born child.

In the radical chart this is signified by the seventh house (centre numbers) which becomes the artificial ascendant from which all other houses must follow in their correct order (outside numbers).

It should be noted that whilst the topic of children in general falls under the umbrella of the fifth house, the native's children are represented separately in the chart according to the sequence of their birth.

For instance, the first born child always takes the fifth house as their own house.

If the chart is turned to determine the affairs of the first born, the fifth house would be the mock ascendant for this chart and the numbers would begin as number one at the fifth house and radiate from there.

The children born to the native after the first child are counted according to the chart being turned for the oldest child.

The second child is a sibling to the first and so three houses are counted from the fifth (5th house is house number one) and the second child is represented by the radical seventh house.

From there the third child is counted as the sibling from the second and takes the radical ninth house, and so on as each new child is born they are counted as three houses from the previous child's house.

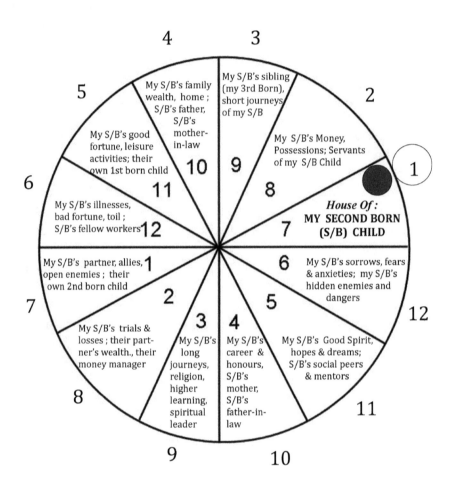

*Fig. 78 The radical chart turned to show the
chart of the native's second born child*

Bonatti's Division of The Houses

Triplicities	FIRE	AIR	EARTH	WATER
DIURNAL	☉	♄	♀	♀
NOCTURNAL	♃	☿	☽	♂
PARTICIPATING	♄	♃	♂	☽

Fig. 79 The Triplicity Lords for the Four Elements

Guido Bonatti (1210 – 1296 CE) introduces a technique which divides each of the houses into three specific topics and then allocates a different planet as ruler of each category to one of the three Triplicity Lords.

He quotes Adila and Alezdegoz as his presumed Arabic sources in Latin translation.

Unfortunately their works are believed to be lost, as neither the translator of the works, Robert Zoller, or its editor, Robert Hand, are familiar with the names provided by Bonatti as the originators of these ideas.

Triplicity is third in the sequence of the planets' Essential Dignities running after rulership or domicile as the first level, and exaltation as the second level of the dignities.

In Triplicity the signs are divided into their four elements and each of the elements is distributed amongst the planets who rule them under the conditions of third level of dignity.

The Triplicity Lords Table *(Fig. 79)* lists the three lords in each of the elements' triplicities with the first two lords being interchangeable, depending on whether the chart is a daytime chart (diurnal) with the Sun above the horizon, or it is a night-time (nocturnal) chart with the Sun placed below the horizon.

Triplicity does not supersede either of the higher levels in a house's rulership as the sign on the cusp can be ruled by either its domicile lord or its exalted lord. Rather, triplicity assists the astrologer by providing additional information on one focus of the house's multiple meanings.

The domicile lord will still dominate as the significator of the house's general condition, but a different planet's perspective can be extremely handy when one house can cover a multitude of areas in the native's life.

Bonatti also recommends the three triplicity lords for time division by splitting the native's life into three separate periods of time.

The triplicity lords are then examined in regards to their nature and their condition in the chart and this leads to information on what the native might expect from each period in life.

The first triplicity lord describes the early period, the second triplicity lord governs the middle period, and the third triplicity lord is in charge of the last period of life.

The three periods are not evenly divided into the same amounts of time but rather are dependent on the rising times of the sign in which the triplicity lord is found.

Robert Hand recommends using the Table of Ascensional Arcs of the Zodiac Signs (known as the AA Table) which are reproduced as *Figs. 82 and 83*.

At first glance the AA Table is difficult to grasp as each sign has a varying list of degrees which alter with a change in latitude as it is not immediately clear as to why certain signs are paired together in the Table.

The AA Table divides the signs into pairs because these are signs which take the equal amount of time to rise across the ascendant,

(Aries/Pisces)
(Taurus/Aquarius)
(Gemini/Capricorn)
(Cancer/Sagittarius)
(Leo/Scorpio)
and (Virgo/Libra).

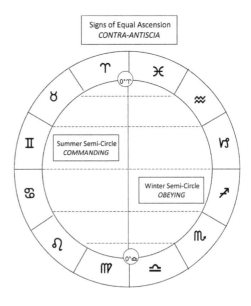

Fig. 80 Signs in Contra-Antiscia

The link between these signs creates the rules for contra-antiscia or signs of equal rising times.

Two points are important here:

> First, to determine the time it takes for the ascendant to be present in an entire sign at any given latitude is calculated by dividing the number of its degrees in the AA Table by the number 15.
>
> This will convert the degrees into time and if you are wondering why it is 15, it is usually an automatic response when roughly calculating the movement of a sign's ascendancy, i.e. 30 degrees divide by 15 = 2 hours (approximately) when the ascendant occurs in one sign.

The AA Table does the same thing, only accurately.

> The second question asks why the odd numbers for each pair of signs' degrees if all signs are 30 degrees when they cross the ascendant?

The amount of the degrees listed in the AA Table under the sign pairings are ***not the number of ascendant degrees,*** but rather, they are the ***number of degrees which cross the Midheaven*** at the same time as it takes for a sign to pass from zero degrees to its maximum thirty degrees across the ascendant.

For instance, when someone is born at 50 degrees northern latitude (Prague, Czech Republic or Winnipeg, Canada), and the ascendant is in the sign of Gemini or Capricorn, then I know that 27 degrees have crossed the Midheaven whilst either of these signs, in their entirety, have crossed the ascendant *(AA Table Fig. 83).*

However, if another person was born at the same place but at a different time during when the full thirty degrees of either Aries or Pisces were crossing the ascendant, then just short of 14 degrees would have crossed the Midheaven.

For someone born in the southern hemisphere the number of latitude degrees still stand true, but the sign must be reversed to get a true reading from the AA Table for the southern hemisphere.

So if the rising sign in the Southern Hemisphere is Pisces, use Virgo in the AA table.

What does this have to do with the three triplicity lords?

If you find that the first house has a water element sign on its cusp and the chart is diurnal, then look for Venus, then Mars and the Moon in the chart to describe the three periods of the native's life.

The signs of each three triplicity lords will give you the number of years if you convert the sign's degrees (according to your latitude) into years, that is, one degree equals one year, then you will have found your three time periods.

Fig. 81 shows four random examples for this method of time measurement using the degrees of contra-antiscia.

Robert Hand has been lecturing on this technique for over twenty years and in a lecture given in 1997 he suggested this method of time period calculation can be used for several of the houses: for the quality of the life (1st house), for the wealth (2nd house), as an indicator of the three periods of life for siblings (3rd house), for instruction on the father's life (4th house) and for the times of change in one's career (10th house).[147]

Random Examples of Timing using Ascensional Arcs for Three-Part Triplicity Lords							
				(charts not included)			
HOUSE	ELEMENT	DIURNAL OR NOCTURNAL CHART	LATITUDE	TRIP NO 1 1ST PERIOD	TRIP NO 2 2ND PERIOD	TRIP NO 3 3RD PERIOD	
FIRST (LIFE)	EARTH	Nocturnal	37 North	MOON in Pisces 19 years	VENUS in Libra 36-37 years	MARS in Taurus 22-23 years	
SECOND (WEALTH)	FIRE	Diurnal	22 North	SUN in Cancer 33-34 years	JUPITER in Capricorn 30-31 years	SATURN in Aries 23 years	
FOURTH (FATHER)	AIR	Diurnal	39 * South	SATURN in Libra * (use Aries) 18-19 years	MERCURY in Taurus * (use Scorpio) 37-38 years	JUPITER in Gemini * (use Sagittarius) 35-36 years	
TENTH (CAREER)	WATER	Nocturnal	43 * South	MARS in Aries * (use Libra) 38-39 years	VENUS in Virgo * (use Pisces) 17 years	MOON in Scorpio * (use Taurus) 20-21 years	

Fig. 81 Time Period Lords using the Table of
Ascensional Arcs (1 degree = 1 year)

The condition of the Triplicity lord, and even the nature of the planet itself will impact on the period of time indicated by the Ascensional Arcs (AA) Table.

In the first example in *Fig. 81* the triplicity lords of a chart with an earth sign ascendant shows the periods of a native's life, robustness, strength and happiness,

> the first period would depend on the Pisces Moon's position in the chart and its dispositor,
> the second period is excellent as Venus is dignified in Libra, but the last period is much harder as it is ruled by a difficult planet in a difficult situation,
> (Mars in detriment in Taurus).

In the second example of a fire sign on the second house cusp, wealth and finances are examined in three distinct periods of time, the early part of the life may be good (Cancer Sun), but the second (Capricorn Jupiter) and third (Aries Saturn) periods have their problems.

Jupiter in Capricorn tries to make ends meet in the second period, but Saturn in Aries has totally let go and is either struggling or finding alternate methods (perhaps not legal) to pay the bills in the last period of life.

In the third example of air on the fourth house cusp, Father does well in the first two periods of life, but struggles in the last period (Jupiter in detriment).

Lastly, in the last example with water on the tenth house cusp, the native's career starts well with Mars in rulership and continues to do well for almost forty years, before being plagued with problems from both triplicity lords Venus and the Moon in fall in the later periods of the career (Venus for 17 years and the Moon for 20 years).

This method allows astrologers to focus on one particular aspect of a house, or to find a general timing framework by considering the condition of the triplicity rulers.

The following two Tables *(Figs. 82 and 83)* list the divisions in the houses according to Bonatti's text.

Five latitudes (22; 37; 39; 43; 50) are tagged and highlighted as these are the latitudes used in the examples above.

LATITUDE	♈♓	♉♒	♊♑	♋♐	♌♏	♍♎
0	27°55	29°54	32°11	32°11	29°54	27°55
5	26°54	29°05	31°51	32°31	30°44	28°56
10	25°51	28°15	31°30	32°51	31°34	29°58
15	24°47	27°23	31°09	33°13	32°26	31°02
20	23°40	26°28	30°47	33°35	33°21	32°09
22	23°12	26°05	30°37	33°45	33°44	32°37
25	22°29	25°29	30°22	34°00	34°20	33°20
26	22°14	25°17	30°17	34°05	34°32	33°35
27	21°58	25°04	30°12	34°10	34°45	33°51
28	21°43	24°51	30°06	34°16	34°58	34°06
29	21°27	24°38	30°01	34°02	35°11	34°22
30	21°11	24°24	29°55	34°27	35°25	34°38
31	20°54	24°10	29°49	34°33	35°39	34°55
32	20°37	23°56	29°43	34°39	35°53	35°12
33	20°20	23°42	29°37	34°45	36°07	35°29
34	20°02	23°27	29°30	34°51	36°22	35°46

Example #2 — *(label pointing to row 22)*

Fig. 82 Time Period Lords using the Table of Ascensional Arcs from 0 to 34 degrees Latitude

	LATITUDE	♈♓	♉♒	♊♑	♋♐	♌♏	♍♎
	35	19°44	23°11	29°24	34°58	36°38	36°05
	36	19°26	22°55	29°17	35°05	36°54	36°23
Example #1	37	19°07	22°39	29°10	35°12	37°10	36°43
	38	18°47	22°22	29°02	35°19	37°27	37°02
Example #3	39	18°27	22°05	28°55	35°27	37°44	37°22
	40	18°06	21°47	28°47	35°35	38°02	37°43
	41	17°45	21°28	28°38	35°43	38°21	38°04
	42	17°23	21°08	28°30	35°52	38°41	38°26
Example #4	43	17°00	20°48	28°21	36°01	39°01	38°49
	44	16°36	20°27	28°11	36°11	39°22	39°13
	45	16°12	20°05	28°01	36°21	39°44	39°37
	46	15°46	19°42	27°50	36°32	40°07	40°03
	47	15°20	19°18	27°39	36°43	40°31	40°29
	48	14°53	18°53	27°27	36°55	40°56	40°56
	49	14°24	18°26	27°14	37°08	41°23	41°25
1st Text Example	50	13°55	17°58	27°00	37°22	41°51	41°55

*Fig. 83 Time Period Lords using the Table of Ascensional
Arcs from 35 to 50 degrees Latitude
– For Northern Hemisphere Latitudes
(Reverse the sign for Southern Hemisphere Latitudes)
Degrees are converted to Years: 1 degree = 1 year*

A Breakdown of the Houses Using Triplicity Rulers

The following Table *(Fig. 84)* lists the division of each house into three categories with each one ruled by a different Triplicity Lord according to the element featured on the house cusp.

HOUSES	FIRST TRIPLICITY RULER	SECOND TRIPLICITY RULER	THIRD TRIPLICITY RULER
First VITALITY	Early Period of Life	Middle Period of Life	Late Period of Life
Second FINANCES	Early Period of Life	Middle Period of Life	Late Period of Life
Third SIBLINGS	Younger Sibling OR Early Period	Middle Sibling Middle Period	Elder Sibling OR Late Period
Fourth FATHER	Father OR Father's Life Early Period	Real Estate OR Father's Life Middle Period	Endings and Prison OR End Period of Life
Fifth	Children and the Enjoyment of Life	Pleasures in General	Giving of gifts for benefit
Sixth	Illness, Bad health and wounds	Servants and Employees	Consequences of servants
Seventh PARTNERS	Spouses OR Relationships - Early Period of Life	Open enemies and contentions OR Middle Period	Partnerships in general OR End Period of Life
Eighth	Death	Old Things	Inheritance from the dead
Ninth	Journeys and their events	Faith and Religion	Wisdom, dreams, premonitions
Tenth CAREER	Work, high rank Promotion OR Early Period	The ability to command OR Middle Period	How well it holds up over time OR End Period of Life
Eleventh	Things given in trust (investments)	Friends	Benefits from both of the above
Twelfth	Secret enemies	Labourers	Large animals

Fig. 84 Bonatti's Triplicity Rulers for The Twelve Houses

Issues With The 'Not-So-Natural' Chart

"Within the contemporary theories of house meanings, there are
presently only two that are given any real credibility. The first
is a rather glib assumption that the houses are associated with,
and take their meaning from, the signs of the zodiac.....At best
this theory is an over-simplification; at worst it blurs the edges of
two quite separate astrological tools resulting in slack symbolism,
so vague as to be of little practical use."

Deborah Houlding, commenting
on the *'macrocosmic chart'*[148]

In contemporary astrology *'the macrocosmic chart'* is the term given
to the conceptual diagram which links Aries with the first house,
Taurus with the second, Gemini with third house and continues with
the signs until Pisces completes the circle at the twelfth house cusp.

It has been referred to as the 'ideal' chart and many modern books
use it as their reference point to justify interchanging houses for zodiac
signs.[149]

The apparent simplicity of twelve signs being the same number as
twelve houses, is as dangerous as placing twelve foxes in a chicken coop
with twelve hens and thinking they will get along fine, simply because
of their numerical similarity.

This concept of a natural correlation between a sign and a house
appears to have started in the 17th century, and unfortunately its
adoption as a valid concept has gone a long way towards undermining
the true meaning of the houses.

Twelve zodiac signs do not directly equate to twelve houses, and no
one chart is more *"natural"* or more *"macrocosmic"* than another.

Hellenistic astrologers would never promote a chart that presented
such a dangerous planet as Mars, a malefic, as having 'natural rights'
to the Ascendant.

Claudius Ptolemy (1st Century CE) allegedly wrote one hundred
aphorisms, or short summations of astrological principles, which became
known as *Ptolemy's Centiloquy.*

Ptolemy's thirty seventh Aphorism clearly states that if Aries is on
the Ascendant, then Scorpio will be on the eighth house cusp, and the

native will cause his own death by his own dangerous or careless actions, as Mars rules both the first and the eighth houses.

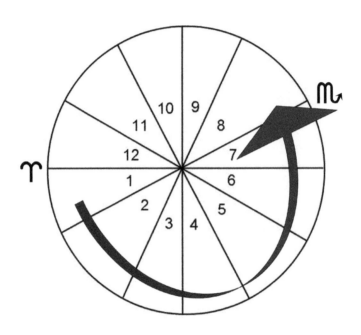

Fig. 85 Ptolemy's 37ᵗʰ Aphorism
"If Aries is on the Ascendant, he will cause his own death."[150]

Obviously, not every chart with Aries rising will conform to this Aphorism. However, it does demonstrate that the ancients were nervous of such a chart and would never have considered Aries to be a safe option for the ideal ascendant's sign.

A contemporary of Ptolemy, Vettius Valens (1ˢᵗ Century CE), states in his chapter on Violent Deaths: *"Aries is destroyed by Scorpio, and both are the dwelling places of Ares (Mars). Since, then, Ares is the destroyer of itself, it is from this that makes suicides and those who throw themselves from heights and those who are ready for death or those who conspire with evil men, piratical, homicidal, those who bring death onto themselves, and those who are destroyed by animals or fire or and an attack; furthermore, those who are destroyed by quadrupeds and blood and seduction."*[151]

Both authors from the Hellenistic period would have considered it very odd to deliberately choose Aries as the ascendant for the perfect chart, as this would mean that Mars is the joint ruler of the first house and the eighth house, the house of death.

In the last century it was common for astrologers to make statements that assumed that the house/sign/planet connection should always begin with the 1st House/Aries/Mars archetype but this particularly aggressive archetype makes delineation very awkward if the astrologer is meant to compare this model to every chart, particularly when the other charts, eleven out of twelve, do not have Aries as their ascendant sign.

In the 'model chart' the parental axis has been turned one hundred and eighty degrees so that father's house has moved from the fourth house to represent the tenth house.

Originally father was the fourth house because he alone had the right to bestow the gift of legitimacy on his children by bequeathing the family property to his offspring.

The argument that father as the sole testator (person who makes a will) is an old fashioned model and no longer has relevance today certainly has some merit.

However, the same criticism can be levelled at the 'natural' chart, when Capricorn on the tenth house cusp is presented as the ideal representation for the Father figure, whilst the fourth house with the productive, caring and nurturing Cancer on the cusp becomes the ideal representative of the Mother figure.

Apparently only father can guide in matters of career and social standing from the top of the chart and mother belongs in the family home in this model.

This stereotypical family structure with the Cancer mother being the nurturing lunar figure in the family, and father is a stern, autocratic, hard working, disciplinarian being the role model as the Saturn's Capricorn head of the family, is not applicable to a large number of family structures, either in ancient or modern times.

Firmicus' one-word model on the meanings of the houses *(Fig. 72)* is not based on a representation of the signs, and he places both parents in the fourth house rather than splitting them into houses of the fourth and tenth axis.

The 'Aries Ascendant' also swapped sex and sexual encounters from the fifth house which connected sex with the procreation of children, and one of the pastimes for the hours of leisure, to the potentially dangerous and treacherous eighth house, simply because Scorpio followed in the order of the signs and landed on the eighth house cusp.

In traditional texts the three water signs were classified as the most fertile of the elements due to the fact that the crab, the scorpion and the fish, all produce a plentiful amount of live progeny.

To the traditional mind it would be sacrilegious (from the Latin *sacrilegium* meaning 'temple robbing, a stealing of sacred things') to waste life by 'stealing' two of the most fertile signs, Scorpio and Pisces, from the fifth and ninth house as they are situated in Thema Mundi.

Even worse to then deliberately place the water signs on dark and non-productive houses such as the eighth and the twelfth where neither house receives light from the ascendant, which would have horrified the ancients.

Life was too precious for such a dreadful waste of the water signs' fecundity.

The 'model chart' proposes Scorpio for the eighth house, which is generally considered to deal with death and matters relative to death, and tends to only relate to the distribution of things, not to the creation of Life as a water sign would indicate from its symbols of prolificacy.

Also, if Pisces presented itself at the cusp of the twelfth, the house of imprisonment, secret enemies and terrible sorrows, it would have been considered an unfortunate and regrettable occurrence for any native, and certainly not one to be lauded or promoted by the astrologer.

When Aries is rising, then Leo, a barren sign, is given to the fifth house and this would raise alarm for traditional astrologers, given that the fifth house is the house of begetting children.

Even deliberately associating the fourth house with Cancer (the third water sign) has problems as the fourth can mean weakness, death, the aged, and the act of drowning.[152]

If there were to be any purpose in creating a model chart, then surely, the Birth of the Universe (Firmicus' Thema Mundi) would seem a more appropriate choice for a *'macrocosmic chart'*, as the Moon-ruled sign of Cancer is more conducive than Aries to represent the archetypal beginnings of life.

The combination of the cardinal modality with the water element creates the sign of Cancer and this is surely the most symbolic zodiac sign for gestation, birth and the survival of humankind, both individually, and collectively.

The Ages of Man acknowledges the Moon's right to have dominion over the initial phase of the lifecycle when the Moon is assigned the first four years of life.

Cancer is jointly governed by two benefics, the Moon by rulership and Jupiter by exaltation, so surely this should add weight to its rightful ownership for the ascendant of the 'natural' chart?

This arrangement of Cancer on the Ascendant would also place the other two water signs on houses which are trine to the Ascendant; Scorpio on the fifth house, and Pisces on the ninth house.

When Maternus wrote: *"Nothing in the individual charts of men should seem different from the birth chart of the universe"*[153]he was not suggesting that Thema Mundi was a 'macrocosmic chart' that should lead the way as an example for every other sign to follow.

Rather, his introductory statement to Thema Mundi, that each human was a tiny universe within a huge universe, underlines the fact that every single chart, regardless of its layout or the reason for its creation, is authentically macrocosmic in nature, and that no single schema need be promoted as more powerful, more productive, or more insightful, than another.

Each chart is distinctive and unrepeatable in its composition, and each individual factor – whether house, or sign, or planet – must be judged separately within the confines of its own unique symbolism.

The Difference between Values and Valuables

One common misconception regularly encountered in contemporary astrology is that 'self-worth and values' are part of the range of matters dealt with in the second house.

The ancient astrologers all clearly identified the second house as describing the native's flow of finances being the services they pay for, and the money they receive for the services they provided.

The second house related to monetary gain and loss, and the accumulation of wealth, pure and simple.

It is reasonable to expect to receive remuneration for personal skills and abilities, but the passive second house with no light from the ascendant is not ideal as the place to look for one's need for fulfilment, emotional feelings, and sense of self-worth.

If one house were appointed to cover this range of specifics, then the ascendant (the house of good health, strength and vitality) may be better equipped to define the characteristics and strengths of the native's state of happiness and well-being.

For those who use the second house to pay their bills on time and gain a certain level of satisfaction by being debt-free, it would be unfortunate to burden the same house with the extra duty of nurturing talents and resources, answering a need for fulfilment, judging self-worth and organising one's sense of values.

Surely it is the planets' responsibility (as a unit) to determine what fulfils an individual, what delivers peace of mind, and what gives personal meaning to life, rather than just those planets which reside in the second house, or the ruling planet of the second house if the house is devoid of planets.

The duty of each planet is to provide the native with their own version of fulfilment, happiness and self-worth, and Macrobius' comments on the Descent of the Soul through the Chaldean Order (Chapter Two) might be a good place to start looking for answers on what satisfies the soul.

Macrobius says that Saturn provides reasoning and theorising so we can surmise that Saturn's level of self-worth is arrived through applying discipline and hard work to a logical process of collecting data.

"Needs must when the devil drives" John Lydgate's *Assembly of Gods* (1420)

The quote above has been modernised but in essence it means "Necessity compels" and when you are desperate, you must do things that ordinarily you would not do.

Saturn is sometimes required to separate love and desire from what it needs to do in order to maintain the native's integrity or honour.

It constantly evaluates, supposedly without fear or favour, and this can be a painful and lonely process, but it provides Saturn with a measuring stick by which it finds its own requirements for happiness and a sense of fulfilment.

Saturn values virtues such as frugality and modesty, and the individual gains self-pride by quietly making do with very little, but virtue is lost, if frugality turns to stinginess or mean-spiritedness, or if Saturn brags about its own humility.

Integrity is another quality valued by Saturn and if the individual weighs up a situation and feels they have not compromised their morals, they gain benefits that no house of money can possibly describe.

Saturn ruling, or situated in the second house, is monetary hardship – not a Saturnian value system.

The individual who uses Jupiter to gain self-worth does so from their acts of generosity, and these acts are not confined to monetary prizes, loans or scholarships, but broaden out far wider into roles as benefactors, teachers, philosophers, priests or shamans.

Jupiter's altruism is far-reaching, but can best be described as Jupiter gaining fulfilment from wanting to spread its wealth of knowledge and its own good luck in every direction possible, so that others think well of the individual and appreciate their efforts to educate, improve or relieve another's difficult situation.

Jupiter either in the second house or ruling the second does not demonstrate an obligation to share its wealth with others, and is more likely to be accumulative with its wealth, rather than generous in its dispersal.

Some other factor, besides second house association must trigger Jupiter's charity, as the house alone is incapable of loosening Jupiter's purse strings.

Macrobius says that the soul collects *"ardent vehemence"* on its arrival at the planet Mars.

The individual who finds their emotional worth and self-esteem through the lens of Mars will value passion, enthusiasm and zeal, and will pride themselves on being true to their convictions.

Mars brings ferocity and sincerity when called to defend its passions, principles or beliefs.

It will value the native's courageous spirit and will urge them to be inventive, tenacious and forceful so that the level by which the native measures these qualities within their own character will indicate their level of Martian self-worth.

If Mars is the ruler of the second house, or resides in the second house, there is nothing here to indicate inner talents or resources, as finances are fought for, and won, within a competitive market, if Mars is in good condition, or are in a constant state of ruin or despair, if Mars is in a poor condition in the chart.

If the Sun resides in the second house, the chart is nocturnal and the Sun must deal with being the second in line after the Moon.

Dealing with self-worth and values is likely to be dependent on the nocturnal planets, not on the Sun itself.

If the Sun rules the second house the individual will want money to show how successful or elevated their position is in society or to buy favours from those in a more influential position than themselves.

Macrobius says the Sun teaches the soul its sensory perceptions and its imagination, so perhaps the individual who pursues the Sun's dreams for self-expression and an honourable value system feels most satisfied and fulfilled through their perception of the world, rather than through the grim world of finance.

Cervantes' novel *"Don Quixote"* was first published in 1605 and told the adventures of an aging minor nobleman who is consumed by books on chivalry and cannot rest until he takes himself off on a quest for glory.

His companions are a skinny old horse named Rocinante and his faithful servant Sancho Panza. Together they embark on Don Quixote's own acts of chivalry and good deeds which ultimately result in physical beatings and terrible humiliation.

Don Quixote has been cited as *"a veritable encyclopaedia of cruelty"*[154], yet the knight errant cannot stop his quest to destroy injustice, even if the injustice is perpetrated by authorities such as the church or state.

Don Quixote regards himself as God's knight, and his creator Cervantes, fashions him as a new kind of hero, who rather than being old, pathetic and quite mad, instead is a man on a journey of self-knowledge, *"one who wills to be himself"*.

The fact that this novel, written over four hundred years ago, still speaks to both the collective and individual soul, is a reminder of the soul's need for fulfilment through the Sun's quest for self-knowledge, especially when the Sun believes that there are worse things in life that *'tilting at windmills.'*

Under the rules of the 'natural chart' Venus, by its rulership of Taurus, is supposedly the significator of the second house, but it would be regretful and somewhat one-dimensional, to restrict this beautiful planet to the singular pursuit of money.

Macrobius says that the soul discovers the *"motion of desire"* when it docks at Venus' portal and emotions ranging from rapture to contentment, love, attachment, impulse, passion and beauty, are where we find Venus' true nature.

Venus is where we see ourselves mirrored in the eyes of a loved one, and whether they over-value or under-value our love, the devotion we are prepared to offer brings the gift of our own self-esteem and our belief in ourselves.

If the native does find Venus is connected in some way through placement or rulership of the second house in their own chart, it may be another's wealth that they rely on, or sadly they may only be able to hold another's affections if they retain their own wealth.

Whatever the situation, it is more a comment on the nature of their relationships than a statement of their own self-esteem or value system.

Mercury is a more suitable lord of money than Venus: *"Of materials, it (Mercury) rules copper and all coins used in buying and selling,"*[155] but he does not have to be confined to the second house to indicate wealth.

Vettius Valens (1st Century CE) states that Mercury yields varied results and commerce can be gained through being paid for knowledge, or through selling, farming, service, trade, teaching or public employment.

Mercury's speed and its tendency to be affected by the other planets means that it can have a drastic influence on finances, changing profit to ruin within a short period of time depending on the whichever planet is associated with Mercury.

Valens warns that Mercury will make everything capricious in outcome and quite disturbed, so it would be wise not to directly associate this planet with values and emotional stability, if it is situated in the second house.

If finances are separated from Mercury's significations, and instead we were concentrating purely on what this planet's version of self-esteem might produce, then Macrobius' text on the Descent of the Soul can provide clues as to where Mercury may cast its spell to create good feelings and peace of mind.

According to Macrobius when the soul alights on the planet Mercury it gains the ability to express and interpret feelings.

Mercury furnishes the soul with one of the vital mechanisms to comprehend, store and vocalise emotions and this skill provides the soul with the potential to make sense of human emotion.

Mercury supplies the soul with the reasoning power and intelligence to comprehend what impact the surroundings and other people will make on the individual's emotional state, and how difficult or easy the individual can absorb this comprehension will have a huge impact on their own self-worth.

Lastly, the Moon (the seventh reason why the second house can never claim the right to our self-worth and value) supplies the soul with sentiment, emotional bonding, nurturing, physical safety, and the desire to serve and be served, but this is only a very small list of the Moon's qualities and its ability to make us feel like we belong on this Earth.

Ptolemy writes in his *Tetrabiblos* that together, Mercury and the Moon, are the joint significators of the mind and soul.

He states that all the spiritual qualities which are rational and intellectual, are contemplated by the situation of Mercury, whilst the appetitive soul which is independent of reason, is considered to be the realm of the Moon.[156]

The different conditions of these planets according to essential and accidental dignities makes them competent to contribute to the properties of the mind, and Ptolemy mentions signs, aspects and sect in his judgement of mind and soul.

In Book Four Ptolemy dedicates a chapter to the quality of employment, and cites the Sun and the sign on the mid-heaven as joint indicators of profession.

There are specific rules as to the type of employment listed by Ptolemy, but generally speaking, it is the respective qualities of the three planets, Mars, Venus, and Mercury which determine the profession.[157]

In the whole sign system, the second house will always possess a trine aspect to the tenth house, thereby creating a natural flow-on effect from the house of profession to the house of wealth.

If all goes well with the lord of the tenth house and planets in the tenth house, then by association, the second house should also benefit from the native's employment.

To complete or formalise the natural arrangement between the two houses, ideally the lord of the tenth or planets in the tenth house should aspect the lord of the second house or planets in the second house.

If this is achieved in the native's chart, then the native can expect that financial security should be assured.

Of course, this is dependent on how quickly or how wisely the individual spends their income, and the methods of attaining wealth or spending it is indicated by connecting factors in the chart.

For instance, the second house squares both the fifth and the eleventh house and these two houses of social commitments, pleasure activities, gambling, leisure pursuits and children can mean the individual is experiencing a rapid and uncontrollable loss of money into areas which cannot be supported by the income.

Likewise, if over-extending one's finances has led to loans with exorbitant rates, or debts to financial institutions, this situation will accentuate the tension in the opposition between second and eighth house.

And the individual will feel financial strain, no matter how much security their employment provides.

The trine from the second house to the sixth house can mean the native works overtime hours, or is required to balance several jobs at the same time, but if their health suffers or they have an accident at work, then the trine can turn from beneficial to difficult and quickly deteriorate into a reduction in finances.

Does the money go on real estate?
Does it disappear without any awareness of where it goes?
Do I spend it on improving my health?
Can I afford my child's overseas school trip?
Is my money pooled with my partner's, or do they control
their own finances?

These are second house questions which keep us awake long into
the night as we fret over finances. Not,

What do I value?
What is my worth?
Why am I here?
Am I satisfied with my life?

All good and valid questions – but none which can be answered by
the chart's second house.

CHAPTER EIGHT

The Whole Sign Chart

"Last night, I spoke to God.
I told Him my plans. He started to cry.
I thought I was great to move the Greatest to tears.
He said that He was crying only because my plans were very
different than His plans for me."

Kamand Kojouri

My own experience of the difference between quadrant-style and whole sign charts through the charts of family, friends, students and clients is best summed up by Kamand Kajouri's poem.

Put simply, the quadrant-style chart reflects what the native wants to happen, whereas a whole sign chart reflects what the planets want to happen, and ultimately, what they will make happen.

It is my opinion that the two charts should lie side by side on the astrologer's consulting desk as each system has enormous merit in understanding the client's past, present and future.

Neither chart should be sacrificed in favour of the other.

Some astrologers suggest that using two house styles at the same time is confusing and counter-productive, but in truth it takes very little time, and very little extra effort, to become familiar with the practice of moving from one style to the other.

Tables such as the ones drawn for the Example Chart: 30th March 2017 *(Figs.94, 97 and 98)*, are easy to recreate as the faster the astrologer can find the information, the more confident they can become at translating the subtle differences between the two house systems.

Historically, the Whole Sign house system was developed during the Hellenistic tradition in the first or second century B.C.E. and was used by astrologers for centuries until reliable Planetary Tables came into print in the later periods. Life then was Fate not Freewill.

Ptolemy (1st century C.E.) uses whole signs for aspect theory, Vettius Valens, a contemporary of Ptolemy, casts dozens of charts in whole sign, and all versions of Thema Mundi, including Firmicus' (4th century C.E.), are naturally whole sign charts as they are theoretically the Birth-chart of the Universe, and therefore, belong to a time before Ephemerides were invented by scientific observers.

Firmicus' explanation on the houses and their meanings *(Fig. 71)* are also set against the backdrop of the whole signs as the ascendant's sign sends aspects to three of the cardinal points by sign (7th, 10th and 4th houses), harmonious aspects to four of the houses (11th, 5th, 9th and 3rd), and has no aspectual relationship with the passive or debilitated houses (2nd, 8th, 6th and 12th) as the signs have nothing in common with one another.

There are many ways to divide space and time, and quadrant-style charts such as Placidus, Koch, Alcabitius or Regiomontanus, use specific rules to arrive at the division of the space between the ascendant degree and the Midheaven degree.

All house systems must agree on these two critical points (ascendant and MC) and the changes are usually quite minor when shifting from one quadrant-style system to another.

In Macrobius' model on the Descent of the Soul in Chapter Two, the soul descends through the seven spheres of the planets and waits at the Moon for its allotted time to descend and physically manifest in human or animal form.

Medieval authors mention the corruption of each planet's essence due to the co-mingling of their energies as the soul arrives on Earth, and the imperfections of physical matter are reflected in the influence that one planet will have over another through the aspects which tie the planets together.

On the physical plane the soul meets matter and form. Matter becomes form, only to have form destroyed, and become matter once more, and this is achieved through the combinations of the changeable characteristics of the four elements of fire, air, water and earth.

Suddenly there are consequences as to where a planet is located according to the elements and the signs as the astrological model sets the planets against the backdrop of the newly-formed chart or horoscope (literally, 'a view of the hour').

Once more the greater Universe has bridged the gap between itself and another tiny universe through the movements of the two luminaries, Sun and Moon, and the five planets, Saturn, Jupiter, Mars, Venus and Mercury, which become immobilized at the moment of birth.

Once the soul arrives, it works out pretty quickly that a physical form has its limitations, and that life on Earth is anything but perfect.

In many ways the beauty of a quadrant-style chart lies in its reflection of Earth's many imperfections.

It highlights differences in Earth's tilting axis which produces season differences in the chart through the rising and setting of the Sun.

The quadrant-style chart accentuates the enormity of Earth's circumference by noting movement away from the Equator in the form of latitude differences.

These discrepancies in latitude and the birth's location on the globe alters house sizes and results in the Midheaven being off-kilter with the ascendant, so that the possibility of a perfect right angle is lost to many signs, pivot points and astrology charts.

Quadrant-style emphasises the differences in the signs' rate of movement across the ascendant, and then swaps them over according to whether the birth occurs in the northern or the southern hemisphere, thereby creating signs of long and short ascension, which ultimately affects the construction of a chart.

In short, quadrant-style charts are messy and up to a point, unpredictable, but then they are supposed to be, simply because they reflect the soul's physical experiences here on Earth.

These differences do not disappear in a Whole Sign chart, but they are neatly tucked away so they are less noticeable to the chart's reader.

Perfection is the criteria of this style of chart, not defects or blemishes which detract from the beauty of the planets which are the main attraction on this austere stage.

For this reason, the native's whole sign chart is not intended to replace their quadrant-style chart, but rather to provide a different perspective on life.

I tend to view the whole sign chart as a cosmic checking system to see whether something is really possible, or whether the promise suggested by the quadrant-style chart does not have the full support of the planets.

If this is the case, the potential in the quadrant-style chart changes direction, it fails to quite reach its benchmark, or it simply fades away from a lack of impetus. The word 'impetus' is derived from the Latin *impetere* meaning both 'assault, force', and *in* – 'towards' and the word *petere* – 'seek'.

The change in a planet's circumstances from quadrant-style to whole sign suits this word perfectly as whole sign chart clearly defines whether the planet will 'seek towards' taking affirmative action or 'force' to achieve its aims in the native's life.

Dual-chart delineation, or the equal participation of two house systems, avoids a tendency to promote a different version of the chart by undermining confidence in another model or by reducing its importance in determining the workings of the native's life by discarding one system in favour of another.

Rather, dual-chart delineation allows for a smooth transition between one model and the other and embraces diversity, appreciates the merits of both systems and combines them to the astrologer's, and the client's, best advantage.

The conversion from quadrant-style to whole sign is a simple task that requires no additional maths, and can be performed on a spare scrap of paper in the time it takes to make a cup of tea.

To convert a chart to whole sign draw a circle with twelve sections (a chart).

Place the ascendant's sign on the first house cusp at zero degrees.

Mark the ascendant's degree as a point in the first house.

Now follow the zodiac signs in their correct order placing each one at zero degrees on each of the house cusps until the return to the first sign and house.

Now place each of the planets, and the Midheaven, within the house which corresponds to the sign in which they are located.

Job done. Chart converted.

Critics of the Whole Sign system say that this house system is contrived and artificial in its orderliness, and that whole sign charts are oblivious to the restraints of physical limitation such as time and space.

I agree that this method of construction simplifies the chart, purely because it eliminates overlapping signs in consecutive house cusps and removes the planets from houses where the sign on the cusp conflicts with the planet's sign.

However, this system should not be discarded off-hand for these reasons.

The beauty of the whole sign chart lies in the purity and singularity of its purpose.

By maintaining the invisible border between the signs and confining the planets to houses, it becomes clear that both planets located in the house, and the house itself, will share the same planet as either the dispositor of the planet's sign, or as the ruler of the house.

This allows focus to remain on one planet – the dispositor of both in situ planets and house ruler – and the condition of this ruling planet will affect both the borrowing planet and the affairs of the house.

In his lecture *On Matter and Form in Astrology,* traditional translator and editor Robert Hand states that the basic difference between the function of an occupant of a house (a planet) and the function of a ruler of a house (and dispositor of a planet) has a great deal to do with the timing of an event as the *"ruled-ruler relationship is a progression in time"*.[158]

In other words, the occupant planet begins the actions within the house in which it is situated, and the ruling planet (of both occupant planet and house) follows through with the action which will complete a given situation.

The ruler shows the outcome of something which was begun in a different part of the chart by a planet whose nature and characteristics are very dissimilar to its dispositor.

Moon in Aquarius may start a situation drawn from a fear of isolation or rejection, and will use the affairs of its placement house to demonstrate its concerns, but Saturn, the ruler of Aquarius, will decide the end result depending on where it is situated in the chart.

The ruling planet has the momentum and incentive to 'finish things off' but if it is stricken by debility or has poor placement in the chart in feeble or debilitated houses, then the end result is unlikely to greatly please the chart's owner.

Writer and translator Demetra George writes in her latest book *Astrology and the Authentic Self,* the use of whole sign houses "*brings the chart into more of an archetypal pattern*"[159] and this is certainly true, given the longevity of the Whole Sign system.

However, on reading the ancient texts and particularly the traditional writers' comments and observations, it becomes clear that humanity and the issues of today are very similar, if not identical, to the issues confronting people in ancient times. If this is true, then the archetypes inherent in the construction of the whole sign chart are as relevant today as they were two millenniums ago.

Clients often wonder why they struggle to manifest their hopes and dreams when the desire is strong but they feel thwarted at every turn.

They will visit an astrologer to find out why, when they have invested time, money or energy into a project, a marriage, a job, a child, or really anything signified by the chart, things have not gone as they had planned.

They suffer disappointment or vexation from plans gone amiss, promises not acted upon or opportunities that ended in a stalemate, and often wonder if they could have done more, or acted differently to achieve a more favourable result.

Rarely do we look at the opportunities that have fallen into our laps, or record times when we have done minimum work for maximum results.

Human nature being what it is, these favourable twists in Fate are easily accepted as our God-given right to happiness or success.

Good fortune is barely acknowledged.

We are more inclined to pack sudden windfalls away in our sub-conscious so that we can return our focus to features of our lives which frustrate or block us.

An astrologer is unlikely to consult with a client who wants to know the reasons behind why they have received unwarranted good fortune – we duck our heads and hope it will last rather than analysing why it happened in the first place.

For reasons beyond our human understanding, the planets in an astrology chart reflect events in our lives, and recasting the quadrant-style chart to a whole sign chart often reveals a significant planet's movement either into a weakened position, or receiving a reprieve from a troublesome position in the initial chart.

If the planet is weakened or lacks the ability to perform well it tends to reflect the nature of, and more closely describe, the events as they have occurred in the individual's life.

Likewise, if the planet becomes fortified, or is released from a dark house into a house of light, than the information gained from the whole sign chart can help the astrologer and the client to map the future a little more accurately, using a combination of the two chart styles.

The Thema Mundi chart is set in the Whole Sign house system and is one of the original archetypal charts.

Thema Mundi identifies the signs which each individual planet rules, and of particular significance to the dual-chart delineations, this symbolic chart has the signs of Jupiter and Venus, both benefic planets, which lie side-by-side with the signs of Saturn and Mars, the two malefic planets.

Usually this phenomenon does not excite much interest.

However, when a whole sign chart changes the sign on a particular house cusp from the one in the native's quadrant chart, then the planet ruling the house changes as well, and this alteration in the condition and power of the house's ruler can have significant ramifications on the native's life.

For instance, Sagittarius and Pisces, both domicile signs of Jupiter, are signs which rest either side of Saturn's two consecutive signs of Capricorn and Aquarius.

If Sagittarius moves forward to take Capricorn's previous house, then the ruler of that house has moved from a malefic planet (Saturn) to a benefic planet (Jupiter) and situations which initially looked insurmountable suddenly clear to provide advantage for the native.

These are the often the good luck stories as under new management (i.e. the whole sign chart), the affairs of this house are brighter than expected from the quadrant-style chart, as Saturn has made way for Jupiter as the house's ruler.

Several houses along Pisces may have moved on from a house cusp, and Jupiter has relinquished its power over that house to become the ruler of the next house.

294

Now Aquarius is on the cusp and Saturn has moved in to become the new landlord of a house which was previously ruled by Jupiter in the native's quadrant chart.

Without the two charts side-by-side the astrologer is likely to be oblivious to these subtle changes, but a conversation with the client will reveal that Jupiter's former house is difficult, restrained and a source of constant restriction to the chart's owner.

This is only one example of the changing parade of house rulerships which can occur when a benefic planet is changed to a malefic planet as the ruling lord of a house, and vice versa.

Pisces (Jupiter-ruled) can replace Aries (Mars-ruled), which in turn could replace Taurus (Venus-ruled), and the opposite axis means Libra (Venus-ruled) replaces Scorpio (Mars-ruled) which replaces Sagittarius (Jupiter-ruled) which in its turn replaces Capricorn (Saturn-ruled).

So it goes on in places all over the chart, where one lord takes over from another, sometimes benefiting a house, and sometimes creating dramas that will only truly reveal themselves in a whole sign chart.

To modern ears, the whole sign attitude of 'what will be, will be' can sound somewhat defeatist, fatalistic or negative in outlook, but this is not the case.

There is a beautifully haunting tune which appears on Chicago-born Celtic artist Liz Carroll and John Doyle's album *Double Play* (2009) which is an amalgamation of three separate Irish tunes collectively called Lament for Tommy Makem/Within a Hen's Kick/The Slippery Slope and it occurs to me that the last two titles, more of a jig than a lament, pretty much describes our journey through life.

We are, all of us, *"within a hen's kick of the slippery slope"* and sometimes, just the tiniest of nudges puts us into a place where we never thought we would be.

Comparing the quadrant-style with the whole sign chart can be hugely beneficial, especially if this is where we meet our *"hen's kick"* – the one that sends us down the slippery slope into who knows where, for good or bad fortune.

Once the practitioner is aware of what is, and what is not possible, they can advise their client on how they may proceed from that base of knowledge.

Even if the specifics of astrology are foreign to the client, they will totally relate to life experiences described when a planet crosses the border from one quadrant-style house to the next house in a whole sign chart, for instance, a planet in the seventh house of relationships sliding into the eighth house.

Or a house which looks like Jupiter (as its ruler) turns out to be more Saturn (Capricorn or Aquarius-ruled) in the events or outcomes of that house.

The expectation of what happens when a planet moves from one house to another, or when the rulership of houses changes dramatically from one lord to the next, are both situations which require careful consideration when recasting charts from the quadrant system to the whole sign system.

In some charts it is possible for a planet to advance by two houses in the whole sign chart, or a planet can take one step backwards into the previous house, and these possibilities are discussed in greater detail later in the chapter.

The shift in signs on houses, house rulerships and the planets' position in the chart all require consideration, when taking this extra step to examine the chart from a slightly different perspective.

In the quote at the start of the chapter the last line is telling:

"He said that He was crying only because my plans were very different than His plans for me."

Personally, I feel the last line of Kamand Kajouri's poem sums up the gap between my plans in the quadrant chart (Freewill), and God's plans as outlined by the planets in the heavens above in the whole sign chart (Fate).

I would recommend looking at both charts simultaneously as this allows a workable and practical bridge to be constructed between the two house systems, so that my client and I, can work together to capitalize on the strengths, and to be aware and allow an expression for the weaknesses which become apparent when the two charts are judged side-by-side.

The whole sign chart relates to the same basic information but applications are less technical, less about the mechanics and the repercussions of the changes, and are more about the subtle shift in the reader's own philosophy on life and the belief systems which support their practice in astrology.

Altering the chart is the easy part.

Even delineating the differences between the two styles of chart becomes easier with practise and observations made within the consulting room, but it is up to the individual astrologer to decide if the practise of dual-chart delineation works for them on a metaphysical level, and to determine if it fits within the framework of their own ethical, moral, philosophical and spiritual beliefs.

One of the trade-offs in changing systems from quadrant-style to whole sign chart is that the former house system forfeits the variable degrees on its house cusps, and often these odd degrees on a house cusp are considered to allow the planets to form aspects, degree to like degree, to a house cusp.

Consulting astrologers can look at this type of aspecting between planet and house cusp to try to find possible ways to activate an otherwise passive house.

For instance, an aspect from a planet's degree to the cusp degree of either the second or the eighth house may stimulate the finances, with the hope that the planet aspecting the cusp can act as a catalyst, especially if it also forms an independent aspect with the ruling planet of either money house.

This kind of planet to house cusp arrangement disappears with the conversion to whole signs as all whole signs houses will begin with zero degrees of a sign.

Even when a planet is placed in the low degrees of a sign it is not capable of forming an aspect to any of the whole sign cusps at zero degrees.

Traditional writers did not view the aspects as mathematical calculations in the same way as modern astrologers apply aspects between planets or from planet to house cusp.

Instead they worked with a planet's moiety, and this could be likened to an energy field which surrounded each of the planets.

This moiety or sensitive area around the planet was activated when the planets moved into areas of Ptolemaic aspects, and could therefore 'behold' or influence one another's behaviour.

Traditional astrologers considered the house cusps were not a repository for energy, and so a planet could not 'see or behold' a house cusp in order to form an aspectual relationship with it.

In traditional practice, the only two critical points in the chart that could be seen and could have aspects formed to them were the ascendant and the Midheaven, and they are the exceptions to the above rule, as, although they are not planets and do not have a source of energy, they are still considered to be powerful, and therefore capable of receiving an aspect from a planet.

These points do not exchange energy with the planets, and the ascendant and Midheaven are one-way recipients of a planet's energy.

There is one more exception to this rule as the Moon's Nodes hold no energy of their own, and do not possess moiety.

However, the North Node (Dragon's Head) augments or enlarges the planet's power if it is placed within reach of the Dragon's Head, and the South Node (Dragon's Tail) diminishes the power of any planet which finds itself conjunct the other end of the Dragon.

The best scenario for the chart's owner regarding the Nodes is if a benefic planet is conjunct the strengthening North Node, then the native's good fortune increases, or if a malefic planet is conjunct the South Node, the damage done by the malefic can be reduced by the weakening Node.

Dual House Systems: Signs Moving Forward...

"Life is a series of natural and spontaneous changes. Let reality be reality.
Let things flow naturally forward in whatever way they like."

Lao Tzu, Chinese philosopher (604-531 BCE)

Certain things are possible when changing from a quadrant-style house system to a Whole Sign house system, and certain things cannot happen.

For instance, a sign can only move forward from one house to the next in a whole sign chart and the sign must retain its place in the order of the signs.

When a chart is converted from quadrant-style to Whole Sign, the signs that are doubled up on consecutive house cusps in the quadrant chart, are released and then the next sign moves to the released house cusp.

The signs which are completely enveloped within the confines of a house (intercepted signs) in the quadrant chart, leave the protection of the enclosing house and move forwards to claim their own house cusp.

The planets have different experiences to the zodiac signs, as they can go backwards by one house, (this is not a reference to a planet's retrograde movement, but is placement in the chart) with the change from quadrant-style to whole sign, but signs never do.

The exception to a planet's ability to go back one house concerns the ascendant and descendant axis.

It is not possible for a planet to cross the horizon line in a backwards motion through the houses from the first house back to the twelfth house, or from the seventh house back to the sixth house (Fig. 106).

Planets also have the capacity to move forwards by two houses, but again, it is not possible to cross over the horizon line by 'jumping' the first and seventh houses. The alteration in house systems will never show a planet moving from a quadrant-style sixth house to a whole sign eighth house, or moving from a quadrant-style twelfth house to a whole sign second house (Fig. 105).

Many quadrant charts will experience disassociate signs on their angles, and this is especially prevalent when people are born in high latitude locations.

In quadrant charts with disassociate signs, the Midheaven's sign is a different modality to the ascendant's sign and the angle between the ascendant and the Midheaven is either considerably less that ninety degrees, or significantly more than ninety degrees.

When this chart is recast in the Whole Sign system, the Midheaven is no longer the tenth sign from the ascendant, and so potentially forfeits its place in an angular house.

Rather than being a lop-sided cusp for the tenth house, now the Midheaven is represented as a point (like a planet), usually in the house either side of the tenth house cusp.

Although the majority of shifts in the Midheaven occur in the eleventh or the ninth houses, I have witnessed charts with extreme size differences in their quadrant-style houses with Midheavens moving to the twelfth house, or shown as a degree in the eighth house, two signs short of the tenth house sign in a whole sign chart.

The Table at the end of the chapter (Fig. 99) lists interpretations on the Midheaven's shift in houses in the whole sign chart.

The following chart is one example of what can happen when house systems change.

The quadrant-style chart is set in the Placidus *(Fig. 86)* method and is converted to the Whole Sign Chart system *(Fig. 87)*.

The chart's two critical points do not alter from one method to the other, as the ascendant remains in Capricorn with the Midheaven situated in Scorpio.

In a Placidus chart, the shortened distance between the Ascendant and the Midheaven (the angles) means there will some signs that feature on two consecutive house cusps, and other signs that do not appear on any house cusp, and accordingly, are fully contained or intercepted in one house.

In the Placidus Example Chart, Aquarius is intercepted in the first house and its opposing sign, Leo, is intercepted in the seventh house. The sign of Gemini is duplicated on the fifth and sixth houses, whilst the same axis features the opposing sign of Sagittarius on eleventh and twelfth houses.

The difference in house sizes is visually obvious in the Placidus chart *(Fig. 86)* but this difference disappears when the chart is converted to the whole sign system.

The houses adopted in the Whole Sign system are equally placed at thirty degree increments around the chart as a representation of the thirty degrees of a zodiacal sign.

The movement of a previously intercepted sign onto the next house cusp will usher the sign which was on the following cusp, onto the next house and every one shuffles along to the next house until the two houses which doubled up on the same sign, no longer have this problem.

In the case of the example chart, Aquarius is intercepted in the first house in the Placidus chart *(Fig. 86)*, but it will move to the second house cusp in a whole sign chart *(Fig. 87)*.

This will require Pisces to move to the third house cusp, and Aries, which was previously on the Placidus chart's third house, moves to the angle (4th house), and also complements the Ascendant as it creates a cardinal square between the signs on the first and fourth house cusps.

Taurus moves Gemini from the fifth house cusp, but Gemini retains possession of the sixth house in both systems.

The Descendant will carry the same sign in both charts, because the Ascendant remains the same in any house system. Leo, which was intercepted in the seventh house in the Placidus chart *(Fig. 86)*, will move forward to the eighth house cusp, and Virgo will move to become the sign on the ninth house.

The cardinal sign of Libra will complete the cardinal Cross on the four angular houses, and Scorpio (and the Midheaven) will move to the eleventh house.

The twelfth house cusp will remain as Sagittarius in both systems.

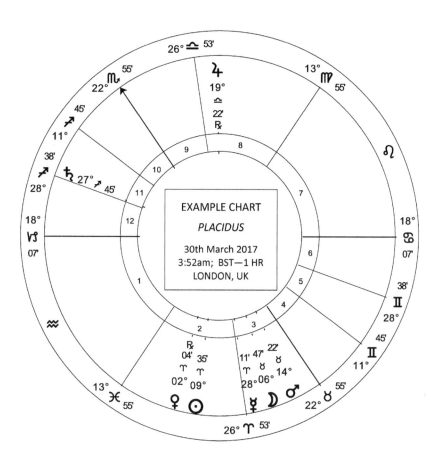

Fig. 86 ***Placidus Chart***
EXAMPLE CHART: 30th March 2017

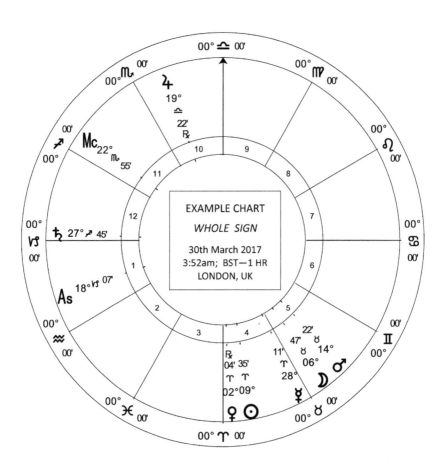

Fig.87 ***Whole Sign Chart*** *EXAMPLE CHART: 30ᵗʰ March 2017*

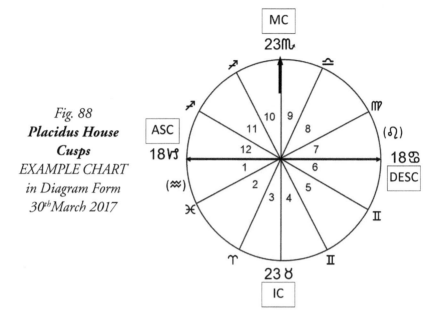

Fig. 88
Placidus House Cusps
EXAMPLE CHART in Diagram Form 30ᵗʰ March 2017

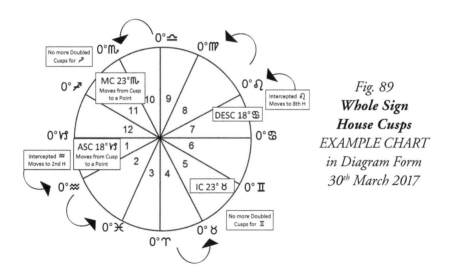

Fig. 89
Whole Sign House Cusps
EXAMPLE CHART in Diagram Form 30ᵗʰ March 2017

The Power of Planets to Rule Houses

	PLACIDUS		CHANGE IN HOUSE CUSPS	WHOLE SIGN	
HOUSE	SIGN	RULING PLANET		SIGN	RULING PLANET
1	♑	♄	No Change	♑	♄
2	♓	♃		♒	♄
3	♈	♂		♓	♃
4	♉	♀		♈	♂
5	♊	☿		♉	♀
6	♊	☿	No Change	♊	☿
7	♋	☽	No Change	♋	☽
8	♍	☿		♌	☉
9	♎	♀		♍	☿
10	♏	♂		♎	♀
11	♐	♃		♏	♂
12	♐	♃	No Change	♐	♃

*Fig. 90 EXAMPLE CHART: 30th March 2017 Signs
on Cusps and the Lords of the Houses*

The forward movement of the signs creates a chart which looks different yet is essentially the same chart, but seen from a different perspective.

New signs on the cusp of several houses have altered the ruling planet of a house, and in fact, there are eight changed house cusps, or more accurately, four house axes have shifted to new signs (2/8; 3/9; 4/10; 5/11).

The horizon will always hold its signs of ascendant and descendant, so the only other unaltered axis is the sixth and twelfth house axis.

All other houses receive new signs and different ruling lords for these areas of life.

The Table *(Fig. 90)* shows the difference between the Placidus and Whole Sign House system according to the changes in signs, houses and ruling planets.

The Whole Sign system is faithful to the order of rulership according to the Thema Mundi chart and the only time that the same planet rules consecutive houses is in the case of Saturn, which rules Capricorn and Aquarius.

However, in the Placidus Example Chart, Mercury and Jupiter rule three houses apiece, and Saturn rules only the first house whilst the Sun does not have rulership over any of the houses.

"The crownless again shall be king."

J.R.R. Tolkien, *Lord of the Rings*

The change in house systems restores a certain balance in house rulership which is absent in charts with doubled house cusps and intercepted signs.

In the Placidus Example Chart Mercury rules the fifth, sixth and eighth house and the opposing houses are under the rulership of Jupiter.

The two lords are in the opposing signs of Aries and Libra, and their house positions in the Placidus chart do not reflect this aspect, as Mercury is in the cadent third house, and Jupiter in the succedent and passive eighth house.

Their opposition is more evident when they move to the angular signs in the whole sign chart.

The Table *(Fig. 90)* demonstrates the angular houses of the fourth and tenth house axis changes in the whole sign chart and house rulership of the fourth house changes from Venus in the chart in the sign of Aries (detriment), to Mars in Taurus (also in detriment). If this was a genuine natal chart the native would experience these changes in house rulership from one system to the other.

Likewise, Mars will hand over to Venus in the opposite tenth house, and this is a major shift in energies from one system to the other.

The exalted Sun in Aries directly benefits from the conversion, as it is now the ruler of the eighth house, and gets extra benefit by moving from the third house in Placidus to the angular fourth house in the whole sign chart.

Accidental Dignity and House Strength

In accordance with his predecessors, eleventh century polymath al-Biruni notes that a planet is accidentally dignified, that is, in a strong and dignified position when it is placed in an angular house.[160]

However, a planet suffers weakness if it is distant from the angles or succedent houses, that is, if it resides in a cadent house.

Fourth century astrologer Firmicus Maternus forgives the third and ninth house their cadent state because both houses favourably aspect the ascendant, and these are also places where the luminaries rejoice, the Sun in the ninth house, and the Moon in the third house, so it is hard to imagine how placement in these two cadent houses would produce a weakened planet.

The remaining two cadent houses, the sixth and twelfth house, are considered to be much worse because they are passive or feeble (no aspect to the ascendant) and debilitated (cadent).

Guido Bonatti writes two centuries after al-Biruni (sometime after 1282 CE) and his text is very clear on where he stands regarding the strength of the houses and their impact on the planets' ability to perform.

Bonatti says that whilst the four angles differ in strength among themselves, collectively they represent the stronger parts of the sky and when an angular planet is something's significator

"it promises the good, and it is said to further (the business)."[161]

The translator uses the word *"further"* in the sense of promoting, or advancing or facilitating the native's undertakings in some way.

The houses which immediately follow the angles are called the succedent houses and they are not as strong as the angles, being judged as half in strength by comparison to the angular house (with the exception of the eleventh house, the house of the Good Daemon).

Bonatti says a planet in a succedent house *"furthers less"* than if the same planet was angularly placed in the chart.

The remaining four houses are cadent from the angles (from *cadere, to fall*), and these 'falling' houses are extremely weak houses.

Bonatti states the cadent houses do not promise good, nor firmness, nor durability, or the prolongation of any matter (with the exception of the ninth house, the house of God).

When a planet is in a house cadent from an angle, *"it is said that the planet fails and is weak and useless."*[162]

Project Hindsight translator Robert Schmidt believes that a planet's placement in one of the three house classifications will affect the ability for that planet to focus on the task at hand.

That is, to concentrate its energies on the purpose of life as promised by the chart, and that angular planets are more effective in accomplishing the business of life.[163]

Firmicus Maternus says the angular houses, or *"four cardines (angles)"* are critical in directing the individual towards divine providence:

"We must always observe them carefully so that we may set forth the most correct revelation of the whole pattern of destiny."[164]

In practical terms, it seems that a planet's angularity keeps it on track through four points of the chart, and that its role in any one of these houses is to keep the native focused on the business of life, in order to fulfil their destiny.

Basically, first house, I can do this by my own actions;

> fourth house, I can benefit from the past and what the fourth house signifies, i.e. father, home, inheritance, family history, hidden treasure;

> seventh house, I can build strong alliances, marry well, form powerful business connections, and keep a cautious eye on my enemies and competitors;

> and tenth house, I can find my own destiny and become powerful in the public arena through my profession and my own actions in my career.

Robert Schmidt says that when a planet is found in a succedent house, it becomes distracted by other influences and therefore becomes temporarily side-tracked.

The succedent houses are the axis of the second and eighth house, and the axis of fifth and eleventh house.

The first of these two axis is passive, because neither house aspects the ascendant.

The second house is usually concerned with balancing finances and making sure that money earned exceeds money spent by the native.

The eighth house can bring money through the partner's finances, through legal or financial institutions, or by inheritance.

However, it can distract the native from the business of life, if money is gathered through the process of grief or separation, in the case of divorce settlements, and can be contentious if others believe they have rights to the deceased's fortune, or to the partnership's joint resources.

Readings from a variety of traditional authors tend to make the planet in a cadent house seem ineffective, weak or their power destroyed in some way, but it would be a mistake to underestimate a planet's ability to be totally engaged in the workings of the cadent houses.

Another term which Robert Schmidt uses for the cadent houses is that they are 'turning away' from life, and that in the case of the favourable cadent houses, it is a matter of the native's choice, rather than disconnecting circumstances which are beyond the native's control.

For instance, the ninth is the house of religion, foreign travel, fate, philosophy or divination and none of these topics strives to promote the interests of the individual, or to deliberately elevate them into the ranks of the powerful, as it would if the same planet was situated next door in the angular tenth house.

The ninth house is more concerned with being left alone to lose oneself in something of a higher principle and planets in the ninth may be ineffective in self-promotion or worldly acknowledgement, but they are not weak or ineffective when it comes to the individual's passion to pursue these interests.

Likewise, some of the most talented individuals have planets in the third house, particularly when these planets aspect other planets in the first sign (by sextile), or a Midheaven degree in the eleventh house (by trine), or a Midheaven degree in the ninth house (by opposition).

Third house choices to turn away from life occur when a skill or passion distracts the native and time melts away without the individual realising that they have stepped away from everyday life for a period of time.

Examples such as playing a beloved musical instrument, practising a skill that envelopes the mind, reading an astrology chart, playing games on the computer – all skills which take time and are often solitary in nature, but are also pleasurable escapes to the cadent third house.

There are times when third house planets distract from life in a less positive way, but they seem to be when other houses are also activated.

An accident or an illness can damage or restrict the individual's physical skills and planets in the third house, and the third house lord, will be required to re-learn or adapt those skills which were lost, in order for the individual to rejoin the flow of life.

A planet in the sixth or twelfth house may be frustrated with its poor positioning, but it is not useless or unproductive when it comes to creating trouble, distress or hidden obstacles.

The Latin name for the sixth house is *Mala Fortuna,* Bad Luck, and the reason that Mars is in its joy here is the fact that it can accelerate from mischief-causing irritation to wreaking havoc within a frighteningly short period of time.

But the same Mars can trine planets in the tenth sign, or even the Midheaven, and this is hardly a weakened Mars.

A more accurate interpretation for the sixth and twelfth house may be that this axis describes cadent as 'falling away' from life because of bad fortune or physical or mental illness or agitation.

The axis which suffers the greatest from its blindness to the ascendant are houses of fear, isolation, danger, sorrow or debility, and rarely are they houses that we choose to enter voluntarily.

Robert Schmidt is reported as saying that a planet in a cadent house is predominantly directed away from the business of the life agenda, and this is likely to be true as misery, heartache, pain or great misfortune separates us from others and the sense of falling into a terrible dark

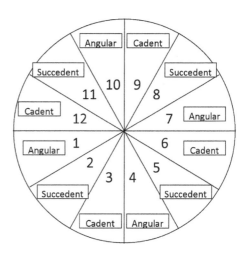

Fig. 91 The Strength of the Houses: Angular, Succedent and Cadent Houses

place takes effort to re-engage with the world around us.

Example Charts: Planets' Changing Houses

In the Example Chart the changes in the planets' house positions show improvement for six of the seven planets.

Only Saturn is weakened by position having moved from the eleventh house to the twelfth, but it will gain accidental dignity as the twelfth house is the house of its joy.

Jupiter has moved forward by two houses from the passive eighth house to the elevated angular tenth house.

A planet's movement by two houses is not unknown and in this chart Jupiter is not the only planet to entirely skip a house when it moves forward.

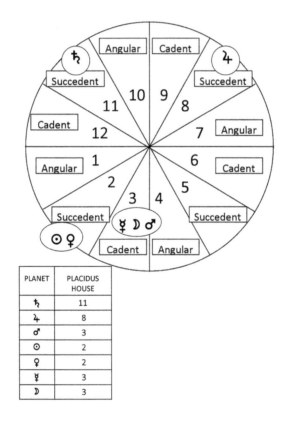

Fig. 92 ***Placidus System***
Planets in the EXAMPLE CHART

Mars moves from the third to the fifth house, and the Sun and Venus move together from the passive second house in the quadrant-style to the angular fourth house in the whole sign chart.

The Moon moves from the cadent third house (house of its joy) to the succedent fifth house, gaining in strength but losing accidental dignity.

Mercury has moved forward by one house and is no longer cadent in the third house, but instead is situated in the angular fourth house.

It is unusual to see all seven planets move houses by changing systems but as the example shows, it is possible.

At the other end of the scale, there are times when the planets' house positions do not alter with Whole Sign and this can be as much a statement about the person as when movement is found between the houses.

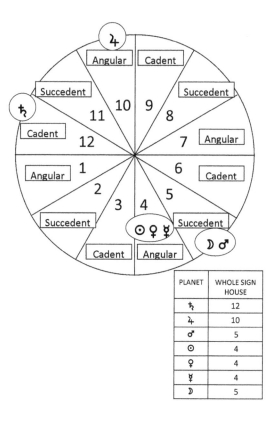

PLANET	WHOLE SIGN HOUSE
♄	12
♃	10
♂	5
☉	4
♀	4
☿	4
☽	5

Fig. 93
Whole Sign Movement
Planets in the EXAMPLE CHART

	PLACIDUS SYSTEM		DIFFERENCES	PLANET	WHOLE SIGN SYSTEM	
PLANET	HOUSE	STRENGTH		PLANET	HOUSE	STRENGTH
♄	11	Succedent	Worse	♄	12	Cadent
♃	8	Succedent	Improved	♃	10	Angular
♂	3	Cadent	Improved	♂	5	Succedent
☉	2	Succedent	Improved	☉	4	Angular
♀	2	Succedent	Improved	♀	4	Angular
☿	3	Cadent	Improved	☿	4	Angular
☽	3	Cadent	Improved	☽	5	Succedent

Fig. 94 EXAMPLE CHART: 30th March 2017
Changes in the Planets' Positions

A Planet's Comfort: Houses in Light or Darkness

"I live and love in God's peculiar light."

Michelangelo

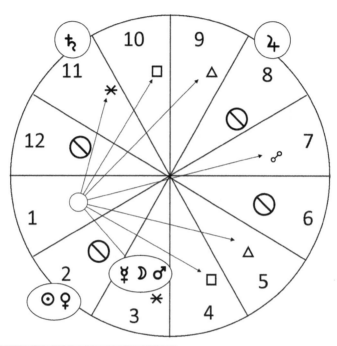

PLANET	PLACIDUS HOUSE	ACTIVE/PASSIVE
♄	11	Harmonious
♃	8	Passive
♂	3	Harmonious
☉	2	Passive
♀	2	Passive
☿	3	Harmonious
☽	3	Harmonious

Fig. 95 ***Placidus Chart***

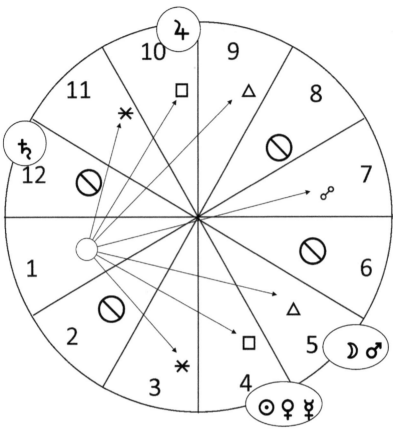

PLANET	WHOLE SIGN HOUSE	ACTIVE/PASSIVE
♄	12	Passive, Debilitated
♃	10	Cardinal Point
♂	5	Harmonious
☉	4	Cardinal Point
♀	4	Cardinal Point
☿	4	Cardinal Point
☽	5	Harmonious

Fig. 96 **Whole Sign Chart**

| PLANET | PLACIDUS SYSTEM | | DIFFERENCES | | WHOLE SIGN SYSTEM | |
	HOUSE	ACTIVE/PASSIVE		PLANET	HOUSE	ACTIVE/PASSIVE
♄	11	Harmonious	*Worse*	♄	12	Passive, Debilitated
♃	8	Passive	*Improved*	♃	10	Cardinal Point
♂	3	Harmonious	*Same*	♂	5	Harmonious
☉	2	Passive	*Improved*	☉	4	Cardinal Point
♀	2	Passive	*Improved*	♀	4	Cardinal Point
☿	3	Harmonious	*Improved*	☿	4	Cardinal Point
☽	3	Harmonious	*Same*	☽	5	Harmonious

Fig. 97 EXAMPLE CHART: 30th March 2017
Table of the Movement of the Planets

The Table *(Fig. 97)* shows the effect on the planets by converting the chart from Placidus to Whole Sign.

Saturn moves from the illuminated eleventh house to the dark house of the twelfth where it supposedly rejoices according to the accidental dignity known as 'the joys'.

Jupiter's move is more successful, moving from the passive eighth house to be elevated in the tenth sign where it opposes fourth house planets Sun, Venus and Mercury in the whole sign chart.

Mars and the Moon have retained their light from the ascendant even though they have moved two houses from the cadent third house (Moon's house of joy) to the succedent fifth house which has an earth sign on the cusp, and is therefore a match in element for the Capricorn sign on the chart's ascendant.

Putting it Together Planet by Planet

"There is a crack in everything, that's how the light gets in."

Leonard Cohen

| PLANET | PLACIDUS SYSTEM | | DIFFERENCES | PLANET | WHOLE SIGN SYSTEM | |
	HOUSE	STRENGTH			HOUSE	STRENGTH
♄ Ruling 1st	11	Succedent Harmonious (Light)	*Worse But in its Joy*	♄ Ruling 1st, 2nd	12	Cadent Passive (Dark) Debilitated
♃ Ruling 2nd, 11th, 12th	8	Succedent Passive (Dark)	*Improved*	♃ Ruling 3rd, 12th	10	Angular Cardinal Active (Light)
♂ Ruling 3rd, 10th	3	Cadent Harmonious (Light)	*Improved*	♂ Ruling 4th, 11th	5	Succedent Harmonious Active (Light)
☉ No Rulership	2	Succedent Passive (Dark)	*Improved*	☉ Ruling 8th	4	Angular Cardinal Active (Light)
♀ Ruling 4th, 9th	2	Succedent Passive (Dark)	*Improved*	♀ Ruling 5th, 10th	4	Angular Cardinal Active (Light)
☿ Ruling 5th, 6th, 8th	3	Cadent Harmonious (Light)	*Improved*	☿ Ruling 6th, 9th	4	Angular Cardinal Active (Light)
☽ Ruling 7th	3	Cadent Harmonious (Light)	*Improved*	☽ Ruling 7th	5	Succedent Harmonious Active (Light)

Fig. 98 EXAMPLE CHART: 30th March 2017
Changes to the Planets' Strengths using Whole Signs

The final Table *(Fig. 98)* collates the material from the previous diagrams and smaller tables so that a full analysis of the two charts can be examined by the reader.

The amount of information gathered can feel overwhelming in this larger table but the process and methods which I have used to find and sort the data can be reproduced in the comparisons for any chart converted from the quadrant-style chart to the whole sign chart.

The chart of Sarah Ferguson is used as an example of dual-chart delineation at the end of the chapter and her natal chart has been cast in both the Placidus house system and the Whole Sign house system.

The Table for the Example Chart *(Fig. 98)* has been reproduced and adapted to suit variances in signs, house cusps and planets in Sarah's natal chart and collated in her Composite Table *(Fig. 115).*

The Mid-Heaven: A Point, Not A House Cusp

The Whole Sign system can create a degree of confusion when the Midheaven is no longer the cusp of the tenth house, and instead, has the potential to land as a point, rather than as a division of houses at the top of the quadrant-style chart.

This will happen with all disassociate Crosses of Matter, and perhaps this is the reason why some astrologers are unwilling to embrace the Whole Sign system, or to include it in their evaluation of the chart.

The tenth house and the Midheaven are very similar in their significations, with the most notable exception being the description of mother, who is definitely tenth house, but is not the Midheaven.

Glory, distinction, honours, reputation, public status, profession, and figures of authority are all significations shared by the tenth house and the Midheaven, but quadrant-style systems promote the *Medium Coeli* (the Latin term meaning 'middle of the skies') which is also known as the MC, as a house cusp, whilst Whole Sign accentuates the difference between an astronomical point, and the tenth sign from the ascendant, in the zodiacal order of the signs.

The idea that the tenth house is the place where one's action culminate, or is the final stage of a process appears in Hellenistic astrology, as Valens uses this method in his chart delineations, and Dorotheus applies the same principle to his chapter on quartile (square) aspects when the planet to the right 'overcomes' the planet to the left.[165]

In the Moon's phases, ten signs away from the Sun marks the waning square, the last opportunity to squeeze the best from the lunation cycle, and the final station of importance or accumulated knowledge before the decrease and death of the cycle, and the commencement of a new cycle.

The following Table *(Fig. 99)* is a guideline for where the astrologer might begin when dealing with this particular quandary when the Midheaven becomes a zodiacal degree, rather than the cusp of the tenth house.

It is worth mentioning that when the Midheaven is not situated in the tenth sign, there will be two ruling planets which become the planetary representatives for honours and public distinctions, one planet ruling the tenth sign, and another planet ruling the Midheaven (with the exception of Saturn), and it will require a full examination of both planets' condition to determine the nature and success of the profession.

Both planets will be equally responsible and there can be times when the native favours one type of career over another in their lives due to the differences in the two ruling planets.

When the Midheaven becomes a degree within a house, it works a little like a planet, in that when it moves position in the shift from one system to another, it can potentially move to a succedent or a cadent house, and this needs to be taken into account in the chart's delineation.

The final Table in Fig. 99 provides suggestions on the Midheaven moving to the twelfth house, and whilst this is unlikely, it is not an impossible scenario.

At the current moment, the second Royal in succession to the English throne is Prince William of Wales, who was born at the summer solstice (and on a lunar eclipse), and his chart is a perfect example of consecutive signs for the two most important points in the chart.

His Ascendant is in late degrees of Sagittarius, and his Midheaven is situated in his Whole Sign twelfth house in early degrees of the previous sign of Scorpio.[166]

When delineating a chart for someone who has their Midheaven contained within the twelfth house, it is generally considered to indicate a person who has reclusive habits or is old-fashioned or unwilling to socialize and they would prefer a simpler, quieter and more private lifestyle.

This option is not available for Prince William, but he is still a young man with a long way to go in life, and it will be interesting to observe his destiny, and the fate of the British monarchy, from an astrological point of view.

Currently, his MC's twelfth house involvement is shown by his desire to illuminate mental health issues in youth and the military, and to bring them out from the collective's twelfth house by removing the social stigma which accompanies this important topic.

MC in the 8th H From angular to passive succedent (dark) house	The aspirations become hidden, confused, or a source of constant drama. Careers can be involved with large money transactions, public funds or insurance, or in crisis management. Counselling or social welfare can be other areas of expertise or training.
MC in the 9th H From angular to cadent (light) house	The pressure to succeed or stay on top can be alleviated as the aspect between the ascendant and the house moves from a square to a trine. The choice is available to remove oneself from public life to pursue further study, or to take time off for long periods of travel for volunteering, work or pilgrimage. Development of spiritual, personal, philosophical interests is often a strong motivation for the native with the MC in 9th house.
MC in the 10th H Stays angular, active in cardinal (light) house	Efforts to gain recognition or receive acknowledgement are well planned, focused and deliberate. The individual's drive is even more prominent if the degree of the MC is closely aspected to the Ascendant by a 90° square. When the MC is in 10th house the signs are identical : the same planet rules both 10th house and the MC. The ruling planet's condition is critical to the native's reputation, life goals and career.

MC in the 11th H From angular to succedent (light) house	The MC appears to be on the rise, rather than at the place of culmination, or having passed the zenith (9thMC). The desire for advancement is fed by hopes and dreams of the future. Mentors and social connection are important to achieve success but there can be a sense of frustration in feeling that life's apex keeps constantly slipping beyond their reach. Often the native's focus or commitment keeps changing or success is difficult to maintain or fully satisfy the native's ideals or expectations.
MC in the 12th H From angular to passive debilitated (dark) house	Movement from 10th to 12th can indicate a fall from grace or imprisonment, removal due to physical, emotional or mental infirmities as darkness is never far removed from the concept of the MC. The desire to distance oneself from public scrutiny or fear of judgement or condemnation is strong. Having to deal with projection, false representation or hidden enemies can be an indicator of the 12th house MC. Self-identification with those in pain, invisible, or caught in a position too difficult for the world to understand is integral to the native's reputation, popularity, or goals in life.

Fig. 99 The Midheaven's appearance in the different houses from Eighth House to Twelfth House

Why Consult Using Dual-Chart Delineation?

There is no doubt that there is a degree of extra work involved in studying the chart differences between two unrelated house systems.

Not only does the look of the chart change when it is converted into Whole Sign, it also alters the reader's mind-set when they change from one system to the other.

It takes some time and practice to accommodate these alterations, which affect both delineation and the philosophy behind the chart, but I believe it is worth the effort.

The older system of Whole Sign has been discarded for many years, perhaps because it was considered too simple, or too old-fashioned, or just no longer relevant to the philosophical development in astrology as astrologers became more scientific in their thoughts, and in the precision of their mathematical calculations.

The Placidean system is the most widely used in modern English astrological circles mainly because most of the available Table of Houses from the 19th century used Placidus, and although the system is accredited to the 17th century astrologer Placidus di Tito, it is believed to be much older, having derived from the tables of 8th century Arabian astrologer ben Djabir (Albategnius System).[167]

My recommendation to use them as complementary systems can best be summed up in the following way.

When I was a child and play was getting out of hand between my siblings and myself, my mother would say, *"What starts in nonsense, ends in tears"*.

I gave the same warning when I became a parent, and I suspect my children will do the same as their own families grow.

It has occurred to me over the years that life in general can be summed up by this phrase.

The tomfoolery of flirting creates the tears of love when relationships develop, and sometimes the hanky-panky of sex brings conception which ends in tears of joy at the birth of a child.

The shenanigans of childhood ends in the tears brought on by adulthood, and the bizarre twists and turns of life ultimately result in the tears of loss, grief and death.

"What starts in nonsense, ends in tears" – but there are both joyous tears and tears borne of heartache.

The quadrant-style charts are uneven, untidy, and often non-compliant with the archetypal ideas of aspectual sign relationship, but I would not recommend completely abandoning them.

The quadrant chart is often nonsensical when houses on one side of the chart are huge and the other side's houses are tiny by comparison, but it is a good place to start.

The Whole Sign chart may well end in tears, but there are good tears and there are bad tears.

Tears of frustration and anger when things do not eventuate in the way they were 'promised' in the Placidus chart.

Tears of relief when planets are reprieved from terrible situations, tears of triumph when things actually do work out, and tears of thankfulness when a deeper level of self-acceptance is possible when the two charts come together beautifully to explain our own tiny universe.

Planets Moving Forwards

The following flowcharts *(Figs. 100 – 108)* illustrate the differences which occur when the chart is converted from one system to the other.

In most cases the planet moves forward by one house and this creates movement from angular to succedent house, succedent to cadent house, and cadent to angular house.

However, it is possible for a planet to move forward by two houses when the shift is made from a quadrant-style chart to a whole sign chart.

In the Example Chart shown above Jupiter moved forward from eighth house to become angular in the tenth because it was found in Libra, the tenth sign from Capricorn, the sign on the Ascendant.

Likewise, both the Sun and Venus are in the sign of Aries, which is four signs from Capricorn, and whilst the extended first house in Placidus placed the conjunction in the second house, the two planets moved forwards two houses to the fourth house in Whole Sign.

Sarah Ferguson's natal Moon also experiences the movement over two houses as her Aries Moon is located in the fourth house in the Placidus chart but moves to the sixth house in the whole sign chart.

The movement of two houses means that a planet in a quadrant-style angular house loses considerable strength by moving to a cadent house in the whole sign chart, a planet in a succedent house moves forward two houses to find itself situated now in an angular house by whole sign methods, and a cadent planet jumps the angular position to settle into a succedent house by whole sign.

It should be noted that whilst a cadent planet can become angular, it will never cross the ascendant to move from twelfth house to second house, nor can a planet straddle the descendant by moving forwards from the sixth house to the eighth house, which is probably just as well since it would mean a move from the house of illness (6th house) to the house of death (8th house).

But this is an impossibility, as the ascendant to descendant axis is the horizon line which sets the entire chart, and planets cannot cross this line by changing house system.

Planets Moving Backwards

"That's the effect of living backwards, it always makes one a little giddy at first," the Queen said kindly, "- but there's one great advantage in it, that one's memory works both ways."

Lewis Carroll, *Through the Looking Glass*

It is unusual for a planet to move back into the previous house when moving from quadrant-style to Whole Sign house system, but it is possible.

In fact, when the Example Chart (30th March 2017) was entered into the computer I moved it forwards at two hourly intervals throughout the day to examine the changes to cusps and to the planets' house positions.

In the 2:00pm chart on the same day Mercury (28degs. Aries) moved back from the tenth house to the ninth house.

In the 4:00pm chart set two hours later Mercury once more moved backwards in the whole sign chart, this time from the ninth to the eighth house.

In most cases, the planet which moves back into a house is found to be in the late degrees of a sign and has just crept into the following house because its degrees exceed the degrees on the house cusp of a quadrant-style house.

When the adjustment to Whole Sign occurs the planet is pulled back into the house which is identical to its own zodiac sign.

Again, two scenarios are not possible: a planet cannot move backwards across the horizon line and thankfully a first house planet cannot move backwards to the twelfth house or a seventh house planet move backwards over the horizon to the cadent sixth house.

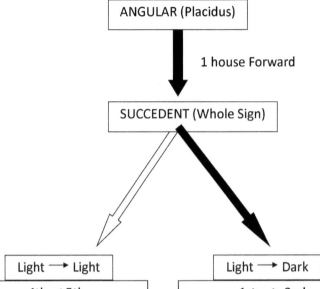

Fig. 100 Angular to Succedent: Moving One House Forward

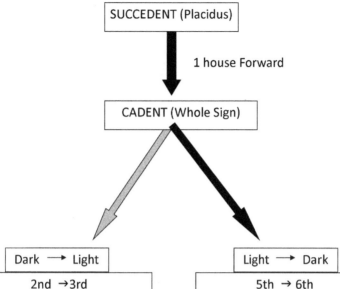

SUCCEDENT (Placidus)

1 house Forward

CADENT (Whole Sign)

Dark → Light

2nd → 3rd
Improvement as planet moves into the light. Link between money and physical skills, early education, siblings, short journeys. Sense of luck or good connections when it comes to making money.

8th → 9th
Planet gets some relief from dark house of crisis, disruption or endings. Moving to good aspect to Ascendant gives a basis of meaning, or a philosophical or spiritual meaning to 8th house experiences. New pathways or opportunities can come from an unexpected ending. Whole Sign allows a planet with sign connection to the ascendant to bring benefit from pain or loss.

Light → Dark

5th → 6th
Planet loses strength moving from a succedent house of light to a dark cadent house. What appears as a benefit has a shadow side. There are strings attached in the form of obligations, hard work or unforeseen complications. Often difficult to get the full joy or pleasure from 5th house; children create toil or poor health, leisure is difficult to gain or enjoy due to commitments or poor timing or work deadlines.

11th → 12th
Hopes turn into disappointments, advantages gained do not bring the benefits promised or are not held long-term. Insecurities, fears and worry mar the hopes and dreams of the house of the Good Daemon. Pull between sociability and privacy

Fig. 101 Succedent to Cadent: Moving One House Forward

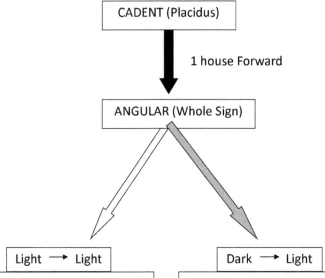

CADENT (Placidus)

1 house Forward

ANGULAR (Whole Sign)

Light ⟶ Light

Dark ⟶ Light

3rd →4th
The skills developed in a good cadent house become orderly, controlled or consistent when the planet moves to angularity. The career or ambitions profit from the planet as it gains vigour, focus or family support. Siblings and family connections are functional or useful and either provide advantage, or become the motivation to succeed. Written communication is readily broadcast and can be damaging ; care needs to be taken depending on nature of the planet.

9th →10th
This can feel like second chances, or a sense of karma at play, with this movement. The desire or conviction to grow through new experiences such as travel, education, or philosophy brings opportunities for leadership, career advantages or public acclaim.

6th → 7th
The movement from dark cadent to angular shows the planet's capacity to resist the pressure to buckle under the misfortunes of life. Complete recovery from illness or accident is not guaranteed, but the native feels they have an inner resolve, or makes the ascendant more determined to overcome opposition (7th), rather than being tormented by events beyond personal control (6th).

12th →1st
A planet appearing hidden or power- less in the 12th gains the benefit of light and clarity when it moves to the 1st house. Its aspirations solidify but its motivation or conduct can come under scrutiny with visibility as the individual finds themselves constantly explaining their actions or motives. Pull between solitude and attention.

Fig. 102 Cadent to Angular: Moving One House Forward

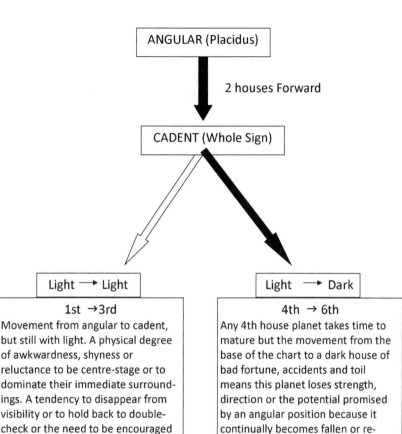

Fig. 103 Angular to Cadent: Moving Two Houses Forward

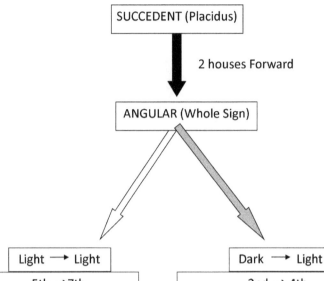

SUCCEDENT (Placidus)

2 houses Forward

ANGULAR (Whole Sign)

Light → Light

5th → 7th
Planet gains purpose or direction
from quadrant-style to whole
sign improvement. The potential
for long-term benefit is increased
and links between the pleasures
and good fortune promised by
the 5th house can strengthen or
create bonds in the 7th house.

11th → 1st
A planet moving from the house
of the Good Daemon to the first
house brings direct advantage or
benefit to the native. The ability
to act on good advice or the
goodwill of others is the reaping
of rewards so long as the original
source from the eleventh house
is acknowledged by the recipient.
However, pride, vanity or poor
behaviour can destroy the good
connection.

Dark → Light

2nd → 4th
The change in house systems links the
two money houses; moveable wealth
(2) and immovable wealth in the form
of real estate or inheritance from the
father or family property (4). Angularity
improves the planet's chances of staying
focussed on the business of life. A good
income from family business is possible,
depending on the planet, and advancement in career (4th/10th axis) can
improve finances for the individual.

8th → 10th
A planet can become easier to manage
when elevation and illumination occurs
with the movement of house systems.
Tenth sign angularity means the planet
gains strength and power from a source
which was otherwise difficult or painful.
The insight gained from a frightening
experience (8th) can add the wisdom or
compassion needed to lead others.

Fig. 104 Succedent to Angular : Moving Two Houses Forward

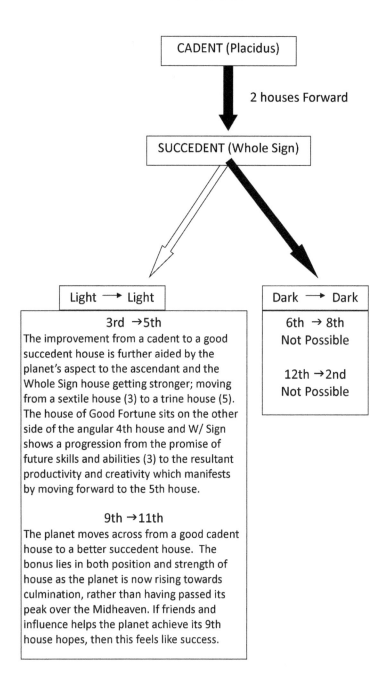

CADENT (Placidus)

2 houses Forward

SUCCEDENT (Whole Sign)

Light ⟶ Light

3rd ⟶5th
The improvement from a cadent to a good
succedent house is further aided by the
planet's aspect to the ascendant and the
Whole Sign house getting stronger; moving
from a sextile house (3) to a trine house (5).
The house of Good Fortune sits on the other
side of the angular 4th house and W/ Sign
shows a progression from the promise of
future skills and abilities (3) to the resultant
productivity and creativity which manifests
by moving forward to the 5th house.

9th ⟶11th
The planet moves across from a good cadent
house to a better succedent house. The
bonus lies in both position and strength of
house as the planet is now rising towards
culmination, rather than having passed its
peak over the Midheaven. If friends and
influence helps the planet achieve its 9th
house hopes, then this feels like success.

Dark ⟶ Dark

6th → 8th
Not Possible

12th →2nd
Not Possible

Fig. 105 Cadent to Succedent: Moving Two Houses Forward
(Impossible to Cross Ascendant/Descendant Horizon)

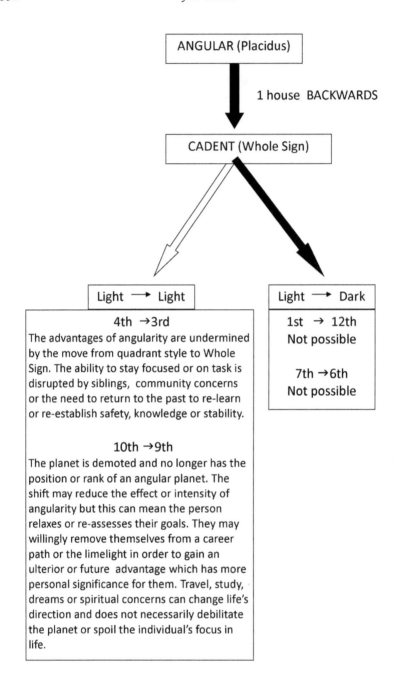

*Fig. 106 Angular to Cadent: Moving One House Backwards
(Impossible to Cross Ascendant/Descendant Horizon)*

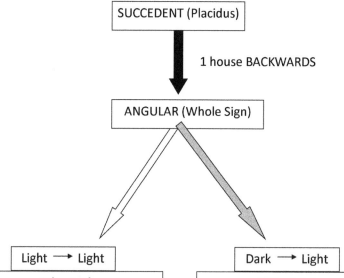

SUCCEDENT (Placidus)

1 house BACKWARDS

ANGULAR (Whole Sign)

Light ⟶ Light

5th →4th
The movement cements the relationship between children and home or
family interests. The leisure, creativity
or good fortune of the 5th can be
productive or valuable if effort and
energy is directed into the opposition
between the 4th and the 10th houses.

11th →10th
The planet appears to rise into the
highest powerful angular house. The
movement between the two houses
elevates hopes and dreams (11) into
the realm of manifestation (10). Good
social or business connections lift the
native to the possibility of reaching
their potential. Depending on the
planet, the movement can cause
confusion between social and
professional interests and resentment
or accusations of being ruthless or
cold can be the result.

Dark ⟶ Light

2nd → 1st
Being the instigator of one's wealth
means the native is resourceful or
clever in taking opportunities and
turning them to financial advantage.
The planet's condition will indicate
if this generates a good result, or if
it creates trouble or frustration.

8th →7th
The planet moving from the dark
succedent house to the house in
the west indicates that it is closer to
setting and although the planet
gains angularity, there may not be
great benefits to this change in
house placement. The planet's sign
will be in opposition to the ascendant and this can be evidence of
others' obstruction to the native's
plans. Legal or financial advice
needs to be treated with care in this
tricky combination .

Fig. 107 Succedent to Angular: Moving One House Backwards

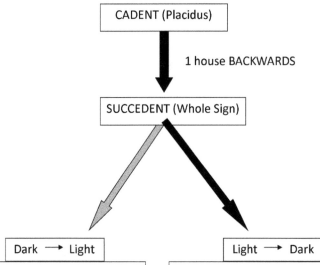

CADENT (Placidus)

1 house BACKWARDS

SUCCEDENT (Whole Sign)

Dark → Light	Light → Dark
6th →5th	**3rd → 2nd**
The move brings some relief for a planet that would otherwise have been confined to a dark and difficult house. The switch back to a house with light means the planet's sign is trine to the ascendant's sign so it can create a situation which begins by looking bleak, but in fact, brings a reprieve or blessing as a result of a poor or frightening experience.	This backward movement removes the planet from light and places it in the house of financial concerns. One favourable outcome can become a link between physical skills and the ability to make money from them.
	However, as the movement is backwards there can be debt rather than financial gain from the connection between siblings, the written word, short journeys or community projects.
12th →11th	**9th →8th**
A planet that looks lost in what is considered to be the worst house rises instead to take its place in a fortunate house. Adversity becomes strength when this happens, and empathy, understanding or insight can instigate a desire to take action on behalf of others who are ignored, fallen, or less fortunate in life.	The planet is inconjunct to the Ascendant and the light which it gained in quadrant style is extinguished by Whole Sign. Worries, drama, endings, money issues beset a planet which is impaired by the move. What looks promising—travel, study, beliefs, new experiences— turns expensive, dangerous or 'murky' in some way.

Fig. 108 Cadent to Succedent: Moving One House Backwards

One Example of Dual-Chart Delineation
Sarah Ferguson: The Logistics

Sarah Ferguson is a British writer, charity patron, public speaker, film producer and television personality.

She is the former wife of Prince Andrew, Duke of York, the second son of Queen Elizabeth II and Prince Philip, Duke of Edinburgh, and as such has maintained her royal title as Duchess of York.

In Sarah's chart, all ten planets, plus her Nodal Axis, have changed position in the movement from Placidus to the Whole Sign house system.

Most have moved forwards by one house, with the exception of the Moon and South Node which together will move two houses, from the fourth to the sixth house, whilst the opposing North Node moves from the tenth to the twelfth house in her Whole Sign chart.

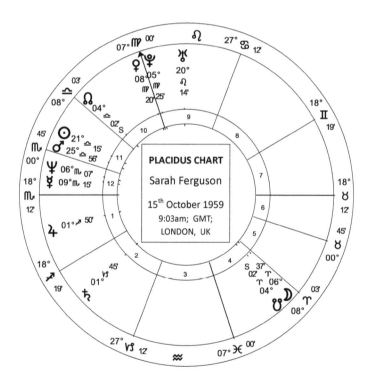

*Fig. 109 Sarah Ferguson, **Placidus Chart***

Technically, Pluto is placed in the ninth house and should be
considered to have moved forward two houses to the eleventh, but as
it is less than two degrees from the Midheaven, it would normally be
considered as angular in the tenth house, rather than residing in the
cadent ninth house of the Placidus chart.

Sarah's Midheaven has moved forward one house, and has moved
from the cusp of the Placidus tenth house it now resides in her eleventh
house in her whole sign chart.

Venus and Pluto will remain conjunct the Midheaven regardless of
the house system changes, but are now also located in the house of friends.

In the whole sign chart the Ascendant is always the first sign and
becomes a point in the first house, and as both Neptune and Mercury are
situated in the same sign as the Ascendant, they too will move to the first
house even though they took a twelfth house position in her Placidus chart.

Two planets have essential dignity, Jupiter in Sagittarius and Saturn
in Capricorn, and both planets will move to the houses they rule in
Whole Sign as Jupiter moves to the second house, and Saturn moves
forward to the third house.

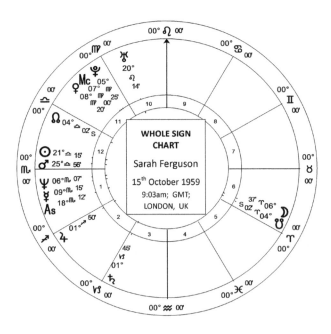

Fig. 110 Sarah Ferguson, **Whole Sign Chart**

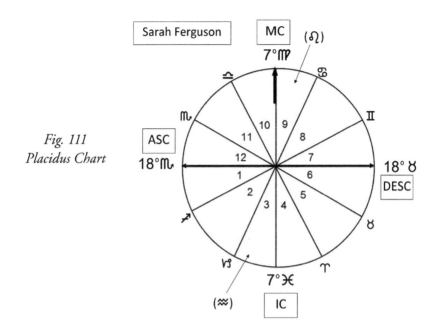

Fig. 111
Placidus Chart

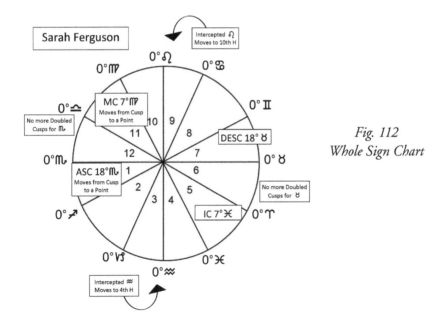

Fig. 112
Whole Sign Chart

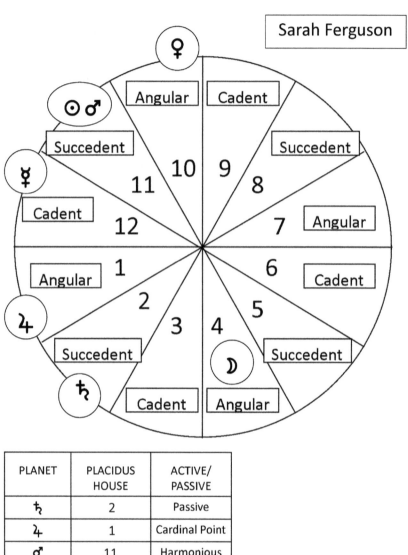

PLANET	PLACIDUS HOUSE	ACTIVE/ PASSIVE
♄	2	Passive
♃	1	Cardinal Point
♂	11	Harmonious
☉	11	Harmonious
♀	10	Cardinal Point
☿	12	Debilitated
☽	4	Cardinal Point

Fig. 113 Sarah's Planets in the Placidus Chart

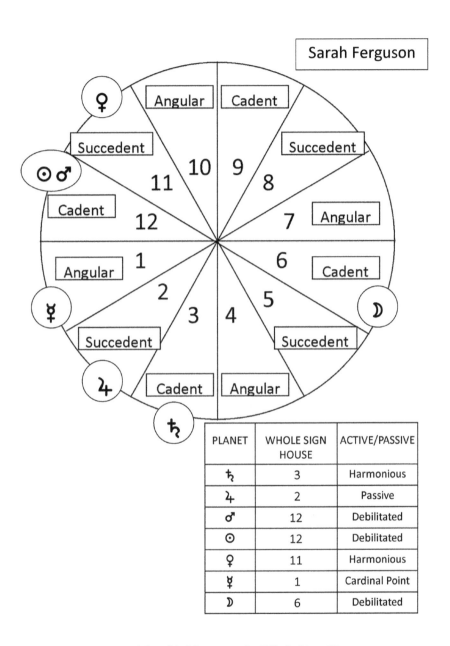

PLANET	WHOLE SIGN HOUSE	ACTIVE/PASSIVE
♄	3	Harmonious
♃	2	Passive
♂	12	Debilitated
☉	12	Debilitated
♀	11	Harmonious
☿	1	Cardinal Point
☽	6	Debilitated

Fig. 114 Sarah's Planets in the Whole Sign Chart

SARAH FERGUSON	PLACIDUS SYSTEM		DIFFERENCES	SARAH FERGUSON	WHOLE SIGN SYSTEM	
PLANET	HOUSE	STRENGTH		PLANET	HOUSE	STRENGTH
♄ Ruling 3rd	2	Succedent Passive (Dark)	Improved	♄ Ruling 3rd, 4th H	3	Cadent Harmonious (Light)
♃ Ruling 2nd, 4th	1	Angular Cardinal Active (Light)	Worse	♃ Ruling 2nd, 5th H	2	Succedent Passive (Dark)
♂ Ruling 1st, 5th, 12th	11	Succedent Harmonious (Light)	Worse	♂ Ruling 1st, 6th H	12	Cadent Debilitated Passive (Dark)
☉ No Rulership	11	Succedent Harmonious (Light)	Worse	☉ Ruling 10th	12	Cadent Debilitated Passive (Dark)
♀ Ruling 6th, 7th, 11th	10	Angular Cardinal Active (Light)	Worse	♀ Ruling 7th, 12th H	11	Succedent Harmonious (Light)
☿ Ruling 8th, 10th	12	Cadent Debilitated Passive (Dark)	Improved In its Joy	☿ Ruling 8th, 11th H	1	Angular Cardinal Active (Light)
☽ Ruling 9th	4	Angular Cardinal Active (Light)	Worse	☽ Ruling 9th	6	Cadent Debilitated Passive (Dark)

Fig. 115 Composite Table for Sarah Ferguson Placidus and Whole Sign Charts

SARAH FERGUSON	PLACIDUS SYSTEM		*DIFFERENCES*	SARAH FERGUSON	WHOLE SIGN SYSTEM	
NODE/ PLANET	HOUSE	STRENGTH		NODE/ PLANET	HOUSE	STRENGTH
☋ No Rulership	4	Angular Cardinal Active (Light)	*Worse*	☋	6	Cadent Debilitated Passive (Dark)
☊ No Rulership	10	Angular Cardinal Active (Light)	*Worse*	☊	12	Cadent Debilitated Passive (Dark)
♅ No Rulership	9	Cadent Harmonious (Light)	*Improved*	♅	10	Angular Cardinal Active (Light)
♆ No Rulership	12	Cadent Debilitated Passive (Dark)	*Improved*	♆	1	Angular Cardinal Active (Light)
♇ No Rulership	9 (♂ MC)	Cadent Harmonious (Light)	*Improved*	♇	11	Succedent Harmonious (Light)

Fig. 116 Nodes and Outer Planets for Sarah Ferguson's Placidus and Whole Sign Charts

Working With Two House Systems
Sarah Ferguson: The Delineation

When Sarah married Prince Andrew in July 1986 she was considered to be a welcome addition to the conservative British royals, given that she had a lineage tracing back to the illegitimate child of King Charles II.

Prince Philip was especially enamoured with Sarah.

Unlike her shy sister-in-law Diana, Sarah had experience in the real world in publishing and public relations, and even the fact that she had lived with former boyfriend racing-driver Paddy McNally, did not dampen the royals' enthusiasm for what they believed would be a 'modern' princess.

The Luminaries: A Good Place to Start

Sarah's chart is diurnal (9:03am, Sun above the horizon) which makes the Sun the chart's main luminary.

The Sun's condition is not good, given that it is in the sign of its fall, Libra, and is conjunct the nocturnal malefic, Mars, which is also not in great condition in the sign of its detriment.

Both planets are disposited by Venus, again, not great, as it is another nocturnal planet out of sect in the sign of its fall, Virgo.

Even though the significant planets, Sun, Mars and Venus, are all situated in signs not to their liking, all three planets are powerfully placed in the Placidus chart.

Sun and Mars are in the beneficial eleventh house, and whilst Mars rules the Ascendant and Sarah's flaming red hair was part of her physical appeal, the Sun's playful antics are somewhat concealed by its rulership sign (Leo) being intercepted in the ninth house.

Venus is conjunct the Midheaven with Pluto and enjoys the angularity and elevation of the tenth house, and indeed, one year after the marriage took place, the press were still singing Sarah's praises.

During this time Sarah gained favourable comparisons between herself and Princess Diana, who had been married to Prince Charles for seven years by then, and the press were beginning to notice the cracks in the longer, more significant, royal marriage.

Sarah was being touted as earthy, lovable *"and far better suited to a royal role than the Princess"*[168] whilst Diana was described in the same article as frosty, complicated and lacking self-control beneath her elegant surface.

By the end of 1987 the press and public had turned against Sarah after she was one of four royals to appear in Prince Edward's ill-judged charity game-show *It's a Royalty Knockout*.

In that moment Sarah went from being *"acceptably unconventional to entirely unacceptable"*[169] and the royal commentators became increasingly vindictive towards her over the next few years.

One paper, *The Daily Mail*, went so far as to call Sarah "the most reviled woman in Britain".

She was constantly attacked and criticised for her gain in weight, reaching a climax when the English press cruelly dubbed Sarah "The Duchess of Pork" and competed amongst themselves to be the one to publish the most unflattering image of the Duchess.

The conversion of Sarah's Placidus chart to Whole Sign begins to support the astrological reasoning behind her downfall from beloved royal to a figure ripe for public ridicule.

Suddenly, the Libran Sun and Mars slip from the protective shield of the eleventh house's Good Daemon into the Whole Sign passive and debilitated twelfth, the house of hidden enemies and a house of sorrow, isolation and imprisonment.

In the Whole Sign chart Leo becomes the tenth house cusp as it is ten signs from the Ascendant's Scorpio.

A twelfth house Sun (in fall) ruling the most elevated house will turn public opinion against any individual, especially when Mars, the chart's Ascendant lord is debilitated in Libra and joins the Sun in the twelfth house of the whole sign chart.

The Venus/Pluto conjunction on the MC loses its angularity in the shift in house systems, and falls into the eleventh house.

With time, the press and public lost patience with the two royal brides, and the previous harmless antics of Sarah and Diana came under fire and their undignified manner, especially when they were in each other's company, became the behaviour of two spoilt and privileged females.

Sarah and Diana had known each other since they were 14 years old, and in fact, Sarah was only twenty months older than Diana.

They appeared to share a close friendship, but Sarah's boisterous nature fed Diana's growing rebelliousness, and Diana was caught out performing silly practical jokes, such as dressing up as a policewoman to gatecrash Andrew's stag party and wearing false breasts at a party with no thought to what repercussions her actions may have on the Royal Family.

Influenced by Sarah egging her on Diana went overboard by impulsively twanging the suspenders of a startled Mario Soares, Portugal's President during the 1980s.

Their extraordinary circumstances made them powerful women, and the press continued to forgive and love Diana, but for Sarah, who became the fallen woman (Venus in Virgo on the MC), there was no coming back, and their friendship lost its innocent eleventh house playfulness as it began to fuel a vicious onslaught from the press and her mother-in-law's loyal subjects.

Sarah's Moon in the Placidus chart is positioned in the fourth house.

This house describes not only her father and his situation, but it is also the house of her partner's mother (ten houses from the seventh by deriving the houses).

If newspaper reports are to be believed, Sarah and the Queen were close at the beginning of the marriage.

Sarah was an accomplished horse-woman and she often accompanied the Queen on her private rides.

She learnt to fly a Piper Warrior which made her the darling of her in-laws, and the Queen even took to waving Sarah to the seat next to her in cars and carriages, at church and at informal dinners.[170]

However, the Moon is debilitated by its conjunction to the South Node, a malefic, and the fact that Sarah's Moon is disposited by her debilitated Mars, gives some indication of Sarah's eventual fall from the Queen's grace.

The fourth house Moon in the Placidus chart describes her own mother's exclusion from the ranks of the privileged classes as Susan

Ferguson made an unforgivable social gaffe by leaving her titled husband for his Argentinean polo coach when Sarah was twelve years old.

Although her father remarried after Susan's disappearance, her mother's scandal did little to help Sarah's cause when photos of the Duchess sun-bathing topless with her financial advisor, John Bryan, were published in 1992 and the English Press, known for its long memory, drew harsh comparisons between the mother and daughter's infidelities and questionable moral fibre.

In the Placidus chart a dignified Jupiter in the first house rules the angular fourth house, but now Saturn in Capricorn takes command of the fourth in Whole Sign, so what begins as a cosy, if somewhat unconventional, relationship between a flighty daughter-in-law and the mother of her husband, turns into an enraged monarch who is embarrassed by her son's terrible choice in a marriage partner.

The degrees of the Sun and the Moon are not close enough to create an aspect, however, they are in signs which oppose one another, so they both fall foul when the house system alters from Placidus to Whole Sign.

The Sun goes into the Whole Sign twelfth house at the same time as the Moon goes into the opposing Whole Sign sixth house, and it appears as though Sarah's fate is doomed so far as achieving honour and respect from her new family, her peers and her countrymen.

For a public figure, the Moon in the chart can sometimes represent public acclaim, notoriety or the love of the common people, and the type of fame Sarah experienced was neither loving nor supportive by the time her marriage had come to an end.

The Whole Sign cadent Moon suffers badly and is not helped by the square to an unforgiving Saturn which has moved from the second house to the Whole Sign third, and represents the Press who used the media to constantly harass, judge and defame Sarah.

Saturn rules the Whole Sign third and fourth houses so that each time the Press drew attention to Sarah's mishaps or her famous spending sprees (dignified Jupiter rules the Whole Sign second house), the dexter square from dignified Saturn over-powering the cadent Aries Moon causes agitation in the Royal Family, and Sarah's marriage is put under further strain as she becomes increasingly isolated from her husband and his family.

Two days after the images of Sarah and Bryan were published in 1992, the Palace announced Prince Andrew's separation from his wife.

The Descendant will not change in the shift, so debilitated Venus in Virgo will rule the seventh house under both systems.

Sarah may have been able to maintain an elevated public position if Venus had retained its tenth house spot, but as soon as it is moves to the following house, either the person does not want to, or cannot, retain its power in the tenth house.

Instead, Whole Sign Venus falls on the mercy of its friends and social set, and this movement best describes Sarah's passionate obsession to maintain the same life-style as her jet-setting friends.

Despite her dignified Jupiter moving to the Whole Sign second house, or perhaps because it feels it should be financially entitled, Sarah has lived above her means for the majority of her life and this has meant she has had to continually turn to Andrew (Venus rules 7th house) for bail-outs to help avoid bankruptcy.

When Sarah and Andrew divorced in 1996, Sarah was reportedly in debt by several million pounds, mostly to the same bank which received her mother-in-law's patronage (Whole Sign Jupiter in rulership in 2nd house), as the Coutts Bank continued to finance her lavish lifestyle four years after the public scandal and Sarah's separation from Prince Andrew.

Sarah claimed at the time of the divorce that she took a mere 15,000 pound a year as a divorce settlement from the Queen, but it was later revealed that a 3 million pound lump sum accompanied her 'pension' as the wife of a retired Navy officer.

In Sarah's Placidus chart, Saturn in Capricorn is in the second house of wealth.

For most people it is hard to imagine how Saturn could be restricting this individual's financial resources, but Saturn in the Placidus second house is more an indicator of Sarah's childhood.

She was nine years old when her father (Saturn) retired after a distinguished military career to the family's country estate and his passion for polo brought him into constant contact with the Royal Family.

Her father's wealth was more about aristocratic connection than cold hard cash as Major Ronald Ferguson was a descendant of King

Charles II via two of his illegitimate sons, and Sarah has been reported as describing her family as "country gentry with a bit of old money."

With a dignified Jupiter in the Placidus first house ruling the second house of wealth Sarah learnt early in life that money was to be made from one's name and the nature of one's environment, and although her family was acutely aware of the royals, *they were actually on the outer edge of that inner circle.*[171]

A more accurate account of Sarah's wealth is gained from comparing her Whole Sign chart to the Placidus chart.

Jupiter retains its rulership over the second house, but now it moves from the Placidus first to the WS second because it is in its sign of rulership.

Sarah's belief that she deserves unlimited wealth in order to support her excessive spending is confirmed by Jupiter in its highest essential dignity.

No dispositor for Jupiter – it is a king in its own sign, and the same rule applies to Saturn in Capricorn.

Jupiter in either the first house of physical appearance (Placidus), or the second house of wealth (Whole Sign) works for Sarah's situation, as she avoided bankruptcy by concentrating on her two million pound a year contract as figurehead for *Weight Watchers* which would be a Jupiter twelve year cycle lasting from 1995 until its expiry in 2007.

Saturn in rulership also helped alleviate the Duchess' financial woes with its combination of second house (Placidus) and third house placement (Whole Sign) when Sarah threw money into building a publishing company to promote her children's books, and spent years on public-speaking tours talking about her relationship with the Queen and her family, whilst developing her own media business within the USA.

Sarah should have achieved financial security for life, but both diurnal and dignified planets, in good sect condition, lost strength, direction and purpose when Jupiter was demoted from the most powerful angular house to a passive succedent one, and Saturn became less effective, but gained light when downgraded from Placidus succedent to a Whole Sign cadent third house.

Saturn in rulership ruling the Whole Sign fourth house shows her mother-in-law's integrity in providing money for Sarah to begin paying off her debts, and a good Saturn in the Whole Sign third should by rights, be capable of supplying Sarah with sound concrete possibilities for her revival.

However, many of Sarah's financial decisions were made with the help of her seventh house financial advisor/companion, John Bryan, and unfortunately, the trine between a solid Saturn and a shady Venus does not provide the sound financial advice the Duchess is seeking from her advisor.

For a time, Sarah became America's adopted sweetheart and the trip between London and California became so constant and regular that it became a 'third house journey' of familiarity.

In America, the Duchess found the love and respect she could not engender from her own people, but eventually her American kingdom also began to falter and collapse under the strain of terrible business decisions and poor professional advice. (Debilitated Sun ruling Whole Sign tenth and debilitated Venus on MC ruling seventh house)

By her 50th birthday, the Duchess was once more in financial difficulties with an estimated 200 creditors in the United Kingdom and the USA.

In 2009 Sarah lost more than 3.2 million pounds in the collapse of Hartmoor, her American lifestyle and wellness company, and by the following year she was preparing to declare voluntary bankruptcy with debts amounting to 5 million pounds.

The Table on the movement of Sarah's planets *(Fig. 103)* indicates that their situation has worsened with the shift from Placidus to Whole Sign.

Of the original seven planets, only Saturn and Mercury have improved, and Saturn may have gained a measure of lightness, but by moving out of the second house Saturn has lost its integrity and its accountability in financial dealings as Sarah Ferguson still owes thousands of pounds to her creditors.

Saturn's removal from the Placidus second house means that a dignified Jupiter has no controlling factor to rein in Sarah's excessive spending.

Second house Jupiter's sinister square to a fallen Venus in the Whole Sign eleventh house describes how debilitated Venus over-powers a dignified Jupiter. Sarah spends large amounts of money on luxuries whilst at the same time taking advice from suspect sources (Venus rules 7th house) as she was recently listed in the Panama Papers, a leaked document naming high profile individuals involved in shady off-shore tax dealings with the South American country.

Mercury, on the other hand, has switched from darkness into the light, from a mostly ineffectual twelfth house (Placidus) to the most powerful one in the chart (Whole Sign first house).

In theory, this should bode well for the native, but in practice, things can go quite wrong when both systems work side by side to determine the individual's fate.

The following episode is a perfect example of how subterfuge and secrecy can lead one to believe they are being cunning when it comes to operating in the dark, when in fact, a planet's actions are about to be shamefully exposed to the entire world.

Mercury sextiles both Saturn and Venus but this 'good fortune' of royal connection and powerful friends can be totally negated by the Neptune which stands alongside a clueless and gullible Mercury.

Such an aspect helps to describe how Sarah was completely blindsided early in her marriage to Andrew by the British press, when her Placidus twelfth house Mercury believed that no-one was paying attention to her thoughtless comments and her inappropriate crude humour, or that her increasingly common social gaffes, would out her to the public, and there was little rejoicing for WS Mercury when it moved into its house of joy.

Her first house Neptune Mercury was once more in play in May 2010 when the Duchess was caught on film accepting a US$40,000 down-payment as part of an apparent cash-for-access deal for introductions to her former husband, Prince Andrew.

The scam was perpetrated by the News of the World's veteran investigations editor, Mazher Mahmood, who posing as a wealthy businessman, approached Sarah to initiate meetings with the Duke of York, then the United Kingdom Special Representative for Trade and Investment.

In the meeting Sarah alleges that it is the Duke himself who has suggested the total amount, 500,000 pounds, be wire-transferred to a British bank account.

Sarah also claims in the secretly filmed footage to have previously arranged introductions for two other tycoons, and that as part of the deal, she is demanding a cut of any future profits accruing from her high-level introductions.

When the film went public, Sarah insisted that Andrew knew nothing of the deal and that it was a serious lapse of judgement on her part but that she was emotionally and financially bankrupt, with "not a pot to piss in".

Sarah's judgement was shown to be seriously impaired by this incident, but instead of her Mercury retreating to the safety of the Placidus twelfth house, Sarah further damaged her popularity in America and destroyed any sympathy the world felt for her, by agreeing to appear in a well-paid interview with talk-show host, Oprah Winfrey.

Sarah's Whole Sign Mercury appeared to be out of control as she made one off-putting statement after another, culminating in the following statement when asked by Oprah how Sarah felt about being removed from the official wedding guest-list for her nephew, Prince William's impending marriage.

Sarah replied, *"I really love the feeling that sort of Diana and I both weren't there"*, totally missing the point that Diana was not present at her son's wedding because she was no longer alive, whereas Sarah had been deliberately snubbed because she had once more brought scandal to the Royals' doorstep.

Every Princess Diana worshipper turned on Sarah at that moment, and any forthcoming advertising endorsements or invitations to speak, dried up immediately for Sarah.

Even with all of Sarah's verbal disasters, there is still some benefit to angularity for her Mercury as it rules the lucky eleventh house in the whole sign chart, where her glamorous, famous or wealthy friends keep inviting her to their functions, perhaps because she is still inclined to be outrageously outspoken, unpredictable, or witty in their company.

In both systems Mercury rules the eighth house, the house of her partner's and other people's money.

By July 2011, Sarah's debts had been cleared by Prince Andrew, with help from his friends, billionaire Jeffrey Epstein, and former treasurer of the Tory Party, David Rowland, and it seemed that Sarah might be permitted to resume her life away from the limelight.

However, controversy from another direction put Sarah back in newspaper headlines, when Turkish authorities asked the British government to help obtain evidence to prosecute the Duchess over allegations that she breached the privacy of children living in state-run institutions.

Three years earlier in 2008 Sarah and her daughter Princess Eugenie had accompanied an undercover reporting team sent into Turkey to investigate living conditions in institutions for abandoned children.

The meddling that Diana could get away with in foreign countries was impossible for Sarah to replicate, as her Whole Sign cadent Moon ruled the ninth house and she would never be acceptable as the unofficial Ambassador for Human Rights which was a mock title that sat so easily on Diana's shoulders.

It may have taken three years for Whole Sign Mercury to reveal the repercussions of Sarah's actions, but the title of the programme, *Duchess and Daughters; Their Secret Mission,* screams Neptune Mercury's involvement with both the Placidus twelfth and the Whole Sign first house.

Although Sarah swore that the segment for ITV had not been politically motivated, the coincidence of its public release at the same time as Turkey's bid for European Union membership, demonstrated how a witless Sarah, had once more been manipulated for purposes beyond her comprehension.

At the time the Turkish government were deadly serious about wanting Sarah extradited to face charges which carried a maximum penalty of over twenty years' imprisonment.

This scenario is not out of the question given Sarah's heavy twelfth house involvement in both charts, Placidus has Neptune Mercury in the twelfth with a debilitated Mars ruling the house, whilst the Whole Sign chart has the North Node, a Sun in fall and Mars, the Ascendant lord, in the twelfth house.

Little wonder that Sarah was genuinely terrified in 2011 that the British authorities' resolve to protect her would weaken, and she would be returned to Turkey for punishment and imprisonment.

Sarah's relationship with the media has always been hit-and-miss.

She has often been misguided when reading the public's reaction to her, and it may be her Neptune Mercury constantly shifting from twelfth house to Whole Sign first house that convinces her she has a special empathy with "the man in the street".

In 2008 Sarah produced and funded two documentaries; one entitled *The Duchess of Hull (2007)*, Sarah's anti-obesity campaign to "stop Britain blowing itself up".

When introduced to one family, it is obvious they have no idea of their visitor's identity, and a rattled Sarah on camera tries desperately to jog the elderly relatives' memories of her marriage to Prince Andrew twenty two years earlier.

It is clear in the documentary that her invisibility distresses Sarah, and perhaps becomes the impetus for her following documentary one year later.

The Duchess on the Estate in 2008 finds Sarah visiting a depressed Northern Moor housing project in Manchester and suggesting to the occupants a variety of ways by which the problems of alcohol, violence and anti-social behaviour could be curbed.

Her suggestion to plant tulips was cringe-worthy.

The Duchess displayed her common touch by orchestrating a game of pool with the locals and drinking the pub's cider, and at one point telling the camera: *"I could sleep anywhere: a park bench, a bedsit, a B&B,"* before revealing she had actually spent the previous night in a nearby upmarket guest-house.

Sarah's Neptune Mercury continues to raise its ugly head and as recently as August 2015 the Duke and Duchess of York jointly purchased a 13 million pound chalet in Verbier, an elite alpine resort in Switzerland as a nest egg for their two daughters.

Speculation abounds as to where the money came from to make the expensive purchase, and Andrew's finances are under as much scrutiny as Sarah's own shaky sources of wealth.

Sarah has since moved there and is seeking to become a Swiss citizen.

Switzerland is famous for its generous tax laws for wealthy foreign residents who pay a lump sum based on their family's cost of living in the country, virtually rent, so long as no income is earned within Switzerland.

It looks as if Jupiter in the Whole Sign second house is finally taking care of business as finances have been on the improve for Sarah since her 55th birthday in 2014 when she appeared 55 pounds lighter and credited the Fusion Xcelerator, a food blender selling for 65 English pounds, for her successful weight loss.

Since then, she has being paid 'a six-figure sum' to endorse the blender, as well as developing her Duchess Discoveries range of hair-styling tongs, a range of teas, and a relaunch of her children's books.

But her creditors are furious that she still owes money and most will never be recompensed for their own losses.

In November 2016 details of a writ filed by the Duchess were made public[172] and the cash-for-access sting by the undercover reporter Mazher Mahmood from 2010 was back in the newspapers.

The Duchess is suing Mahmood's employers, the News Group Newspapers, for 25 million pounds in lost income, plus an undisclosed amount for compensation for the serious distress and upset she suffered after the exposé.

Her lawyers claim Mahmood invaded her privacy and "used deceit to induce her to make unguarded statements to her detriment", a Neptune Mercury statement if ever there was one, arguing that her comments were innocent and taken completely out of context when replayed by the Press.

Sarah also claims that when the News of the World ran her story it caused "serious embarrassment, humiliation, distress and reputational damage" plus huge financial loss for the Duchess.

Sarah allegedly joked to the undercover reporter: *"I'm a complete aristocrat. Love that. Don't you? I love it. It's tremendously fabulous!"*

She has her own coat of arms so perhaps she is an aristocrat, but Sarah needs to take heed of the motto written beneath the family shield in Latin:

Ex Adversis Felicitas Crescit – From Adversity grows Happiness

If Sarah truly intends to adopt her family's motto and apply it to the remainder of her life she still has sufficient time to take responsibility for her actions (dignified Saturn at the bendings of her Nodal Axis) to gain the best from both charts, and perhaps access some humility along the way to finding happiness.

Endnotes

1   Julius Firmicus Maternus: *Matheseos Libri VII* (Eight Books of the Mathesis, or Theory of Astrology), *Liber Tertius,* trans. Jean Rhys Bram, Spica Publications, Aust, 2001 (orig, 1975, Noyes Press), p. 61

2   Ibid, p. 63

3   Ibid, p. 63

4   Ibid, p. 64

5   Macrobius Ambrosius Theodosius *"Descent of the Soul from the Height of Cosmos to the Depths of Earth",* Book One, Ch 12

6   Maurus Servius Honoratus (365 CE), Commentary on Virgil's AEneid, vi, 714. G.R.S. Mead on the Tradition of Servius : *"Servius, however, in his Commentary on Virgil's AEneid, vi, 714, hands on another tradition, in which the spheres were regarded as inimical to the good of the soul, its evil propensities being ascribed to their energies."*

7   Omar of Tiberius, trans. Robert Hand, Ed. Robert Schmidt *Three Books on Nativities* (Project Hindsight Latin Track Volume XIV, 1995), Introduction by Robert Hand, p.i

8   Ibid, p.93

9   Guido Bonatti, *Liber Astronomiae, Books One, Two and Three,* trans. Robert Zoller, Ed. Robert Hand, Spica Publications, 1998, Australia, Third Tractate, Ch 65, p. 106

10 Omar, p. 93

11 Bonatti, p. 115

12 Omar, p. 93

13 Ibid, p. 93

14 Claudius Ptolemy, *Tetrabiblos or Four Books of the Influence of the Stars,* trans. J.M. Ashmand. 1822,Ballantrae Reprint, Ontario, Canada, Book IV, Chap 10, p. 138

15   Bonatti, Ch 65, p. 122

16   Ptolemy, Book, III, Ch. 13, p. 107. Also available online courtesy of http://www.classicalastrologer.com/, Forward by Prof. Peter J. Clark, Victoria, British Columbia, Feb 2006, p. 86

17   Johannes Schoener, *Opus Astrologicum,* Trans. Robert Hand, Project Hindsight, Latin Track, Volume IV, addendum by Robert Hand, Conference on Cos, 25/4/1996. Part I – The Seven Ages of Man – Schoener – Concerning the General Governors of the Seven Ages

18   Ptolemy, p. 138

19   Schoener, p. 1

20   Ibid, p. 1

21   Ptolemy, p. 139

22   *Corpus Hermeticum, The Divine Pymander of Hermes Trismegistus, Book I. 24-26,* This version published by The Editors of the Shrine of Wisdom, Manual no 7, Finitry Brook, Surrey, UK, Chapter 6 Regeneration, p. 45

23   Johannes Schoener, *Opus Astrologicum,* Trans. Robert Hand, Project Hindsight, Latin Track, Volume IV, Canon V. Making the Significations of the Twelve Houses of Heaven Known in Brief, p. 35

24   Bonatti, p. 106

25   Schoener, *Opusculum Astrologicum* p. 34

26   Bonatti, p. 112

27   Vettius Valens, *Anthologies, Book II, Part I* Translation by Robert Schmidt, Ed. Robert Hand, Project Hindsight, Greek Track, Volume VII, The Golden Hind Press, 1993, p. 3 http://www.csus.edu/indiv/r/rileymt/vettius%20valens%20entire.pdf

28   https://plato.stanford.edu/entries/socrates/

29   Avraham Ibn Ezra (1092-1167), *Five Medieval Astrologers,* Translated and Edited by James Herschel Holden, American Federation of Astrologers, Arizona, USA, 2008, from *The Centiloquy of Bethen,* No. 15, p. 112

30   Avraham Ibn-Ezra, *The Beginning of Wisdom,* Translated by Meira Epstein, ARHAT Publications, USA, 1998, Chapter Eight, Note 87, p. 136

31   Robert Hand, *On Matter and Form In Astrology,* transcription by Oya Vulas from a lecture given at the York conference in 2005. Available from the website http://www.ncgr-turkey.com/on_matter_and_form. htm, Accessed 26th Jan 2015. P. 8

32   Benjamin Dykes, *Introduction to Traditional Astrology; Abu Ma'shar & al-Qabisi,* The Cazemi Press, Minnesota, USA, 2010

33   Benjamin Dykes, notes from *Traditional/Medieval Astrology Seminar,* www.bendykes.com, 2010, p. 1

34   Avraham Ibn-Ezra, *The Beginning of Wisdom,* Note 86, p. 136

35   Ibid, Note 88, p. 136

36   Firmicus Maternus: *Matheseos* Book 2, Ch. 3, p. 25

37   Avraham Ibn-Ezra, *The Beginning of Wisdom,* Note 78, 79, p. 135

38   Bonatti, Second Tractate – Part Two, Ch. 26, p. 30

39   Firmicus Maternus: *Matheseos,* Note #25 on Book III by translator Jean Rhys Bram, quote from Porphyry, p. 289

40   Guido Bonatti, *Liber Astronomiae,* Second Tractate – Part Two, Ch. 36, p. 42

41   Valens, p. 106

42   Al-Biruni, *The Book of Instruction In the Elements of the Art of Astrology,* Written in Ghaznah, 1029A.D., Reproduced Brit. Mus. MS Or. 8349, Trans. R. Ramsey Wright, Luzac & Co. London, 1934, Note 445, p. 259

43   Bonatti, Second Tractate, p. 74

44   Ibid, p. 47

45   William Lilly, *Christian Astrology, Volume One,* http://mithras93.tripod.com/, Copyright 1999, p. 115

46   Guido Bonatti, *Liber Astronomiae,* Second Tractate, Chapter 35, p. 40

47   Avraham Ibn-Ezra, *The Book of Reasons,* Translated by Meira Epstein, Ed. Robert Hand, Project Hindsight, Hebrew Track, Volume I, 1991, p. 39

48   Guido Bonatti, *Liber Astronomiae,* Second Tractate – Part Two, p. 44

49   Avraham Ibn-Ezra, *The Beginning of Wisdom,* Note 80, p. 136

50   Ibid, p. 136

51   Guido Bonatti, *Liber Astronomiae,* Third Tractate, p. 115

52   Ibid, p. 1

53   Claudius Ptolemy, *Tetrabiblos,* Ashmand translation from Proclus (1822), Book I, Chap. 17, p. 39

54   Ibid, Book I, Chap. 5, p. 14

55   George, Demetra, *Asteroid Goddesses,* ACS Publications, San Diego, California, 1986, p. 7 *"The Sun, Mercury, Venus, Moon and Mars are known as the personal planets because they rule the personl qualities of identity, intellect, values, emotions and drives. Jupiter and Saturn function as the social planets, signifying the ethics and laws by which a society operates."*

56 Avraham Ibn-Ezra, *The Beginning of Wisdom,* Note 90, p. 136

57 Ibid, Note 89, p. 136

58 Firmicus Maternus, *Matheseos,* Footnote: Book II, Ch. VIII by translator Jean Rhys Bram, p. 29

59 Ibid, Footnote, p. 30

60 Avraham Ibn-Ezra, *The Beginning of Wisdom,* Note 98, p. 137

61 Ibid, Notes 94, 95, p. 136, 137

62 Ibid, Note 91, p. 136

63 The first statement made by Ibn-ezra appears in *The Beginning of Wisdom,* Note 92, p. 137 and the second is from *The Book of Consultations of the Stars,* featured in James Herschel Holden's *Five Medieval Astrologers,* Note 2, p. 111

64 *The Centiloquy of Hermes Trismegistus,* featured in James Herschal Holden's *Five Medieval Astrologers,* Note 89, p. 105

65 Ibid, Note 90, p. 105

66 *The Centiloquy of Hermes Trismegistus,* featured in James Herschal Holden's *Five Medieval Astrologers,* Note 66, p. 102

67 Guido Bonatti, *Liber Astronomiae,* p. 95

68 Ibid, p. 95

69 Avraham Ibn-Ezra, *The Beginning of Wisdom,* Note 84,85, p. 136

70 Vettius Valens, *Anthology.* Trans. Robert Schmidt, Ed. Robert Hand, Project Hindsight, Greek Tract, Volume VII, Book II, On Trigons, p. 1

71 Ibid, p. 2

72 James Herschel Holden, *Five Medieval Astrologers,* published by the American Federation of Astrologers, Inc, 2008, contains *The Centiloquy of Hermes Trismegistus* (pg. 93) translated from Arabic sources by Stephen of Messina in c. 1262 CE

73 Ibid, p. 94

74 Rhetorius The Egyptian, *Astrological Compendium Containing His Explanation and Narration of the Whole Art of Astrology,* trans. James H. Holden, publ. American Federation of Astrologers, 2009, p. 7, Footnote by translator in a reference to Firmicus, *Mathesis,* Book ii, Ch 3,

75 Nicholas Campion, *The Book of World Horoscopes,* Cinnabar Books, Bristol, UK, 1995: Chart 458, The Sassanian Horoscope for the First Man, p. 531

76 Ibid, p. 521

77 Julius Firmicus Maternus: *Matheseos Libri VII* (Eight Books of the Mathesis, or Theory of Astrology), Book Two, p. 25

78 Deborah Houlding, *Centiliquium of Hermes Trismegistus, http://www.skyscript.co.uk/centiloquium2.html,* Notes and References, No. 3. Referenced from Antiochus, *The Thesaurus,* trans. R. Schmidt, ed. R. Hand, Project Hindsight Greek Track Vol II-B, Berkeley Springs: Golden Hind Press, 1993

79 Ibid, Notes and References, No. 3. Referenced later by Rhetorius The Egyptian, *Astrological Compendium,* trans. James H. Holden, p. 7

80 Ibid, p. 7

81 Al-Biruni, Notation 447, p. 260

82 Ibid, p. 261

83 Avraham Ibn-Ezra, *Beginning of Wisdom,* p. 125

84 Claudius, *Tetrabiblos,* Book III, Chap 18, p. 110

85 Gettings, Fred, *The Arkana Dictionary of Astrology,* Penguin Books 1985, London, UK, p. 87

86 Heraclitus, Fragment 76, Accessed on 1st July 2017 https://en.wikisource.org/wiki/Fragments_of_Heraclitus#Fragment_76

87 Aristotle, *On The Heavens* trans. W.K.C. Guthrie (Loeb Classical Library, Harvard University Press, London, England, pub. 1939, reprint 2000), Introduction xi

88 Aristotle, *On The Heavens* trans. W.K.C. Guthrie, translator's note, p. 258

89 Heraclitus, Fragment 126, Accessed at http://philoctetes.free.fr/heraclite.pdf

90 Pythagorus' Table of Opposites, http://www.britannica.com/EBchecked/topic/430268/table-of-opposites Accessed 12th Dec 2014

91 Al-Biruni, Notation 347, p. 210

92 Ibid, p. 211

93 Ibid, p. 211

94 http://www.greekmedicine.net/b_p/Four_Humors.html

95 *The Centiloquy of Hermes Trismegistus,* Translated by James Herschel Holden, *Five Medieval Astrologers,* AFA Publications, Phoenix, USA, Notation 8, p. 94

96 Claudius Ptolemy, *Tetrabiblos,* Ashmand translation from Proclus (1822), Book I, Chap. 16, p. 26

97 *The Centiloquy of Hermes Trismegistus, Five Medieval Astrologers,* J. H. Holden, Notation 89, p. 105

98 Johannes Schoener, *Opusculum Astrologicum* trans. Robert Hand (Berkeley Springs,WV: The Golden Hind Press, 1994) p. 18

99 Manly Palmer Hall, *Astrological Keywords,* copyright 1958, The Philosophical Research Society, Inc, reprinted 1978, Littlefield, Adams & Co., p. 34

100 Fred Gettings, *The Arkana Dictionary of Astrology,* Penguin Books, London, 1985, p. 101

101 Vettius Valens, *Anthologies,* Book 1, Riley Translation

102 Claudius Ptolemy, *Tetrabiblios,* J. M. Ashmand Translation, orig. 1822, Ch. 4, p. 14

103 http://www.ncbi.nlm.nih.gov/pubmed/224184

104 R.L. Rubens (1996) "The unique origins of Fairbairn's Theories", *Psychoanalytic Dialogues: The International Journal of Relational Perspectives* 6 (3) :413-43

105 Fred Gettings *The Arkana Dictionary of Astrology* (Penguin Books, London, England, 1985, reprint 1990) p. 276

106 Vincent van Gogh, Dutch artist in late 1880s. (van Gogh has Jupiter Moon conjunction in Sagittarius)

107 Thomas Hobbes (5th April 1588 – 4th December 1679) was an English philosopher and founder of modern political philosophy and political sciences. (Hobbes' Venus conjuncts Saturn in Taurus)

108 Barton, Tamsyn, *Ancient Astrology,* Routledge, London, 1994, reprint1998, p. 41

109 For a full discussion on Manilius' work see Jim Tester's *A History of Western Astrology,* The Boydell Press, Woodbridge, UK, pp. 30-48

110 Manilius, Marcus, edited by G.P. Goold, *Astronomica,* Loeb Classical Library, Harvard University Press, 1977, reprinted 1997, p. 239, Footnote *(d)* : Servius Sulpicius Rufus, extolled as the greatest of jurists by Cicero, *Brutus* 151-153

111 Ibid, p. 239

112 Amy Mowafi (born 3rd July 1980) is a writer, editor, on-line entrepreneur and author of best seller *"Fe-mail: the trials and tribulations of being a Good Egyptian Girl"* and *"Fe-mail 2".* (Amy has Saturn conjunct Mars in Virgo).

113 Thomas Hobbes (1588-1679)

114 Ingersoll, Robert Green, *The Works of Robert G. Ingersoll, Vol 2: Lectures.* Ingersoll (1833-1899) was an American atheist and abolitionist who toured the US for 30 years lecturing on religion and politics, and was considered by many to be one of the best known advocates of free thought in the 19th century.

115   Desmond Morris, English scientist (1928-)

116   Samuel Beckett

117   Samuel Beckett (13th April 1906-22nd December 1989) was an Irish avant-garde novelist, playwright, theatre director, and poet who lived in Paris most of his life.

118   Thich Nhat Hanh (born 11th October 1926) is a Vietnamese Zen Buddhist monk, teacher, author, poet and peace activist. Nhat Hanh has published more than 100 books, including more than 40 in English. He lives in the Plum Valley Monastery in the South of France (Nhat Hanh's Mars is in Taurus).

119   Sivananda Saraswati (8th September 1887 – 14th July 1963) was a Hindu spiritual teacher and a proponent of Yoga and Vedanta. A prolific writer, Sivananda wrote 296 books in his lifetime on a wide variety of subjects. (Sivananda's Sun is conjunct Mercury in Virgo trining Moon in Taurus)

120   Dorotheus of Sidon, *Carmen Astrologicum*, Translated by David Pingree, published in 1993 by Ascella Publications (Deborah Houlding), p. 67

121   Firmicus Maternus, Book Two, Diagram V, p. 40

122   Ibid, p. 39

123   Ibid, p. 38

124   Ptolemy, Claudius, *Tetrabiblos,* Ashmand Translation, Book I, Ch XVI, Mutual Configurations of the Signs, p.26

125   Ibid, p. 41

126   Ibid, p. 41

127   Maternus: *Matheseos* Book Two, p. 40

128   Johannes Schoener, *Opus Astrologicum*, p. 34

129   Valens, p. 11

130   Maternus: *Matheseos* Book Three, p. 84

131   Ibid, p. 79

132   Bonatti, Guido, *Liber Astronomiae* p. 95

133   Julius Firmicus Maternus: *Matheseos Libri VII* Book Three, p. 87

134   Ibid, p. 41

135   Schoener, *Opusculum Astrologicum* p. 34

136   Julius Firmicus Maternus: *Matheseos Libri VII* Book Three, p. 66

137   Ibid, p. 41

138   Houlding, Deborah, *The Houses: Temples in the Sky,* The Wessex Astrologer, Bournemouth, UK, 2006, p. 23

139   Maternus: *Matheseos Libri VII* Book Seven, p. 167

140   Bonatti, Guido, *Liber Astronomiae* p. 95

141 Ibid, p. 94

142 Maternus, Book Two, p. 40

143 Bonatti, p. 95

144 Maternus, Book Two, p. 40

145 Robert Hand, *On Matter and Form*, Accessed Jan 2015

146 Bonatti, Guido, *Liber Astronomiae*, Chapter 54, pp. 64-75

147 Transcription of a lecture given by Robert Hand at the Australis '97 Conference held in Adelaide, Australia. Available in *The Congress Papers, Astrology: An Ancient Art in the Modern World*, edited by Mari Garcia, Robert Hand, *The Triplicities*, pp. 78-98

148 Houlding, *The Houses: Temples of the Sky*, Introduction p. *x*

149 Gettings, Fred, *The Arkana Dictionary of Astrology*, Arkana Penguin, London, 1985, p. 299 ***macrocosmic chart :*** *A term derived in modern astrological circles to denote the standard configuration of the schematic heavens with Aries on the Ascendant, Taurus on the cusp of the 2ⁿᵈ house, and so on, without particular reference to space or time: it is the ideal chart, the schematic chart. Every geocentric chart – be it natal, horary, progressed or otherwise – is really a variation, set in space and time, of the macrocosmic chart.*"

150 James Herschel Holden, *Five Medieval Astrologers*, published by the American Federation of Astrologers, Inc, 2008, contains *Ptolemy's Centiloquy* (Attributed), pg. 75

151 Vettius Valens, *Anthology, Book II, Ch. 41*, pg 14

152 Houlding, *Temples in the Sky*, p. 10

153 Maternus: *Matheseos* Book Three, p. 62

154 Harold Bloom The Guardian, article *"The Knight in the mirror"* reviewing Edith Grossman's English translation (2003) of Cervantes' Don Quixote https://www.theguardian.com/books/2003/dec/13/classics.miguelcervantes

155 Vettius Valens, *Anthologies*, Book I

156 Ptolemy, Claudius, *Tetrabiblos*, Ashmand Translation, Book III, Ch XVIII, The Quality of the Mind, p. 108

157 Ibid, Book IV, Ch IV, p. 120-121

158 Robert Hand, *On Matter and Form*, Accessed Jan 2015, p. 11

159 George, Demetra, *Astrology and the Authentic Self*, published by Ibis Press, Lake Worth, FL, USA, 2008, p. 48

160 al-Biruni, *The Book of Instruction In the Elements of the Art of Astrology*, Notation 512, p. 315

161 Bonatti, *Liber Astronomiae,* Chapter LIII, p. 63

162 Ibid, p. 63

163 Robert Schmidt, *PHASE Conclave 2006 Lecture,* Cumberland, MD. Reference (Endnotes, Chapter 2, p. 299, ref. 8), Demetra George, *Astrology and the Authentic Self,* p. 50

164 Maternus, Book Two, p. 37

165 Dorotheus of Sidon, *Carmen Astrologicum,* Trans. David Pingree, published by Acella Publications, Deborah Houlding, 1993, ISBN 1-898503-00-1, Book Two, Chapter 15

166 Prince William of Wales' Chart Details: 21st June 1982, 9:03pm, BST – 1:00, London, UK. Asc 27Sagittarius, MC 2 Scorpio

167 Gettings, Fred, *The Arkana Dictionary of Astrology,* Arkana Penguin, London, 1985, p. 377

168 http://www.vanityfair.com/style/2013/08/princess-diana-sarah-ferguson-relationship

169 https://www.theguardian.com/uk/2010/may/24/feel-sorry-for-sarah-ferguson

170 http://www.vanityfair.com/style/2013/08/princess-diana-sarah-ferguson-relationship

171 Ibid

172 https://www.theguardian.com/uk-news/2016/nov/20/duchess-of-york-damages-mazher-mahmood-sting

CPSIA information can be obtained
at www.ICGtesting.com
Printed in the USA
FSHW02n0405220918
52379FS

9 781543 403770